The State, Society,
and Limited Nuclear War

SUNY Series in the Making of Foreign Policy:
Theories and Issues

Alex Roberto Hybel, Editor

The State, Society, and Limited Nuclear War

Eric Mlyn

State University of New York Press

Published by
State University of New York Press, Albany

For information, address State University of New York Press,
State University Plaza, Albany, N.Y. 12246

Production by M. R. Mulholland
Marketing by Nancy Farrell

Library of Congress Cataloging-in-Publication Data

Mlyn, Eric, 1961–
    The state, society, and limited nuclear war / Eric Mlyn.
        p.   cm. — (SUNY series in the making of foreign policy)
    Includes bibliographical references (p.   ) and index.
    ISBN 0-7914-2347-6. — ISBN 0-7914-2348-4
    1. United States—Military policy. 2. Nuclear weapons—Government
policy—United States. 3. Nuclear warfare—Public opinion.
4. Public opinion—United States. 5. Pressure groups—United
States. I. Series.
UA23.M5853 1995
355.02′17′0973—dc20   94-10966
                                                                            CIP

10 9 8 7 6 5 4 3 2 1

To Judy

Contents

Acknowledgments   ix

List of Acronyms   xiii

1. Introduction: An Overview of U.S. Nuclear Weapons Policy   1
2. U.S. Nuclear Weapons Policy and Theory Development:
     The Dominance of Bureaucratic Politics   19
3. The State and U.S. Nuclear Weapons Policy   35
4. The McNamara Years: The Shift to MAD?   55
5. Shifting Sands?   85
6. A Radical Departure? PD-59 and Forward   113
7. Conclusions: State, Society, and U.S. Nuclear Weapons Policy   151

Notes   175

Bibliography   211

Index   229

Acknowledgments

This book has been long in the making. When I first began to pursue this study, the Cold War was in full force. Both the United States and the Soviet Union were adding to their already bulging nuclear arsenals. The threat of strategic nuclear war between the superpowers seemed to be increasing. Now, many years later, the Cold War is over. The nuclear arsenals of the United States and the former Soviet Union have been greatly reduced. In this midst of all this change, many people and organizations have provided support and guidance; I would like to acknowledge them here.

Brian Job and Terry Hopmann provided useful advice throughout this study. I am fortunate to have had their support and wise guidance. Fellow graduate students at the University of Minnesota stimulated my thinking by reacting to earlier drafts of this project. They include Michael Barnett, Christopher McGrory-Klyza, Eric Selbin and Alexander Wendt. Others have reacted to various ideas associated with this study. They include William Arkin, Bruce Blair, Ben Frankel, Fred Kaplan, Jack Levy, Timothy McKeown, Eric Nordlinger, David Rosenberg, Scott Sagan and Robert Toth. Three anonymous reviewers for SUNY Press made excellent suggestions for change, and SUNY editor Clay Morgan has been quite helpful with many details along the way to the final preparation of this manuscript. Megeen Mulholland was instrumental in preparing the final version of the manuscript.

Thanks are in order to the Center for Foreign Policy Development at Brown University for awarding me a predoctoral research fellowship, which provided the time to work on this study along with interesting and fulfilling intellectual diversions along the way. In particular, I thank the Center's former Director Mark Garrison for bringing me to the Center, and Research Director Richard Smoke for showing interest in this project. My colleagues at the University of North Carolina, Chapel Hill, have provided a comfortable and supportive environment in which to finish this project.

I would like to thank the Graduate School of the University of Minnesota for providing travel funds for my research. I was also fortunate to have the assistance of the National Security Archives for the filing of Freedom of Information Act requests. William Arkin of the

Institute for Policy Studies and later Greenpeace shared with me his excellent files on the history of U.S. nuclear weapons policy.

I am also grateful to all those former government officials who took time from their schedules to talk to me about this project. I hope that I have accurately reflected their thinking in this study.

I also thank Mara Mlyn and Michael Sullivan for their hospitality on my frequent trips to Washington, D.C.

Finally, I would like to acknowledge the role played by my wife, Judy Byck. She has withstood moves around the country and my uneven moods as I have tried to "finish this thing." She has not read most of what follows. But without her, the words on these pages would have no context and would represent too much of my life. For making sure I realized that there was more to the world than the history of U.S. nuclear weapons policy, Judy deserves my greatest debt and love. This book is dedicated to her.

Any flaws that remain must have somehow slipped through the cracks. Don't ask me how; nevertheless they remain my responsibility.

For granting permission to reprint short excerpts from their publications, I thank the following publishers and authors.

Aaron L. Friedberg, "A History of the U.S. Strategic Doctrine," *Journal of Strategic Studies*, 3:3, (March 1980). Used by permission of Frank Cass Publishers.

David Rosenberg, "Reality and Responsibility: Power and Process in the Making of United States Nuclear Strategy, 1945–1968," *Journal of Strategic Studies*, 9:3, (March 1986). Used by permission of Frank Cass Publishers.

Robert Jervis, "Security Regimes," *International Organization*, 36:2, (Spring 1982). Used by permission of MIT Press.

David Lake, "The State and American Trade Strategy in the pre-Hegemonic Era." *International Organization*, 42:1, (Winter 1988). Used by permission of MIT Press.

G. John Ikenberry, "Conclusion: An Institutional Approach to American Foreign Policy," *International Organization*, 42:1, (Winter 1988). Used by permission of MIT Press.

Matthew Evangelista, "Issue-Area and Foreign Policy Revisited," *International Organization*, 43:1, (Winter 1989). Used by permission of MIT Press.

Desmond Ball, "U.S. Strategic Forces: How Would They be Used," *International Security*, 7:3, (Winter 82/83). Used by permission of MIT Press.

Graham Spinardi, "Why the U.S. Went for Hard Target Counterforce in Trident II (And Why it Didn't Get There Sooner.") *International Security*, 15:2, (Fall 1990). Used by permission of MIT Press.

Stephen Van Evera, "The Cult of the Offensive and the Origins of the First World War," *International Security*, 9:1, (Summer 1984). Used by permission of MIT Press.

Paul Nitze, "Atoms, Strategy and Foreign Policy," *Foreign Affairs*, 34:2, (January 1956). Used by permission of *Foreign Affairs* and the Council on Foreign Relations.

Melinda Beck and David C. Martin, "A New View of Nuclear War," *Newsweek*, August 18, 1980. Used by permission of Newsweek Inc.

List of Acronyms

ABM	anti-ballistic missile
ABRES	Advanced Ballistic Re-Entry System
ACDA	Arms Control and Disarmament Agency
ALCM	Air Launched Cruise Missile
CBO	Congressional Budget Office
CEP	Circular Error Probable
CIA	Central Intelligence Agency
CINCSAC	commander in chief of Strategic Air Command
CRP	Coordinated Reconnaissance Plan
CRS	Congressional Research Service
DoD	Department of Defense
DPM	Draft Presidential memorandum
DSTP	Director of Strategic Target Planning
FOIA	Freedom of Information Act
FY	fiscal year
GAO	General Accounting Office
GPALS	Global Protection Against Limited Strikes
ICBM	intercontinental ballistic missile
IOC	initial operating capacity
IRBM	intermediate-range ballistic missile
JCS	Joint Chiefs of Staff
JSCP	Joint Strategic Capabilities Plan
JSTPS	Joint Strategic Target planning Staff
LNO	Limited Nuclear Options
MAD	Mutual Assured Destruction
MARV	maneuvering re-entry vehicle
MIRV	multiple independently targetable re-entry vehicle
MPS	multiple protective shelter
MRBM	medium-range ballistic missile
NATO	North Atlantic Treaty Organization
NESC	Net-Evaluation Sub-Committee
NSAM	National Security Action Memorandum
NSC	National Security Council
NSDD	National Security Decision Directive
NSDM	National Security Decision Memorandum

NSSD	National Security Study Directive
NSSM	National Security Study Memorandum
NSTAP	National Strategic Targeting and Attack Policy
NSTL	National Strategic Target List
NTPR	Nuclear Targeting Policy Review
NUTs	Nuclear Utilization Theory
NUWEP	Nuclear Weapons Employment Policy
OTA	Office of Technology Assessment
PD	Presidential Directive
PRM	Presidential Review Memorandum
SAC	Strategic Air Command
SALT I	Strategic Arms Limitation Treaty
SALT II	Strategic Arms Limitation Talks
SDI	Strategic Defense Initiative
SIOP	Single Integrated Operational Plan
SLBM	submarine-launched ballistic missile
SOPs	Standard Operating Procedures
START	Strategic Arms Reduction Talks

1

Introduction: An Overview of U.S. Nuclear Weapons Policy

This study confronts the issue of U.S. nuclear weapons policymaking with the goal of clarifying what this policy has been and identifying those forces that have been most important in shaping it. My goal is to investigate the nature of the relationship between those who have formulated U.S. nuclear weapons policy (the state) and those who are outside the state as members of society. Has U.S. nuclear weapons policy been democratically controlled, with input from society, or has it been determined by a policy elite insulated from the demands of society? I will argue that strategy, devised by central state decision-makers, not bureaucratic interests, was the dominant factor driving the development of U.S. nuclear weapons policy

In order to accomplish this I look at the state, society, and limited nuclear war. I argue that the history of U.S. nuclear weapons policy is best explained by viewing the state as a coherent whole, with the resulting strategy a reflection of state interests rather than bureaucratic or parochial interests. Furthermore, I will show that the relationship between the various levels of U.S. nuclear weapons policy, specifically the disjunction among them, is best explained as an attempt by the state to maintain autonomy from society rather than as a result of conflicting bureaucratic interests.

I confront two "common wisdoms," one that concerns the substantive aspects of U.S. nuclear weapons policy, and the other that concerns understandings of nuclear policymaking within the U.S. For the former, I will investigate the history of U.S. nuclear weapons policy from 1960 to 1993, with particular attention to the relationship between the three levels of U.S. nuclear weapons policy. For the latter, I will address the assumption that the state is autonomous from society in the formulation of nuclear weapons policy. Of particular interest is the existence of the catch-22 faced by state policymakers. If they embraced limited nuclear options and war-fighting nuclear strategies, societal forces became agitated and threatened state autonomy. This is linked to societal perceptions of the likelihood and dangers of nuclear war. On the other hand, if state policymakers did not embrace these controversial nuclear plans, they were unable to procure those weapons needed to fulfill such a strategy. This study documents that catch-22.

The Three Levels of U.S. Nuclear Weapons Policy

The literature in security studies has not always recognized the three levels of nuclear weapons policy or the importance of the relationship between them. The first level, *declaratory policy*, is the nuclear weapons policy state policymakers publicly express. This is most often articulated by the president or the secretary of defense, and can be found in major policy addresses or in the Defense Posture Statements issued annually by the Department of Defense. Declaratory policy has several different audiences, including U.S. allies, the Soviet Union, and the American public. It is the latter audience that is of particular interest for this study.

The second level, *force development policy*, indicates the actual capabilities that exist within the U.S. nuclear arsenal. This level is operationalized by looking at the specific characteristics and force structure of U.S. nuclear forces. It is crucial because it indicates the actual capabilities of the strategic nuclear arsenal.

Finally, the third level is *action policy*, the highly classified targeting plans contained within the Single Integrated Operational Plan (SIOP). The SIOP contains U.S. nuclear strategic targeting plans, and is issued by the Joint Strategic Target Planning Staff (JSTPS) of the Joint Chiefs of Staff (JCS). Though highly classified, enough leaks and insider accounts have occurred to follow the operationalization of the SIOP and its evolution over the years.[1]

The relationship between these three levels of policy is complex and has varied over time. The three levels have very often been different from each other. *It is the relationship between these three levels of policy that is the substantive focus of this study. It is my hypothesis that the state has pursued disjunctions between these levels to enhance its autonomy from society.*

The following table summarizes the levels of U.S. nuclear weapons policy and the primary forces that go into shaping each level. Of particular interest is the disjunction between action and declaratory policy. Many have believed that U.S. nuclear weapons policy has always embraced Mutual Assured Destruction (MAD). MAD maintains that nuclear deterrence rests on one side's ability to destroy a significant

Policy	Proximate Influence	Operationalized
Action	Joint Chiefs Military Civilian Decision-Makers	SIOP
Force Development	President Congress Military	Force Characteristics
Declaratory	President Secretary of Defense	Annual Defense Posture Statement Major Policy Addresses

percentage of the other side's population and industry after withstanding an initial strike. Such targeting aims at populations and cities. The last decade or so has seen the increasingly common recognition that this was not the case. Though U.S. declaratory policy has often embraced such a posture, action policy has rarely embodied MAD targeting. Briefly, U.S. action policy, which became coordinated under the SIOP in 1960, has since the early 1950s called for a much higher level of counterforce targeting than a MAD strategy calls for.[2] This strategy is often referred to as NUTs, or Nuclear Utilization Theory. This will be documented in the case studies that follow.[3]

The United States has never had a MAD targeting policy. According to Aaron Friedberg:

The United States has never adhered to a doctrine of mutually assured destruction. Indeed, by any reasonable definition of the word, the U.S. has never had a strategic nuclear doctrine. Or, perhaps more precisely, the United States has had a strategic doctrine in the same way that a schizophrenic has a personality...[4]

Similarly, Robert Jervis, wrote:

First, American procurement and targeting policies have never followed the strictures of Mutual Assured Destruction. Instead the U.S. has not consistently shunned postures that provided at least some capabilities for defense. Similarly, American weapons have always been aimed at a wide range of Soviet military targets as well as at Soviet cities.[5]

Policymakers have also noted this disjunction, though not as often as scholars. In 1956 Paul Nitze criticized the gap between the declaratory policy of massive retaliation announced by John Foster Dulles in 1954 and the actual targeting. He wrote, "[T]he more we can bring our action policy and our declaratory policy into line with each other the more effective both become."[6] Similarly, a report by the Commission on the Organization of the Government of Foreign Policy (The Murphy Commission) offered explicit recognition of this disjunction in 1975. Henry Rowen wrote:

> The existence of large gaps between policy and operational behavior is a common phenomenon. High officials place great weight on policy statements. They do so because formulating policy goals and communicating them to the public, to Congress, and not least, members of the bureaucracies, is one of their principle responsibilities. Officials in the Executive Branch are also responsible for the execution of policies...the aspect of policy over which presidents and other high officials have greatest control is making speeches and issuing policy statements. Just about everything else is harder to do.[7]

More recently, former Secretary of Defense Harold Brown wrote " [T]he declaratory policies of Western governments must mirror actual nuclear policies more closely than has been the case in the past."[8]

State-Society Relations

The second "common wisdom" that appears in the literature posits that nuclear weapons policy (dubbed "high politics") lies in a privileged sphere of public policy. According to this view, strategic nuclear policy is insulated from domestic politics. The Realist paradigm in international relations reflects this common wisdom. Realists have never paid explicit attention to the role of domestic politics in the formulation of foreign policy. In this sense, this is a crucial case study because it seeks to test the degree of state autonomy from society where autonomy has been assumed to exist. If the state is not autonomous from society in this issue area, we may begin to question state autonomy in other issue areas as well. This common wisdom has also resulted in a paucity of literature concerned with the domestic political context of U.S. nuclear weapons policy. Security issues have been left to scholars within international relations.

Because of the above concerns, the theoretical focus of this study will be on notions of the state, state structure, and state autonomy. The United States is often seen as a "weak state," unable to pursue policy without the interference of society. However, scholars assert that for national security policy the United States is a strong state not significantly constrained by society. I begin this investigation with the strong suspicion that the state does not enjoy the wide degree of autonomy that has often been assumed to exist within this policy area and that this autonomy has been gradually decreasing over time. Furthermore, I will investigate the mechanisms used by the state as it seeks to achieve and maintain autonomy from society. Also of concern is the resistance that the state encounters in its quest for autonomy. Even if the state is autonomous from society, or has been for a large part of the nuclear age, such autonomy is not automatic—it is not inherent to security issues as has often been assumed.

Although I focus primarily on the internal workings of the state and the state's relationship to society, external factors are important as well. I will use the nuclear balance between the United States and the Soviet Union as the external context for the exploration of the case studies. External factors may determine the degree to which domestic political factors become important for U.S. nuclear policymaking. Here I focus on the impact the nuclear balance has had on the relative importance of domestic political factors for the formulation of U.S. nuclear strategy. I will consider whether state autonomy was easier to maintain in times of U.S. superiority.

What Is U.S. Nuclear Weapons Policy—MAD vs. NUTs

During the 1960s and early 1970s there was widespread belief that U.S. nuclear targeting embraced MAD.[9] A pure policy of MAD would target population, or countervalue targets. Advocates of such a posture hold that the United States can maintain an effective and credible nuclear deterrent only by holding populations hostage. Opponents of this posture endorse NUTs. They argue that MAD, because of the condition of mutual vulnerability, is not credible and that the United States must have limited and flexible nuclear options. These latter options would include the targeting of nuclear forces and other military targets. Advocates of such postures claim that this type of targeting makes for a more credible nuclear deterrent and can, in case deterrence fails, enable policymakers to keep nuclear war limited. Though this study will not seek to evaluate this debate, the differentiation of these two strategies is crucial for understanding the development of U.S. nuclear strategy.[10]

For advocates of MAD, there is little discussion of fighting a nuclear war, of "winning" or "prevailing." Deterrence rests on the threat of the destruction of civilization. Advocates of MAD do not move beyond thinking about what will deter. Instead, once nuclear weapons are used this policy has failed. No other options are endorsed by MAD advocates.

This debate, however, is sometimes confused because MAD is often used not to describe a set of policies or strategies (though this is the meaning of term that is of interest within the study) but instead is used to describe a condition that is simply a fact of the nuclear era. Jervis, in differentiating between MAD as a policy and MAD as a condition, notes:

> Not only does MAD mean different things to different people, but the term is used sometimes for description and sometimes for prescription. It may also refer, either descriptively or prescriptively, to different aspects of policy, to declaratory policy, procurement policy, or war planning. Since the elements are not always consistent, one aspect of policy may be accurately described as MAD while others might not be.[11]

Jervis shows that MAD may exist at some levels and not at other levels of U.S. policy. Second, he points out the descriptive rather than the prescriptive nature of some discussions of MAD. As used in its descriptive sense, MAD does not differentiate one type of targeting policy from another. Rather, it says that if nuclear weapons were used, mutual destruction would be assured no matter which type of nuclear targeting is adopted. From this perspective, MAD is a condition that cannot be avoided, despite the best efforts of nuclear strategists to devise war fighting plans that might keep a nuclear war limited. Targeting or war planning that attempts to keep a nuclear war limited is misguided in its attempt to deny the essence of the nuclear age. For those who see MAD as a condition of the nuclear age, MAD is usually, though not always, advocated as a policy.[12]

Those who advocate NUTs strategies believe that nuclear weapons could be used as military tools. Unlike advocates of MAD, NUTs advocates see nuclear weapons has having more utility than simply deterrence. They reject MAD as both policy and condition. They usually argue that MAD really did not address what would happen should nuclear war occur. It is not my claim that NUTs advocates desire to fight a nuclear war any more than those who advocate MAD. Instead, they argue that NUTs strategies could better deter the outbreak of nuclear war and could contain such wars should deterrence fail. The deterrence is seen to be enhanced through this kind of strategy by making a nuclear response more credible. After all, if NUTs advocates did not think that the use of nuclear weapons would result in the destruction of the planet, nuclear response would seem more credible.

As will be documented below, NUTs strategies shared the belief that nuclear wars could be fought short of total destruction. However, NUTs strategies have manifested themselves in various ways over the course of the nuclear age. Despite the different terms, all NUTs strategies share a desire to target nuclear weapons against counterforce targets, and thus required accuracy. In addition, they all require that options be developed to use only small parts of the nuclear arsenal to meet contingencies short of all-out nuclear war between the United States and the Soviet Union. These policies are referred to as damage limitation, flexible options, limited nuclear options, and the counter-vailing strategy. Though these each emphasize a different part of the overall NUTs agenda, they all believe that nuclear weapons could be employed as rational instruments of state policy. The details of these policies will emerge in the case studies below.

Those who advocate counterforce NUTs options disagree with MAD advocates.[13] Advocates of counterforce options are skeptical that countervalue targeting is an effective and credible nuclear deterrent against an opponent's actions that are less than an attack on the U.S. homeland. The credibility of the United States extending deterrence to European allies had been the driving force behind the acquisition of limited counterforce nuclear options. It has never seemed credible to say that we would trade New York for Bonn if the Soviet Union attacked Western Europe.[14]

MAD and NUTs are ideal types. Strategies and policymakers rarely advocate a pure counterforce or pure countervalue strategic nuclear policy. Instead, these are opposite ends of a continuum, with most policies falling somewhere between these two. Nevertheless, the emphasis and underlying beliefs of varying strategies usually embrace one of these schools. For clarity, I will treat these as ideal types throughout this study. In the case studies that follow, the tension between these two ways of thinking about nuclear weapons will become apparent. Of particular interest is the belief that U.S. nuclear weapons targeting policy has embraced MAD as a policy. There is a lingering misconception that the United States has not traditionally targeted Soviet nuclear weapons. The belief holds that the United States has traditionally targeted Soviet populations and industry—primarily countervalue rather than counter-force targeting. In fact, at each point when declaratory policy embraced counterforce limited nuclear options (1962, 1974, 1980), the press, Congress, and many interested observers greeted these public declarations as radical departures in U.S. nuclear weapons policy. However, these announcements were more evolutionary than revolutionary.

Declaratory policies of MAD do not talk about the use of nuclear weapons, and thus tend not to frighten the public. They do not make nuclear war seem likely. Talk of counterforce options, limited nuclear war and the like brings the horror of nuclear war all too close to home. As one observer put it, a "rationalized nuclear doctrine appeared more usable" and thus took away the sugar coating from our policy and alarmed forces in society as they began to think about the horror of nuclear war.[15]

The predominant explanation for the disjunction between action and declaratory policy draws on the bureaucratic politics model. Some of these explanations seek to legitimize the disjunctions between these levels of policy by claiming that it would be impossible to achieve coherence in such a complex policy area.[16] The very size of the national security state makes such explanations intuitively appealing, and make disjunctions or lack of policy coordination appear to be the natural unavoidable state of affairs. Others claim that the disjunction is intentional, designed to mislead the American people.[17] Finally, one interpretation posits that cognitive psychology offers an explanation for the lack of continuity between the various levels of nuclear policy.[18]

Some assert that disjunctions between force levels, targeting, and doctrine should not exist. The idealized version of how these levels of policy should be made posits that civilian inputs determine targeting, and that all three levels should be the same.[19] As a result, the existence of this disjunction poses several problems for nuclear weapons policy. First, it has at times affected the ability of the state to procure those weapons that it views as necessary for the U.S. nuclear arsenal to fulfill targeting plans. It is difficult for the state to procure increased counterforce capabilities when declaratory policy embraces a countervalue logic. Second, and perhaps more important, the inconsistencies among these different levels of nuclear policy affect the ability of the public and Congress to influence the course of nuclear weapons policy.

The Myth of MAD

It is useful here to outline briefly the type of misperceptions held by the press, politicians, and scholars about nuclear weapons policy. The most important period is the early 1960s when Secretary of Defense Robert McNamara initially rejected MAD as declaratory policy. Later, he embraced it at the declaratory level while leaving action policy dedicated to limited counterforce options. In assessing the weapons build-up of this period, Graham Allison and Frederic Morris conclude, "[A]merican strategic forces in the nineteen-sixties were being driven by something other than official strategic doctrine and estimates of enemy capabilities seems inescapable."[20] They reached this conclusion because they misperceived U.S. policy as MAD. They write, "[B]y the end of Robert McNamara's tenure as Secretary of Defense, the primacy of 'assured destruction' as the central American strategic objective had been established."[21] By failing to recognize that MAD was declaratory and not action policy, the authors are forced to figure out why the United States had acquired so much more nuclear capability than required by a pure MAD posture. Because McNamara appeared to move away from MAD in the early 1960s, Allison and Morris conclude that the United States had an excess of capabilities because decisions for the force development level had already been made. Had Morris and Allison recognized that U.S. action policy had been dominated by counterforce targeting, regardless of McNamara's shifts in declaratory policy, the U.S. nuclear force posture would have been better explained. This will be further documented in chapter 4.

Similarly, Stephen Van Evera, in criticizing changes in U.S. declaratory policy in the early 1980s, warned of the danger of abandoning MAD for counterforce targeting. He wrote:

"Assured Destruction" leaves much to be desired as a nuclear strategy, and the world of "mutual assured destruction" ("MAD") which it fosters leaves much to be desired as well. But 1914 warns that we tamper with MAD at our peril: any exit from MAD to a counterforce world would create a much more dangerous arrangement, whose outlines we glimpsed in the First World War.[22]

Van Evera claims that the United States was abandoning MAD for NUTs, and that such a move was dangerous considering the offensive doctrines that he believed were responsible for World War I. However, he exaggerates the extent to which the United States had relied on a policy of MAD in the past. Edward Luttwak displays similar reasoning in his attempt to account for the perceived decline of the United States from strategic nuclear pre-eminence. He writes that it was "by deliberate policy that the United States allowed its once great advantage to wane, and this policy was not dictated by budgetary stringencies but was rather the result of a pervasively influential and dogmatic belief in the theory of 'assured destruction.'"[23]

Rand analyst Carl Builder wrote in 1979:

> For almost twenty years of public discussion, the strategic thinking in our country has been tightly gripped by a marvelously logical concept called Assured Destruction. An idea that was originally intended only as a yardstick for "How much is enough?" soon became the cornerstone of U.S. strategic policy.[24]

This leads Builder to conclude that counterforce capabilities had become a nonsubject in U.S. strategic discourse.

Richard Betts notes the prevalence of the myth of MAD in his review of the Council on Foreign Relations' edited volume *Nuclear Weapons and World Politics*. Though he commends a piece in the volume by Michael Mandelbaum, he points out that Mandelbaum offers a flawed assessment of how much the United States actually emphasized MAD in its targeting plans. He notes "[T]he disquieting extent to which so much of the essays' reasoning hinges on MAD is underlined not only by doubts about Soviet adherence to the conception, but by the fact that it has never been exclusively embraced by the United States either."[25]

Many scholars have compared the supposed U.S. adherence to MAD to the nuclear strategy advocated by the Soviet Union. Such assessments, usually put forward by hawks, argued that U.S. adherence to MAD in combination with a Soviet belief in war-fighting made for a dangerous nuclear relationship. For example, Richard Foster notes:

> There are basic asymmetries in the strategic doctrine and objectives between the United States and the Soviet Union that give the Soviet Union a superior strategy as well as strategic superiority. The Soviets speak of survival and victory in nuclear war, while Americans speak only of a nuclear stalemate, based on a prediction of mutual assured destruction of the superpowers in the event of nuclear war. Thus, the Soviets are assuring their survival: the United States may be assuring its own destruction—or capitulation.[26]

Many cited the myth of MAD to show that the Soviet Union pursued an aggressive nuclear policy. This may have provided further domestic political motivations for the myth of MAD.

Scott Sagan, in his book on U.S. nuclear policy, writes of the "two myths about MAD."[27] The first one is the myth documented above, namely the misperception that action policy was driven by MAD. In addition, Sagan refers to the "experts' myth about MAD," which is the belief that MAD was mere rhetoric used either to placate the public or to somehow cap Air Force requests for additional intercontinental ballistic missiles (ICBMs).[28] He argues that MAD did inform actual U.S. strategy and notes that although counterforce was the emphasis during the McNamara period, destroying cities was also seen as a high priority. In addition, a major part of U.S. strategy continued to involve holding cities hostage, either as counter-recovery targets or as a way to destroy Soviet society.

This is a question of nuance. A pure policy of MAD would not have counterforce targeting. The fact that the actual capabilities of a U.S. arsenal built for counterforce purposes also can be consistent with MAD is not necessarily evidence of the desire for targeting cities as part of nuclear strategy. Instead, it is better seen as evidence that the collateral damage (the killing of populations) involved in "surgical" strikes is indeed difficult to limit and that we do in fact live in a MAD world. It is also evidence that a huge nuclear arsenal designed for counterforce purposes can also be used to destroy cities. Here, the distinction between MAD as a policy and MAD as a condition becomes important. The evidence cited by Sagan in support of his view that MAD did inform U.S. targeting policy might be better attributed to the fact that we live in a MAD (again, MAD as a condition rather than as a policy) world. His point is instead best seen as recognition that the destruction of cities would be inevitable, even if not desired, if a nuclear exchange were to take place.

Scholars are not alone in misassessing the announced changes in the late 1970s and early 1980s as a shift from MAD to NUTs. The press misperceived the degree to which there was a revolutionary rather than evolutionary change in U.S. strategic policy. In *Time* magazine, Burton Pines wrote, "the U. S. has relied on what policymakers term 'mutual assured destruction (MAD).'"[29] He goes on to say, "[I]n addition, Soviet military literature has been emphasizing a 'war-fighting' nuclear doctrine—something missing from U.S. strategy." This misperception stems from Pines' belief that McNamara "flirted with the concept of counterforce but abandoned it mainly because it was too costly, given the state of technology in that era."[30] Pines misperceives the shift in U.S. policy because of the mistaken belief that McNamara had abandoned counterforce in actual U.S. war plans. Other popular newsweeklies made similar observations. One wrote that PD-59 represented "a departure from the former strategy of...an all-out attack against major Soviet population centers." Another wrote, " [U]ntil now, the United States has relied on a Strangelovian concept in which it would respond to a 'first strike' with an all-out attack that annihilated major Soviet cities and industrial areas as well as military centers."[31]

Such misperceptions were not limited to the press. Members of Congress have operated under similar delusions. Representative Ron Dellums (D-CA) greeted the change in declaratory policy in 1979 by saying that the targeting of "populations and industrial bases, which has been our historical targeting approach" was a dangerous shift in U. S. policy.[32] Sen. Claiborne Pell (D-RI), of the Senate Foreign Relations Committee, noted during hearings on the Strategic Arms Limitation Talks (SALT II) treaty, "some years back, it was understood that the policy we had in the United States was a policy of mutually assured destruction (MAD)."[33] Sen. Malcolm Wallop (R-WY) wrote that "over the past fifteen years, at least four American Presidents, and their leading defense advisers, have built weapons and cast strategic plans well nigh exclusively for the purpose of inflicting damage upon the enemy's society."[34] These misperceptions are not easily explained by political party or view toward defense. Both hawks (such as Wallop) and doves (such as Pell and Dellums) made this mistake.

Policymakers who should have known better have also misrepresented U.S. nuclear weapons policy. After having been involved in changes that took U.S. nuclear weapons policy away from a posture of MAD, Henry Kissinger, in a September 1979 speech, said, "[I] believe it is necessary that we develop a military purpose for our strategic forces and move away from the senseless and demoralizing strategy of massive civilian extermination."[35] And in as late as 1985, President Reagan told a group of correspondents from *The New York Times* that "[T]he only program we have is MAD—Mutual Assured Destruction. And why don't we have MAS instead—Mutual Assured Security."[36]

Members of the military made such assertions as well. Retired Admiral Thomas Moorer and other retired flag officers condemned the United States for adhering to "the concept of Mutual Assured Destruction (MAD) which has shaped the U.S. policy since the 1960s" and warned against the "adherence to the obviously bankrupt doctrine of Mutual Assured Destruction (MAD)."[37]

Case Studies

This study considers three periods of U.S. nuclear strategy. The first is the period beginning in 1960 and the changes in policy implemented by Secretary of Defense Robert McNamara. The second is the announcement of selective nuclear options by Secretary of Defense James Schlesinger in 1974. The third is the announcement of the countervailing strategy and Presidential Directive 59 by the Carter administration and its implementation in the Reagan administration. In the last chapter, I also will look at later events in order to bring the story up to the beginning of 1993.

I will not focus on the period before 1960 for two reasons. First, historians and political scientists have extensively explored this period. Second, the nature of U.S. nuclear policymaking, including institutional changes within the defense establishment, mark the previous period as an anomaly. U.S. nuclear plans became coordinated within the SIOP in 1960. Before this, the problems that policymakers faced for the coordination of U.S. nuclear policy were different from those after 1960. A brief summary of the three cases follows:

City-Avoidance

The first case study will focus on the changes in U.S. strategic nuclear weapons policy that took place during the Kennedy administration, largely during the tenure of Secretary of Defense Robert McNamara. In 1962, McNamara told U.S. allies at the North Atlantic Treaty Organization (NATO) and then said in a commencement address at the University of Michigan that the United States would avoid targeting cities. The goal was to keep a nuclear war limited and civilian damage to a minimum. McNamara expressed the hope that by moving U.S. targeting policy toward a no-city posture, the Soviet Union would be encouraged to do the same. An abandonment of the nuclear policy of massive retaliation announced by John Foster Dulles in 1954, this shift was in part an attempt to add credibility to U.S. strategic nuclear policy.

The announcement met with much opposition, both at home and abroad. Many interpreted this as indicating that the United States was contemplating fighting a limited nuclear war. Critics complained that the announcement of the no-city doctrine made it sound as if the United States were seeking to gain a disarming first strike capability against the USSR. This did not sit well with the public. As Peter Wagstaff concludes, "[T]he illogical public description of the cities-avoidance theory simply served to conceal the uncomfortable subject of limited strategic war and its ramifications from the public."[38]

McNamara backed away from the rhetoric of city-avoidance in favor of flexible response and MAD. By 1964 the Military posture statement did not refer to city-avoidance. However, despite the public adherence to a policy of MAD, the SIOP contained targeting plans that were consistent with city-avoidance that had been abandoned at the declaratory level. Thus, this case study focuses on a period when the gap between declaratory and action policy was particularly pronounced. It is during this period that the myth of MAD planted firm roots.

Limited Nuclear Options

No major executive branch official saw it as desirable to talk again about limited nuclear options until Secretary of Defense James Schlesinger renewed this debate. In the winter of 1974 he announced that the president needed a more refined set of nuclear options.[39] Schlesinger acknowledged that the United States had previously targeted the USSR's military operations. This acknowledgment came as a surprise to some who had thought that the SIOP had embraced countervalue targeting and MAD as McNamara indicated during this early years as secretary of defense.

There are many reasons for this declaratory shift. Davis writes that while "no single objective lay behind the new doctrine, a remarkably widespread consensus in favor of change developed within the government."[40] This widespread consensus developed around the idea that not only should counterforce targeting be an important part of both the SIOP and declaratory policy but a president should have multiple and flexible options in the event he chooses to use nuclear weapons.

PD-59 and Forward

Though it was the Reagan administration that heard much of the public outcry for its emphasis on counterforce targeting, moves toward this began in 1977. This culminated in the summer of 1980, when President Jimmy Carter signed Presidential Directive 59 (PD-59) which called for the targeting of Soviet military and political assets.[41] In the public explanations of this policy, Secretary of Defense Harold Brown was careful to note that he did not view PD-59 as a radical departure from previous U.S. nuclear policy. Instead, he stressed that it be viewed as a refinement of previous U.S. targeting plans. He wrote in the fiscal year (FY) 1981 report:

> For nearly 20 years, we have explicitly included a range of employ-
> ment options—against military and nonmilitary targets—in our

strategic nuclear employment planning. Indeed, U.S. nuclear forces have always been designated against military targets, as well as those comprising war-supporting industry and recovery resources. In particular, we have always considered it important, in the event of war, to be able to attack the forces that could do damage to the United States and its allies.[42]

Though this renewed emphasis on counterforce targeting began in the Carter administration, it was the Reagan administration that began an all-out effort to procure the weapons systems necessary for such a targeting scheme. Debates over these systems, including the MX missile, were often acrimonious, as Congress and the public were reluctant to go along with the new declaratory policy emphasizing counterforce and limited nuclear options. This period thus provides an excellent case study for the relationship between the three levels of nuclear policy discussed above. It is during this time that the state had the most difficult time keeping U.S. strategic nuclear weapons policy relatively autonomous.

This last case study concludes with a consideration of U.S. nuclear weapons policy during the later 1980s and early 1990s. Here, I will show that though the Cold War was over, the historical pattern of U.S. nuclear weapons policy proved difficult to break.

Methodology and Sources

My methodology is informed by the work that has focused on the use of case studies for developing theory in history and political science.[43] This controlled comparison research strategy will allow the examination of the relationship between the levels of nuclear policy by asking a series of questions of each case. This as an iterative process, informed by both induction and deduction. It is deductive in that it draws from existing theory to frame the cases examined and to posit the initial set of questions that informs the focused methodology. It is inductive in that new questions will be shaped as I investigate the cases. The conclusions drawn will be based on the application of these questions to each case. As such, there is not the clear demarcation between theory testing and theory formation associated with pure scientific approaches.[44] This approach is appropriate because of the lack of theoretical work previously done on the relationship between state and society as regards the formulation of U.S. nuclear weapons policy.

Case studies have yielded rich results for both the testing and the building of theory. However, because of the controversy surrounding this methodology, the case study approach must be conducted systematically to provide for valid inference and analysis. This study addresses these concerns in several ways. First, the selection of cases is not capricious. By looking at three cases that span the years 1960 to 1993, I am looking at the entire universe of cases for the evolution of U.S. nuclear weapons policy. Second, my approach utilizes what George and others have called a "process-tracing" procedure.[45] This approach pays special attention to decision-making procedures where the investigator "assembles bits and pieces of evidence into a pattern."[46] Such an approach does not focus on a specific point of data, but instead looks at an entire set of behaviors that encompass a specific decision-making process.

Finally, the focused nature of the case study process is of crucial importance.[47] This method has the researcher focus only on those aspects of the case that are relevant to the objectives of the study. I do not intend to present a comprehensive picture of the history of U.S. nuclear weapons policy. Instead, I focus on the relationship between the three levels of this policy and state-society relations. Of crucial importance for the structured comparison methodology are well-defined questions used to inform each case study. These questions are asked of each case study and will delimit the amount of information considered for each case. The case studies are not complete and exhaustive accounts of the periods in question, but instead are used to explicate the theory of state behavior that I develop in this study. The questions to be posed of each case study are listed in chapter 3.

The sources used are varied. Many excellent secondary sources focus on the evolution of U.S. nuclear weapons policy, and I utilize many of these to inform my case studies. I use many previously classified documents. Some of these have been obtained through the Freedom of Information Act (FOIA) by other scholars doing research in this field, and some have been obtained through my filing of requests through the FOIA. I have also relied on government documents. Of particular interest for my research has been the annual reports issued by the secretary of defense. In addition, I have relied on the testimony before Congress by Executive Branch officials on the evolution of U.S. nuclear weapons strategy.

Finally, I have conducted more than thirty open-ended interviews with former government officials who had a role in the formation of U.S. nuclear weapons policy. These interviews were all taped and conducted on a not-for-attribution basis, though subjects did agree that they could be quoted anonymously. I did this on a not-for-attribution basis to ensure candor on the part of those interviewed. I interviewed both military and civilian officials, and decision-makers from the Department of Defense, Department of State, the National Security Council, and the Arms Control and Disarmament Agency.

Overall Implications of the Study

This exploration has important consequences for our ideas on the relationship between democracy and the conduct of foreign policy and U.S. nuclear strategic policy. There have been times, particularly in the late 1970s and the early 1980s, when government declaratory policy began to match the war-fighting, limited nuclear options plans contained in the SIOP. Talk of counterforce and limited nuclear options led to the greatest domestic political turmoil concerning the formation of U.S. strategic policy that this nation has ever seen. Such concerns culminated in the movement for a nuclear freeze.

Descriptive and normative criteria are relevant here. For the former, there is no consensus as to whether U.S. nuclear weapons policy has indeed been responsive to public opinion. Bruce Russett has written that "evidence tends to support the hypothesis that in a democracy governments do tend in some sense to respond to the voice of the people."[48] Conversely, Robert Dahl asserts that our system has failed to allow citizens control over nuclear weapons policy. Dahl writes that an elite guardianship has maintained control over nuclear weapons policy. He concludes that nuclear strategic issues "have largely escaped the control of the democratic process."[49]

Nuclear weapons no doubt pose some of the most difficult policy questions that state and society must face. Acknowledging that nuclear weapons may be the most important question to face the populace does not, however offer guidance on the normative questions concerning whether nuclear weapons policy should be democratically controlled. Analysts have taken the extreme importance of this issue as evidence that nuclear weapons policy should be democratically controlled (as Dahl concluded) and, conversely, that society should not influence or control this policy. For those who have very little faith in the wisdom and capabilities of the populace, leaving matters as important as the future of the planet subject to the frivolous opinions of the masses is extremely dangerous. Conversely, others argue that because nuclear weapons confront us with the most important issue of our time, they must be subject to the control of those whose security is ultimately in question. I will return to these questions in the concluding chapter.

2

U.S. Nuclear Weapons Policy and Theory Development: The Dominance of Bureaucratic Politics

This is a study of both American politics and international relations. It looks both inward into the nature of the state and U.S. domestic politics and outward toward external forces that establish the parameters for the former. U.S. nuclear weapons policy must respond to the demands of both the international system and domestic politics. This chapter discusses the way political scientists have written and theorized about the formulation of nuclear weapons policy. I will present, discuss, and critique the bureaucratic politics approach. This is followed by a brief discussion of the process of U.S. nuclear targeting. I will introduce the statist theoretical framework in chapter 3.

An obvious void in security studies has come to the fore in recent years. This absence of systematic theorizing about the evolution of U.S. nuclear weapons policy and its relationship to domestic politics is partially a result of the separation in political science between those who study international relations and those who study American politics. This separation has led to the development of two separate strands of literature. The first, found in the literature of security studies, offers much theorizing on the external aspects of nuclear weapons, including a well-developed theoretical literature on nuclear deterrence.[1] The second strand is a well developed theoretical literature on the sources of power within the domestic political arena. Developed by those who study American politics, this literature has not addressed the evolution of U.S. nuclear weapons policy. This study has the goal of uniting these disparate literatures.

It would be nothing short of folly to say that political scientists have ignored the importance of domestic politics for the study of foreign policy or defense policy. Instead, the point here is that there have not been theoretically grounded explorations of the domestic politics of nuclear weapons policy.[2] Much of the literature within international relations that does focus on domestic political processes deals with economic, not security issues.[3] The study of international relations has never taken seriously the role of domestic politics for the formulation of the high politics of security policy.

Such is especially true for the paradigmatic Realist conception of international relations, the dominant perspective employed by security scholars. This is also true for Neo-Realism. Realism accords theoretical primacy to states as unitary rational actors and thus largely ignores the inner workings of states and domestic politics. To Realists, the state is of primary interest not in reference to its domestic political context or its relationship to society but for its relationship to other states and its position in the international system. The classical Realist perspective attributes state action, particularly the tendency for states to engage in conflict, to human nature. These aspects of human nature are transposed to the international system and are seen as determining the behavior of states externally.

Neo-Realism accords theoretical primacy to the anarchic structure of the international system. Here, too, the actions of states are not determined by domestic politics. The state is of interest not as an actor in the domestic political arena but instead for its role in the international system.

Realism has both descriptive and normative appeal for scholars. The Realist framework is useful for scholars not only in analyzing relations between states but for its normatively appealing description of how security policy is made. This is summarized by the notion that for foreign policy, "politics stops at the water's edge." Hall and Ikenberry write, "[R]ealists generally find the state capable of acting purposively in pursuit of larger economic or geopolitical goals; and they clearly regret those occasions on which the state is not autonomous, believing in particular that this adversely affects the conduct of foreign policy."[4] As Graham Allison and Morton Halperin note, "[W]hat public expectation demands, the academic penchant for intellectual elegance reinforces."[5] The political compromise that is an important part of the democratic process is seen as inappropriate for the development of a consistent and coherent foreign policy. This view is particularly true for nuclear weapons policy. Realism satisfies what many would like to believe about the formulation of foreign policy.

The Bureaucratic Politics Approach

The bureaucratic politics approach presented the Realist paradigm with a serious challenge. Graham Allison and others called into question the idea that a nation's foreign policy is the result of a rational, optimizing decision-making process that resembles the perfect cost-benefit analysis presumed dominant in much economic analysis. Allison and other scholars put forward the idea that a nation's foreign policy is not the result of a unitary state acting with optimal rationality. Instead, policy is the result of the bargaining and negotiation of bureaucracies within the nation's foreign policymaking apparatus. The results of this process are seen as suboptimal. The actors involved in the decision-making process come to it with views determined largely by the role that they play within the government, rather than by the national interest. Implicit within the bureaucratic paradigm is that process is linked to outcome: suboptimal process equals suboptimal outcome. This suboptimal outcome does not reflect the national interest, but is instead a reflection of the political power of various foreign policy bureaucracies.

In *Essence of Decision*, Allison attempts to explain U.S. and Soviet policy in the Cuban missile crisis. Allison rejects the rational actor model, which, consistent with the Realist paradigm, looks to the government as a unitary rational actor. In its place Allison examines two other models of decision-making. Model II, an organizational process model, sees foreign policy decisions "less as deliberate choices and more as *outputs* of large organizations functioning according to standard patterns of behavior."[6] The most important actors in this model are government agencies that act consistent with standard operating procedures in pursuit of certain, predefined goals. Model III, the governmental politics model, makes individuals within the government bureaucracy the main players, and sees decisions largely as the political result of the bargaining and negotiation among these players. According to this model, political maneuvering becomes the most important way for advocates to push policy options within the government bureaucracy.

Later, Allison and Halperin combined and refined models II and III and developed the bureaucratic politics model.[7] In summing up this approach, they wrote:

> Players choose in terms of no consistent set of strategic objectives, but rather according to various conceptions of national security, organizational, domestic and personal interests. Players make governmental decisions not by single rational choice, but by

pulling and hauling. (This by no means implies that individual players are not acting rationally, given their interests.)[8]

Allison and Halperin recognize that organizations are players in the game and that individual perspectives may derive from their membership in organizations. This bureaucratic politics model broadens the original Model III, though with more of a role for organizational mandates than the original form of the model allowed.

Bureaucratic Politics and Weapons Procurement

The bureaucratic approach is the dominant paradigm for studying weapons procurement decisions. Many case studies of the development of specific weapons systems were published after the bureaucratic approach was developed. While these studies vary in their scope and conclusions, they all focus on the role that bureaucracies play in the various stages of weapons development. This focus on procurement illustrates how the bureaucratic perspective has been used to explain force development, the second level of policy of interest to this study.

One of the first such studies investigated the development of the Thor-Jupiter intermediate-range ballistic missiles.[9] Armacost focuses on the bureaucratic bargaining over who would build intermediate range ballistic missiles. He draws an analogy between these "quasi-sovereign" bureaus and agencies and the behavior of nations in the international system. Armacost also draws analogies to the legislative process, equating these bureaus with the pressure groups that function within a pluralist framework. He maintains, "[C]ompared with the formulation of agricultural policy, tax policy, and other domestic legislation, the politics of weapons innovation is evidently closed."[10]

Harvey Sapolsky studied the shift from the *Polaris* to the *Poseidon* submarine, particularly the call for the more accurate B-3 submarine launched ballistic missile (SLBM) on the *Poseidons*. He stresses that the decision to move from the noncontroversial *Polaris* to the more controversial *Poseidon* was an internal bureaucratic decision kept from the public.[11] Though Congress did get involved after the decision was made, Sapolsky maintains that it remained within the confines of the bureaucracy.

In response to the fact that the bureaucratic politics approach was popularized through a case study of a crisis event, Edmund Beard studied the decision to build the ICBM. Beard asks why the ICBM decision extended over a decade.[12] One crucial factor is that the Armed

Forces, particularly the Air Force and the Strategic Air Command (SAC), were reluctant to give up the manned bomber as the primary means to deliver nuclear weapons. Beard, rather than viewing *Essence of Decision* as a crucial case study, maintains that studying a crisis situation actually tilts the balance in favor of a bureaucratic perspective because there is not enough time for policymakers to conduct an optimal decision-making process. According to Beard, the decision to build the ICBM provides the crucial case study because it covers a longer period and thus should have allowed for more rational influences.[13] Critiquing the bureaucratic model, Beard writes:

> If the "bureaucratic politics" model is taken to state that organizations pursue organizational goals and that such pursuit alone determines foreign (or defense or other) policy, then the theory is clear. Unfortunately, it is also incorrect. If the model says, on the other hand, that policies are influenced to a greater or lesser degree by organizational and personal interests, which operate generally within a broad set of shared images or constraints, the theory is probably irrefutable. It is also less clear.[14]

In his story of the more controversial development of multiple independently targetable re-entry vehicles (MIRVs), Ted Greenwood notes that politicians are reluctant to acknowledge that factors other than those based on rational strategic calculations influence weapons procurement decisions. He notes, "[N]o matter how important parochial interests actually are in determining policy, internal and public justifications must be made on the basis of national interest."[15] Greenwood acknowledges that bureaucratic factors are only one of many influences on public policy. He cites the importance of bureaucratic politics (conflict), bureaucratic process, standard operating procedures (SOPs), technology, strategic analysis, and the action/reaction phenomenon for the development of weapons systems.

Finally, Morton Halperin tackles the issue of the anti-ballistic missile (ABM) system, the most controversial weapons development decision of the 1960s or 1970s.[16] Halperin pays particular attention to the role of the president. According to Halperin, though the president is a powerful actor in the nuclear policymaking process, he does not control the process. Halperin also pays a good deal of attention to the role of Congress and the public, noting that President Lyndon Johnson could not afford to ignore domestic politics with the presidential election less than a year away. The speech announcing the decision to build the ABM was seen as odd since McNamara had justified the deployment on the basis of the Chinese nuclear threat, a threat that had not been the primary concern of policymakers. This has been explained as resulting from the balancing of the interests and views of several governmental constituencies that had some interest in deploying an ABM.

In a study that places these weapons procurement studies in a wider context, Lauren Holland notes that the bureaucratic politics approach is particularly useful for explaining the beginning stage of weapons development.[17] She writes, "[T]he resistance that builds during later stages of the procurement process is primarily a product of the broadening of the arena of conflict that occurs as the decision becomes more visible to a wider audience."[18]

This point is also stressed in an analogous critique of the bureaucratic politics model, which claims that the approach, by ignoring the important influence of the public and Congress, is too circumscribed. In an apt analogy, Holland notes that these bureaucratic studies of procurement decisions provide an understanding of the tree, but not of the entire forest. For example, it can be seen from the above studies that it was those developments that were politically salient that involved a wider variety of actors. However, explaining weapons procurement is different from explaining the evolution of U.S. strategic policy. Attention to bureaucracies may help explain the beginning stages of weapons systems development, but it is too narrow to explain the main topic of this study—the evolution of U.S. nuclear weapons policy.[19]

A related approach is illustrated in the social construction approach applied by Donald MacKenzie, who has written a detailed history of the development of missile guidance, and specifically the enhancement of missile accuracy. MacKenzie argues that accuracy did not develop in response to state interests (as I argue) but instead resulted from a combination of organizational and social factors. In fact, he explicitly rejects the type of statist approach that I put forward here.

> I have always had to disaggregate "the state," identify the often conflicting preferences of its different parts such as different armed forces or even subgroups within these services. So the state should not be thought of as unitary.[20]

I will respond to this general sentiment below.

Critiques of Bureaucratic Politics

Critics of the bureaucratic approach have pointed out that Allison's formulations perhaps were neither new nor innovative.[21] Nonetheless, he should be given credit for making the assumptions of the approach explicit. By claiming paradigmatic status for it, Allison not only operationalized the bureaucratic approach but opened it up to extensive exploration and criticism. Earlier bureaucratic approaches were not so widely heralded or attacked because they did not make great claims for their theoretical power. Instead, these were often narrative histories that included bureaucracies as explanatory threads in a complex policy-making process.

The development of the bureaucratic approach has led scholars and policymakers to look to bureaucracies as important sources of influence. The problem with the approach is that many of its adherents and critics pitch it at the level of metatheory, as a paradigm that can explain all foreign policy decision-making, or as the best possible explanation for state decisions. This is unfortunate, because even some of the strongest proponents of the approach recognize that it is best used as just part of an explanatory framework. Morton Halperin, in introducing his influential work on the bureaucratic approach, says many factors explain a government's actions in foreign policy. He writes, "[W]e focus only on one part of this process—that involving the bureaucracy and the President as he deals with the bureaucracy."[22]

Art notes that while the first generation of bureaucratic theorists considered the role of the public in the formulation of policy, the second wave theorists (Allison et al.) did not have enough of a role for these forces. Caldwell, in criticizing this omission, notes, "[E]ven in the Cuban missile crisis itself, domestic political considerations played a role. Perhaps overstating the potential consequences, President Kennedy told his brother during the crisis that if he did not act decisively, he would be impeached."[23]

Policymakers desire the scope of conflict to remain as narrow as possible. This is particularly true for bureaucrats who desire to do their work and make policy within the narrow confines of bureaucracies. To broaden the scope, to have more actors involved in the process, is to lose bureaucratic power.

As Francis Rourke writes:

The amount of power that bureaucratic organizations actually exert over foreign policy decisions depends not only upon their own resources for extending their influence, but also upon the passivity of other participants in the policy process. When public opinion is aroused, as in the case of Vietnam, the authority of bureaucracy diminishes.[24]

Stephen Krasner stresses these concerns in his critique of the bureaucratic approach.[25] Krasner is troubled by the notion that a permanent government (bureaucracy) maintains control over the formulation of foreign policy. He criticizes the bureaucratic model by asserting that the notion that "the Chief Executive is trammeled by the permanent government has disturbing implications for any effort to impute responsibility to public officials."[26] The bureaucratic approach concludes that elected decision-makers have lost control over the policymaking process. This criticism is echoed in many of the works that critique the bureaucratic approach by saying that the approach does not attribute enough power to the President and other central decision-makers.

Desmond Ball wrote that many of the adherents of the bureaucratic approach pushed the model to explain the faults of their own governmental experience:

> This suggests a general point about the bureaucratic politics theorists. Allison's and Halperin's colleagues are a reasonably identifiable group. Many of them enjoyed power at the sub-Cabinet level during the 1960s, principally during the Kennedy Administration; they were academic theorizers about policy and power before they entered the Administration, and they were profoundly disillusioned with their governmental experiences: for this they blame the bureaucracy.[27]

He goes on to note that the idea of political responsibility is missing from the bureaucratic literature.

Application of the Bureaucratic Approach to U.S. Nuclear Strategy

Applications of this approach to specific foreign policy decisions have been numerous; the weapons procurement decisions discussed above are one example. Because I will be exploring the evolution of the various levels of U.S. nuclear weapons policy, we must investigate the relationship between U.S. strategy and weapons development. In the ideal model of foreign policy decision-making, one that posits rational decision-making, a strategy would be decided upon and then the appropriate weapons would be procured to fulfill that strategy. According to such a model, the weapons procured would fit the overall strategy. However, developments have not always been consistent with the ideal type.

While these theorists have important things to say, they fail to recognize that U.S. nuclear weapons policy is multidimensional. Certain weapons systems that may not make sense for a MAD declaratory policy may make sense for a NUTs action policy. Put another way, the lack of congruence between the characteristics of the weapons procured and declaratory policy may be due not to the suboptimal outcomes associated with bureaucratic politics but instead to the fact that the weapons did make sense when seen in terms of U.S. action policy.

The predominance of these bureaucratic explanations for the disjunction between action and declaratory policy is to be expected and is easily explained. Scholars in the 1960s and 1970s offered bureaucratic explanations for the suboptimal outcomes that have often been associated with the development of nuclear weapons systems. As Desmond Ball notes:

Studies of the major U.S. force development decisions of the 1950s through the 1970s—the decisions to develop the ICBM, the decisions to deploy a long-range strategic ballistic force of 1,000 Minuteman ICBMs and 656 SLBMs, and the decision to develop the MIRV—all indicate the outcomes were, more than anything else, the product of intramural bargaining, negotiation, and compromise between these quasi sovereignties, with the quality of the arguments and the strategic analysis being decidedly secondary to the political power of the respective adversaries.[28]

Though it is most often applied to the development of weapons systems or specific discrete decisions, rather than the evolution of a broad policy area such as the evolution of U.S. nuclear weapons policy, this disjunction has been explained by those who relied almost solely on the bureaucratic approach.

Analysts who use the bureaucratic approach for explaining the disjunction between declaratory and action policy posit that the president is unable to coordinate policy between the declaratory and action (implementation) stages. Some of these explanations maintain that the disjunction exists because the military thinks in traditional military terms and thus targets counterforce, or traditional military targets.[29] Conversely, civilians such as the president and his close defense policy advisors think in terms of deterrence, and call for threats of destruction rather than counterforce targeting. Here there is an assertion of a lack of civilian control. Arkin and Pringle note, "in retrospect, the lack of presidential knowledge about or control over nuclear war planning at the operational level is stunning. The executive branch had no clear idea of where America's nuclear policy, or lack of it, was leading."[30] As another commentator has written, "Omaha [the location of the SAC] is a long way from Washington."[31] David Rosenberg explains:

> Each of the four levels of strategic planning can head in a direction different from the others, as each responds not just to guidance from levels above, but to separate organizational needs and restraints. These bureaucratic strictures help account for contradictions and divergences that emerge between the president's stated policy, the Defense Department's force posture, the plans of the Joint Chiefs of Staff, and the final implementation of plans by the Joint Strategic Planning Staff and the Military commands.[32]

Desmond Ball echoes this point: "[C]omplete rationality and coherence is too much to expect in any area of public policy, let alone one as complex and involving such large, powerful and disparate bureaucratic entities as U.S. national security policy."[33] Ball and like-minded analysts correctly assert that the coordination of these various levels of policy is difficult and that the disparate and powerful bureaucracies that make up the U.S. national security establishment make coordination difficult. However, it is not that difficult for the public pronouncements of the president and secretary of defense to embrace the war plans that make up U.S. strategic nuclear targeting. If policymakers saw it as within their interests to do so, declaratory policy could describe actual U.S. war plans. The explanation that this policy area is too complex is insufficient to explain the disjunction between the three levels of nuclear policy.

Scott Sagan offers an explanation somewhere between the conclusions espoused by the bureaucratic school and the idea that the disjunction was in fact allowed to exist.[34] A true bureaucratic explanation posits that the lack of coordination between the various levels of policy is not intentional, but instead represents a suboptimal outcome that policymakers prefer to avoid. Sagan concludes that the persistence of counterforce targeting in U.S. action policy was not driven by the parochial interests of the U.S. military, and thus the disjunction was not of bureaucratic origin. Contrary to some of the authors discussed above who note that civilian authorities did not pay significant attention to the targeting that was being done by the military, Sagan believes that "civilian authorities have approved of the basic targeting doctrine."[35] My research strongly confirms this. Furthermore, Sagan maintains that civilian control over such policy has been increasing in the last decade or so. My research confirms this as well.

Sagan also implies that civilian authorities did not have total control over such policy. He reaches this conclusion because the targeting had unintended consequences. Sagan's evidence shows that the unintended consequences result not from a lack of control by central decision makers but instead from the inherent difficulties in formulating limited nuclear war-fighting strategies. These unintended consequences follow from the fundamental essence of the nuclear age. For example, Sagan notes that McNamara was shocked by the indistinguishability of counterforce strikes and countervalue strikes. While this may in part be due to the overzealousness of the military, it is more the result of the fact that in the 1960s the technological characteristics of nuclear weapons did not allow for the kind of limited and precision war-fighting that McNamara sought. This does not however mean, as Sagan implies, that the military did not cooperate or that civilians lacked control. Thus, Sagan may be correct that "[A]merican political authorities made their own nuclear doctrine, but...they did not make it just as they desired."[36] However, it draws from the inherent nature of nuclear weapons, not the inability of central decision-makers to control the military and nuclear targeting.[37] It is to the process of targeting that we now turn.

U.S. Nuclear Weapons Targeting

There is no agreement in the literature on how civilian inputs are translated into targeting doctrine. This is partly because the targeting process is classified. Some claim that targeting is based on the capabilities of the existing force structure. According to this view, targeters are presented with the forces that they have to work with and then target opposition forces according to civilian guidance.[38] Others say that targeters put so many targets on the list that they then propel the force structure to expand because of the increased need for target coverage.[39] According to this scenario, the number of targets that need to be covered has always been greater than the force structure can actually cover. This then creates pressure for the force structure to grow. Evidence I have gathered shows that the process is more consistent with the former.

The bureaucratic ruminations surrounding the formulation of U.S. nuclear weapons policy are shrouded in acronyms and numbers and incomprehensible titles. The complex web of government bureaucracies that deal with the formulation of U.S. nuclear weapons policy comprises parts of the State Department, the Department of Defense, and the military bureaucracy, including the Joint Chiefs of Staff and its Joint

Strategic Target Planning Staff. Congressional activity also must be included in the overall picture.

The formulation of targeting policy has followed a standard pattern, a pattern that I divide into three phases.[40] Phase 1 takes place largely within the executive branch, centered in the White House and the Department of Defense. Civilians, with varying degrees of help from the military, occasionally conduct studies that culminate in a presidential decision. This decision is then translated into general guidance for the military. This leads to phase 2, in which the JSTPS translates this broad guidance from civilian leadership into actual targeting plans. This culminates in the creation of the SIOP. The degree to which civilians have overseen the implementation of their guidance has varied, though civilian oversight of this process has increased over time. This will be traced in the case studies that follow.

Though Congress does not have an explicit role in the formulation of action policy, it becomes an integral actor in phase 3 when appropriations for weapons have to be approved. It is here that the state must confront what U.S. nuclear weapons policy is and what types of weapons are needed for that policy. The details of the phases of policy are as follows:

Phase 1—Civilian Activity

At times during the evolution of U.S. nuclear weapons policy, civilians have created plans to reshape U.S. nuclear weapons targeting. The secretary of defense, or sometimes forces more directly related to the president such as the national security adviser, initiates a study that examines past U.S. nuclear weapons plans and what types of changes might be desirable. This can involve guidance on both targeting and procurement.

Though the process has remained largely the same, the names of the mechanisms have changed as various administrations have stamped their own imprimatur on internal policy reviews and decisions. The first activities are studies and presidential decisions. The results of these executive branch studies had no specific name during the Kennedy administration, but were routinely issued as National Security Study Memorandums (NSSM). These were referred to as Presidential Review Memorandums (PRM) during the Carter administration and National Security Study Directives (NSSD) during the Reagan administration. The decision documents (that result from the study process) were referred to as National Security Action Memorandum's (NSAMs) during the Kennedy and Johnson administrations, National Security Decision Memorandums (NSDMs) during the Nixon and Ford administrations,

Presidential Directives (PDs) during the Carter administration and National Security Decision Directives (NSDDs) during the Reagan administration. Though the process itself usually followed the pattern that studies would be codified by decisions, sometimes the studies led to other studies.

After a decision memorandum has been formulated it is passed to the secretary of defense, who issues a Nuclear Weapons Employment Policy (NUWEP). The NUWEP translates the presidential guidance into a statement on how nuclear weapons should actually be used in the case of war.[41] The NUWEP is transmitted to the Joint Chiefs of Staff where phase 2 of the process begins. Ideally, this presidential decision is also translated into broad Defense Guidance, a statement on which weapons should be procured and maintained. Military input on this guidance is also achieved through Annex C of the Joint Strategic Capabilities Plan prepared by the JCS.

To put this process in the language used in this study, the NUWEP serves as the link between broad civilian guidance on action policy to the Joint Staff elaboration of this action policy. The Defense Guidance represents force development policy. Changes in declaratory policy result from the culmination of these periods of study and reflect presidential decisions at the highest level. Whether these actually change action policy is a difficult question. The relationship of these to force development policy is also a little more difficult to understand, though changes in declaratory and action policy often change the type of weapons needed.[42]

Phase 2—On to Omaha

After the studies and the guidance are decided upon and a NUWEP is issued, civilian inputs are translated into actual target lists and war plans. This takes place at Offutt Air Force Base in Omaha, Nebraska, where the Joint Staff develops detailed guidance from the NUWEP. Though the JSTPS is theoretically "a single, multiservice nuclear war planning agency," SAC has dominated the organization.[43] The director of strategic target planning (DSTP) has always been the commander in chief of SAC (CINCSAC). As a balance to this, the deputy director has traditionally been from the Navy. The JSTPS does not have its own weapons; instead, the JSTPS coordinates nuclear forces under the command of branch commanders.

When first created by Secretary of Defense Robert Gates in August 1960, the JSTPS was to formulate U.S. nuclear weapons targeting policy with the input of all of the armed forces and NATO.[44] The task was clearly difficult enough in 1960; it has multiplied in complexity ever since for three reasons. First, the number of targets that had to be covered in the Soviet Union and the Eastern bloc multiplied, because of both an increase in important targets and improvements in intelligence. Second, the increase in the number of warheads in the U.S. nuclear arsenal has also complicated the task. Finally, civilian demands for an increasing number of limited nuclear options have made the task of nuclear planning more difficult. The JSTPS staff grew from two hundred to over six hundred in the early 1980s. As Colonel Richard Lee Walker writes:

> Over the years since JSTPS was established, both the target system and the weapon arsenal have increased in number. These increases translate into an exponential increase in the potential calculations required. As increased flexibility is introduced, the burden increases in at least linear fashion. An attack option significantly different from existing options could add a new dimension contributing to the exponential growth of the necessary calculations.[45]

The JSTPS is split into two parts, the National Strategic Target List (NSTL) division and the SIOP division. The different tasks of these divisions are summarized by O'Malley, as follows: "the NSTL division analyzes overall weapons against overall targets in the allocation process, and the SIOP division is concerned with each delivery vehicle during force application."[46] While the NSTL division is concerned with target coverage and the capabilities of U.S. weapons to accomplish that coverage, the SIOP division is concerned with the actual feasibility of certain options and missions, and deals with issues such as Designated Ground Zeros. The NSTL contains all data on possible targets for U.S. nuclear forces. Overall, the NSTL division provides computer support, analysis and evaluation, intelligence estimates, and information on targeting, while the SIOP division is concerned with combat plans, tactics, reconnaissance, and SIOP analysis.

The NSTL division issues a National Strategic Target List, a National Strategic Target Data Base, and a National Strategic Designated Ground Zero list. The SIOP division makes contributions to this concerning timing, tactics, force posture, and a Coordinated Reconnaissance Plan (CRP). These two divisions combine their contributions into the SIOP.[47] The JCS also issues a Joint Strategic Capabilities Plan (JSCP), which instructs commanders and the JSTPS on how to match forces to targets. Annex C, which is part of the JSCP, contains detailed instructions on how to do this.[48] Though periods when civilians have sought to change the U.S. SIOP are of particular interest for my work here, continuous efforts are made to update the SIOP and keep it current. Every six months the SIOP is revised based on these types of changes.[49]

The difficulties of translating ambiguous civilian guidance into targeting plans cannot be underestimated. The military has sometimes deemed civilian guidance impossible to follow, and civilians have sometimes appeared shocked by the results of their guidance. Walker has proposed improvements in this process so that the gap between guidance and actual targeting can be reduced. One of his suggestions is for civilian authorities to become more familiar with the JSTPS process and the limitations that are involved in the targeting of nuclear weapons.[50]

Phase 3—The Role of Congress

Congress plays an important role as part of the national security state, though the degree to which it has influenced U.S. nuclear weapons policy has varied over the years. Congress's role in the formulation of U.S. nuclear weapons policy increases as we move to the latter case studies. Though Congress does not have a direct role in the process of U.S. nuclear targeting, it can have an indirect impact in the long run by affecting force development policy. Since action policy is really a capabilities plan (because only currently procured weapons can be allocated to targets) the amount of weapons available to targeters can be influenced by Congress.

Congressional involvement in U.S. security policy takes place primarily in the House and Senate Armed Services Committees and the defense subcommittees of both chambers' Appropriations Committees.[51] And though Congress has no veto per se over U.S. declaratory policy, through its power of the purse it debates declaratory policy. In considering funding for new capabilities and weapons systems, Congress can inquire as to what is guiding the acquisition of certain weapons and why certain capabilities are necessary given current doctrine.

The Senate Foreign Relations Committee has at times summoned members of the executive branch to testify about nuclear weapons policy. Finally, as will be seen in the latter two case studies, as the state loses more of its autonomy, the floor of both the House and the Senate become a place where the state itself debates policy. These are times when societal forces exert influence. These debates on the floor of both chambers have come over the controversial deployments of specific counterforce weapons systems.

Conclusions

Bureaucratic approaches leave very little role for society—they also leave very little room for the influence of Congress. The view that Congress and the public have little influence over foreign policy and defense policy may have normative appeal, but should not hinder a realistic assessment of the nuclear policymaking process.

Bureaucratic approaches have been useful for explaining some parts of nuclear weapons policymaking, particularly for the development of specific weapons systems, and particularly for the beginning stages of these projects. The bureaucratic approach can be of some utility in looking at the formation of all these levels of nuclear policy that are of concern here. However, this is not the same as saying that the bureaucratic approach is most useful for describing the relationship between these various levels of policy. They present interesting glimpses of part of the picture. Thus, in the next chapter I develop the statist paradigm, which provides a more useful model for explaining U.S. nuclear weapons policy.

3

The State and U.S. Nuclear Weapons Policy

When the state comes up in current social scientific discourse, non-Marxists, at least, are usually referring to it in this sense: as an actor whose independent efforts may need to be taken more seriously than heretofore in accounting for policy making and social change.[1]

This chapter summarizes the statist approach that informs the case studies to follow, reviewing the statist literature, defining central concepts and terms, and then indicating the utility of the statist approach for understanding the evolution of U.S. nuclear weapons policy. It is the argument of this chapter that statist theory enables us to understand the relationship between the three levels of nuclear policy better than the bureaucratic approach outlined in chapter 2.

The importance of the state-society relationship has been of interest to those who have examined the development of the state's ability to wage war. Here the relationship between the state and society has been investigated along two important lines of inquiry. First is the state's ability to extract resources from society to build the instruments of war. Second has been the ability of the state to call upon those from society to fight wars.

The creation of nuclear weapons changed both. First, nuclear weapons are inexpensive, at least relative to the amount of spending that would be necessary to gain a comparable amount of firepower through conventional means. Such concerns were pivotal during the 1950s, when the United States cut its defense budget but expanded its nuclear arsenal. And calls during the 1970s for the United States to rely less heavily on nuclear weapons for the defense of Europe often met with domestic opposition because such a shift could have lead to increases in defense spending. The advent of nuclear weapons has, in terms of monetary extraction, decreased the links between society and the state for the acquisition of war-making capabilities.

The same general conclusion can be drawn as we think about the issue of conscription. The advent of nuclear weapons has allowed the United States to extend its global reach without having to draft or hire large numbers of men and women for the armed forces, which would have been needed without nuclear weapons. Thus nuclear weapons have allowed the United States to protect distant lands without getting the approval of society in the form of participation in the armed forces.

Nuclear weapons policy poses special problems for maintaining the link between state and society. Perhaps the link is found in the state's use of society as a hostage. In this sense, society is linked to this policy area as never before. From such a perspective, all of society is recruited and called upon for the conduct of U.S. nuclear weapons policy. However, the nature of the link between state and society explored here is more direct, focusing on the reaction that society has to the nuclear weapons policy pursued by the state. In addition, changes in this policy—or "improvements"—sometimes require the type of financial commitment that makes the extraction issue relevant. It is to these issues that we now turn.

Explaining the State

The dominant modes of explanation within political science look to society as the ultimate source of public policy. Pluralists focus on the actions of groups within society. Marxists emphasize class. For the latter, the capitalist class holds a privileged position in seeing its policy desires adopted by the state. Conversely, at the root of the statist tradition is the idea that states are not merely the recipients of policy impulses but can initiate as well. Though some pluralists acknowledge that the state is an important actor that at times initiates policy, the debate between statists and pluralists is one of emphasis.[2] However, to classify this debate as one of emphasis is not to denigrate its pivotal importance. The statist paradigm incontrovertibly allows for a wider degree of initiation by the state than does the pluralist paradigm.

The last decade or two has seen a resurgence of interest within both political science and sociology in the statist paradigm. This paradigm posits that social scientists should pay more attention to the state as an important force in policymaking. Such approaches usually assume that the state can act autonomously from society in the formulation of public policy. Statists do not look to society as the ultimate arbiter of public policy, as do pluralists and Marxists. While there is debate among proponents and critics of this paradigm about what it is that makes up the state and what differentiates the state from society (these questions are explored later in this chapter), one of the keys to understanding the statist approach is the notion of constraint and autonomy. The statist paradigm contends that the state is not necessarily constrained by domestic political actors (be they individuals, organizations, groups, or classes) but instead can act autonomously upon its preferences. Statists do not seek to determine the impact that society has on government, but instead how the state can affect society to pursue its own goals.

Most statists are concerned with foreign economic policy.[3] This is partially in reaction to the historical tradition of analyses of trade and foreign economic policy that attributes the actions of the federal government to either the push and pull of pluralist politics or the dominance of the capitalist class. The statist paradigm has not been applied to the study of national security because it has been assumed that the state enjoys autonomy from society in this issue area. Many who have written on the utility of the statist approach have ruled out its application for the study of national security. For example, Eric Nordlinger notes:

> On these issues [national security], not only is there a distinct tendency to defer to state preference, in addition, the secrecy surrounding intended state actions, the relative absence of information sources other than the state itself, and the often times great gap between authoritative actions and consequences constitute advantageous contextual conditions that extend the applicability and heighten the effectiveness of the state's options to reinforcing societal deference.[4]

Similarly, Stephen Krasner asserts, "[A] state that is weak in relation to its own society can act effectively in the strategic arena because its preferences are not likely to diverge from those of individual societal groups."[5] Nettl wrote over two decades ago, " [W]hatever the state may or may not be internally...there have in the past been few challenges to both its sovereignty and its autonomy in 'foreign affairs.'"[6] David Lake states:

> [T]hat the foreign policy executive is an important actor in the national security issue-area is readily accepted by most international relations scholars. Foreign policy decision-makers, after all, make war, develop strategic nuclear doctrine, conduct

diplomacy, and handle crises with little input from society. On these issues, the rational actors and bureaucratic politics models appear as valid simplifications of reality.[7]

Finally, Evangelista writes, "[E]ven proponents of domestic structural approaches who seek to demonstrate the relative autonomy of the state...do not view security policy as germane to their concerns."[8]

The assertion that the state is autonomous from society in the formulation of national security policy is not a very controversial claim within the academic orthodoxy in international relations—such is the rough approximation of the Realist paradigm. Sometimes this is implicit, other times explicit. Domestic politics and the influence of societal groups have not been deemed crucial for the high politics of nuclear weapons policy. As a result, some might claim that the application of the statist paradigm to the study of national security does not cover new ground. Instead, it in some ways resurrects the Realist paradigm and applies it to foreign policy decision-making.

However, the statist paradigm is different from the Realist paradigm. It leads to a different type of exploration, with a different research methodology and different questions guiding the analysis. Realists focus on the state as an actor in the international system; statists focus on the state as an actor in the domestic political arena. However, while the Realist paradigm simply assumes state autonomy, those associated with statism pay particular attention to the state structures and capabilities that allow for or hamper autonomy. The assumption of state autonomy has precluded an investigation of this area. In this sense, statism seeks to investigate Realist assumptions and measure their validity.

My application of the statist paradigm posits that the state must act in both the domestic and international settings, and that its actions in these two arenas are related.[9] The relative position of the state within the international system can affect the degree to which domestic political variables become important. The power of the state in the international arena may be closely related to the power of the state in the domestic political context.

My goal is to apply these notions of state autonomy, to see how the state attempts to achieve autonomy in the national security policy area, and to verify whether the state does enjoy the degree of autonomy that is posited by national security scholars. That I am testing this assumption is evidence that I suspect that it may not be correct. My hypothesis is that the state is not autonomous from society in the formulation of U.S. nuclear weapons policy, and has gradually been losing its autonomy.

The Statist Paradigm: What (Who) Is the State?

What is the state? I accept Nordlinger's definition of the state as "all public officials—elected and appointed, at high and low levels, at the center and at the peripheries—who are involved in the making of public policy."[10] The answer to this question is a source of contention among both proponents and critics of the statist approach. For critics of statist approaches, this definitional muddle serves to invalidate the approach. The literature yields a variety of ways to define the statist approach. I classify these to clarify my approach.

Benjamin and Duvall argue that statists have viewed the state in five different ways.[11] The first, the narrowest conception, looks to the state as a unit of action, consistent with the assumptions made by behaviorists. They note that this is probably the most concrete way to view the state. The second conception is concerned with structure. Rather than looking at the state as composed of various separate institutions and individuals, this view looks to the structuring principles of the state as a whole. From this perspective the state is viewed with a sense of abstract coherence. The third way of viewing the state is also concerned with structural principles, but emphasizes the social relations of political power and control in society. A neo-Marxist formulation, this view looks at the state as an entire ruling class. The fourth way the state is viewed in the literature is broader still and views it as an entire legal-institutional order. The fifth view of the state is as the dominant normative order in society.[12] Benjamin and Duvall favor the second and fourth conceptions of the state for their conceptual and empirical utility. Though the authors provide some useful conceptual distinctions about the nature of the state, they do not clearly define the state in empirical terms. This may be because the authors are not using the concept in any specific research design but instead seek to make conceptual distinctions.

The difference between the first and second conceptions of the state is of most interest for this study. It illustrates the conflict between bureaucratic and statist approaches. I will use the second conception, though it is crucial that we more clearly differentiate this from Benjamin and Duvall's first conception of the state. As Krasner also notes in a review article on various conceptions of the state, the first conception is consistent with pluralist approaches.[13]

Furthermore, it is also consistent with the bureaucratic approach outlined in chapter 2. This is because it looks at the state as made up of several different units acting on their own. This is analogous to the atomized view of the state that is central to the bureaucratic approach.

Differentiating these first and second views of the state, Krasner recognizes that Robert Dahl (and pluralists in general) have used the first approach. He comments "[T]he most critical difference is that Dahl views the state as a collection of individuals occupying particular roles, not as an administrative apparatus or legal order."[14] Thus, though some pluralists might see the state as able to initiate policy, the statist approach is different because it views the state as a structure rather than as actors fulfilling different roles.

The Importance of State Structure

While the authors cited above focus on definitions of the state, others spend more time focusing on other conceptual issues of equal importance.[15] The notion of state structure (often called domestic structure) is crucial for an understanding of how statists view the state-society relationship. Ikenberry offers a useful typology of different forms of state structure.[16] The narrowest definition of structure considers administrative, legislative, and regulatory rules. A broader conception of structure deals with the degree of centralization or diffusion of power within the state. Among other things, this level deals with the balance of power between Congress and the executive. Finally, the broadest conception of state structure deals with boundaries between state and society. My work will focus on the middle and broadest level.

Questions of state structure raise important empirical questions. I will explore the nature of the defense policymaking institutions to identify the structural components that either enhance or diminish the opportunities for the state to fashion strategic nuclear weapons policy without interference from society. It is state structure that can determine how much interference or resistance the state gets from society in formulating policy. This is accomplished by allowing for more or fewer access points through which society can have an influence over policy. Also, we want to consider how the state attempts to limit these access points.

The idea of structure also leads statist research in another direction. The institutional structure of the state can determine the efficacy of the state's actions. As Ikenberry notes, "[O]rganizational structures influence the types of policies likely to be generated and successfully implemented by influencing the access groups and individuals have to policy making and the resources they are able to wield."[17] Thus, we should not view state structure as merely determinant of which inputs the state receives. State outputs shape societal interests and in turn their ability to influence the state. The nature of the structure of the state can thus affect how groups seek to influence it.

Structural questions have been seen as important by authors who look to state building and the evolution of institutional development in the United States.[18] The development of institutional structures to handle new issues that confront society is an important phenomenon. Following such developments for U.S. nuclear weapons policy adds insights into how the state attempts to deal with new issues and how society can influence policymaking for these issues. I follow these developments as we watch the U.S. state develop institutional mechanisms to deal with issues such as strategy, doctrine, weapons deployment and the coordination of targeting.

State Capacity and Autonomy

Two other concepts are crucial for this discussion. The first is the concept of state capacity and the second state autonomy. The concept of capacity is usually used to indicate the strength of the state. This strength is the ability of the state to act autonomously vis-à-vis society. Addressing the issue of state autonomy, Skocpol writes that the state "may formulate and pursue goals that are not simply reflective of the demands or interests of social groups, classes or society."[19] Similarly, Krasner also focuses on the state's ability to overcome domestic resistance as the primary measure of state autonomy. While these definitions by Skocpol and Krasner describe what is meant by state autonomy, Nordlinger notes that the state may be autonomous even if it is implementing policy without the opposition of societal forces. In these cases, societal interests may be coincidental with the state or may simply not exist. In such cases, it is important to explore why such views do not exist or why they are coincidental with state interests. It may in fact be that the actions of the state have led to the existence of one or both conditions. These concerns are particularly relevant for this study.

The determinants of state autonomy are both the capacity and structure of the state. Though some definitions of state capacity conflate state autonomy with state capacity, state capacity can foster state autonomy or inhibit and prevent it. This is determined by state structure. While capacity can facilitate autonomy, it also can limit it. The two concepts are not the same. For example, a state structure that allows for many access points on a particular issue will probably not have a large degree of autonomy. The relationship among these concepts should be viewed in this way:

STATE STRUCTURE→STATE CAPACITY→LEVEL OF STATE AUTONOMY

The structure of the state determines state capacity, which in turn determines state autonomy.

Such conceptualizations of the state are closely linked to the notions of strong state and weak state that are important concepts in both pluralist and statist approaches to foreign economic policy. The pluralist conception is that the United States is a weak state, particularly regarding foreign economic policy. Such a view has evolved from the perception that important trade bills were the result of compromise and the pressure of domestic interest groups. The state is seen as weak because it remains permeable at several levels. For such studies, the point of access for the state has most often been Congress. Such views classifying the United States as a weak state would, to use the language presented above, assert a low level of state capacity and thus a very low degree of autonomy. The prevailing wisdom has been that although the United States is a weak state in most policy areas, it is a strong state for the formulation of foreign policy, particularly defense policy. In nuclear weapons policy, state capacity and state autonomy are assumed to be high.

One of the problems with the strong state/weak state distinction is that it is viewed as a constant rather than as a variable. When state strength is treated as a constant, the United States is always seen as weak relative to certain issue areas. This is an inaccurate view of the nature of state strength. State strength should be seen as variable, the degree of strength varying according to temporal and issue area considerations. The degree of strength or weakness of the state depends, in part, on developments related to the structure and capacity of the state. This allows us to look at the evolution of state structures to trace the relationship between structure, capacity and autonomy over time.

We can look at the power of the state and judge it according to three criteria.[20] The first, and perhaps easiest, task for the state is to resist societal pressure. Here, in one way or another, the state can insulate itself from societal pressures. Second, and more difficult, is to change the behavior of private interests. Here, a strong state can shape private interests. Finally, a very strong state can actually change the social structure and change the makeup of society. Such a change might mean that the state is so powerful that groups that at one time pressured the government no longer exist, or are significantly weakened so that they no longer represent a force the state needs to respond to.

Though Ikenberry, Skocpol, and Krasner pay varying degrees of attention to structure and its relationship to state autonomy, Nordlinger explicitly rejects this structural approach to state autonomy.[21] He argues that the state is made up of individuals; individuals act but structures do not. Nordlinger's view of the state is more consistent with a pluralist or even a bureaucratic perspective because it offers an atomistic view of the state. It does not accept the notion of the state as a structure. Since it is difficult to speak of a structure acting, an in-depth investigation of this conceptual quagmire would demand that we delve into the nature of the agent-structure problem that has plagued the social sciences. Such an investigation is clearly beyond the scope of this study. Suffice it to say that individuals within bureaucracies are the fundamental units of action for the state. Nevertheless, this does not mean that we cannot talk about the state and operationalize its views and actions.

Congress and the State

One of the most contentious issues for the statist approach is the place of the legislature in definitions of the state. Is Congress best viewed as part of the state or part of society? Statists disagree on this score. Krasner defines the state as the president and central executive branch actors; most important in his case the State Department. This definition of the state excludes Congress. I differ with Krasner on this point. Krasner has stacked the deck in favor of his own statist interpretation, which posits that the state acts with relative autonomy in the area of raw materials investment policy. By not including Congress in the state, the state appears more autonomous than it probably really is, because the legislature, at least within the U.S. state, serves as the entry point of society. It is the least autonomous part of the state.

Actors on Capitol Hill are powerful elected officials. Of course, some legislators are more powerful than others, but this is also true of the executive branch. Instead of placing Congress outside the state, I place it in the state but as an entrance point for society. If we were to picture the various components of the state on a continuum, the figure below indicates the nature of the state for the issue of U. S. nuclear weapons policy.

The State   Society

←——→

Department of Defense   Congress
Military Bureaucracy
   President
National Security Council

For U.S. nuclear weapons policymaking the state includes the president, the National Security Council, the Joint Chiefs of Staff, the Department of Defense, and Congress. These actors are important in the development of U.S. nuclear weapons policy. Although analysts could define the state similarly across issue areas, the structural components of the state might be different. That is, if we define the state as the primary authoritative actors responsible for public policy, these actors are different for different policy areas. With this conceptualization, the definition remains the same but the institutional components of the state change, depending on the issue area under consideration.

Others echo this approach. Regarding U.S. trade policy, David Lake writes that

the state can be usefully disaggregated into two principal components. The representative elements of the state include the legislature, which serves as the principal link of the state to society, and the constituent agencies, such as the Departments of Agriculture, Commerce and Labor in the United States....[T]he foreign policy executive constitutes a second component of the state.[22]

This conception recognizes that some parts of the state are more autonomous from society than are other parts. Congress is the least autonomous part of the state and as such serves as a gatekeeper between state and society. Nonetheless, it must be seen as part of the state.

Congress and Defense Policy

Congress was relatively inattentive to foreign policy until the early 1970s. This congressional resurgence resulted from dissatisfaction with its role in the Vietnam War. The bipartisan foreign policy consensus that emerged at the end of World War II was the result of both U.S. preeminence in the international system and an inattentive Congress. And these two factors are closely related. Rarely did Congress question major foreign policy initiatives undertaken by the executive branch, and even more rarely did Congress initiate policy.

Explanations for this reassertion focus on the breakdown of the post–World War II domestic political consensus on foreign policy. There were also changes in congressional capabilities that facilitated the growth of congressional involvement. Perhaps the most important change was the Congressional Budget and Impoundment Act of 1974. This act created the House and Senate Budget Committees, which enabled Congress to establish its own expenditure and revenue levels for all policy areas, including defense.

Important staffing changes enabled Congress to have a more significant role in defense policy. The first was an increase in congressional and committee staff, which has given Congress the resources to challenge the Pentagon and the executive branch. Technical support for this increased role has come from the Office of Technology Assessment (OTA), established in 1972 as a source of scientific expertise for Congress. In addition, the General Accounting Office (GAO) was given expanded power in 1970 and 1974 as congressional watchdog. For example, the GAO issued reports showing that by 1974 the cost of major weapons systems has exceeded estimates by 23 percent.[23] The Congressional Budget Office (CBO) provided Congress with important budget review capabilities. The Congressional Research Service (CRS) has served as an important resource as well.

At the same time that Congress became a more active participant in this policy area, public interest groups concerned with national security grew and became more active. Internally, Congress organized Members of Congress for Peace through Law, and externally, the Arms Control Association, Council for a Livable World, and the Center for Defense Information began to work with Congress on nuclear arms issues.

There is disagreement over whether the United States can pursue a coherent and effective foreign policy when Congress challenges executive branch dominance. Those who oppose congressional involvement assert that foreign policy should be pursued with one coherent voice from the executive branch. In fact, advocates of an executive-dominated foreign policy blame public opinion, and in turn Congress, for the U.S. defeat in the Vietnam War. The logic here is that the executive could have mustered the large amount of resources that were needed to achieve complete victory in Vietnam had it not been for the restraints imposed by Congress and society. Those who see congressional involvement in foreign policy as inappropriate usually note that it is even more inappropriate for the high politics of nuclear weapons policy.

In his classic work on the subject, Samuel Huntington posits that the best way to understand congressional involvement in foreign policy is to differentiate between strategic and structural policy.[24] Strategic policy, which involves the formation of broad doctrine, is seen by Huntington as dominated by the executive. These decisions are influenced primarily by the demands of the international environment. Decisions on structure, which involve the actual procurement and deployment of forces, seem to be open to both congressional and executive influence.

Though the dichotomy between these two types of policy is useful, the subject matter of this study demands that we re-evaluate this conceptual tool. Since there are three levels of nuclear weapons policy, some are strategic and others structural. For instance, declaratory policy states the broad strategic goals of U.S. nuclear weapons policy, and thus is strategic. The force development level, which involves the allocation of money and decisions over weapons procurement, is clearly structural. Action policy, which involves the targeting of U.S. nuclear weapons, does not fit neatly into either of these categories, though it is more strategic than structural.

These various levels of policy are interconnected and cannot develop entirely independently of each other. Declaratory policy (strategic) must at some point relate to the force development level (structural). The United States cannot forever pursue a certain policy if Congress does not fund the forces needed to fulfill that policy. Congress can affect strategic policy, especially over the long run. Strategic policy cannot be isolated from structural policy.

There have been various assessments made of the importance of the congressional role in strategic nuclear policy. An increased capability and even an increased involvement does not necessarily lead to an increased impact on policy. The ABM decision is the watershed for congressional involvement in strategic nuclear policy. On August 6, 1969, the U.S. Senate approved by one vote the proposed ABM system. As arms control lobbyist Thomas Halsted said, "[T]he ABM debates have brought about some fundamental changes. The public has become involved to an important degree in national security decision making. The days of congressional rubber-stamping may be over."[25]

However, in his survey of Senate involvement in arms control policy, Platt notes that although members of Congress spent more time on strategic issues in the 1970s and had more staff to deal with these issues, they had little impact on overall U.S. arms control policy. However, Platt does find that the Senate was involved and did have some impact on the development of counterforce weapons in the mid-1970s. This latter point is discussed more extensively in chapter 5.[26] In sum, arms control policy is different from overall strategic nuclear weapons policy, with the latter more relevant to the substantive focus of this work.

An extensive literature traces the increasing role of Congress in the formulation of strategic policy in the 1980s.[27] This literature clearly shows that over the 1980s, congressional involvement in nuclear weapons policy percolated down to the floors of the House and Senate.

Many executive branch proposals for major weapons systems received intense scrutiny. This literature also makes clear that congressional scrutiny over strategic force modernization went beyond a concern for budgetary matters and to issues that directly dealt with policy concerns. These details will emerge in the case studies below, and will be documented more fully for the 1980s.

The International System

I close this chapter on the state with a discussion of the importance of external variables. This chapter has emphasized that the main contribution made by this study is its focus on the state as an actor in the domestic political arena rather than as an actor in the international system. However, the state does not cease to exist as an actor in the international system.

The state's position within the international system is of crucial importance for looking at the state-society relationship. My approach views the external context as creating the environment within which state society relations are conducted. The nature of the perceived nuclear balance between the United States and the Soviet Union is a crucial variable in this study. Internal and external explanations do not compete with each other. The external environment may be best seen as providing the situational context for policy outcomes, but explanations for the nature of the policy choices themselves need to rely more heavily on variables that reside within nation states.

In the first case study on McNamara's "city-avoidance" in 1962, the United States enjoyed nuclear superiority. In James Schlesinger's "limited nuclear options" in 1974, the Soviet Union was catching up with the United States and the Strategic Arms Limitation Treaty (SALT I) codified rough parity. At the announcement of PD-59 and the countervailing strategy in 1980, the Soviet Union was at least on a par with the United States in some measures of the nuclear balance, and ahead in other areas.

The onset of parity and the relative decline of the United States regarding the nuclear balance led to the increasing importance of the domestic political arena.[28] In the age of nuclear superiority, the United States did not need to worry about bringing declaratory policy into line with action policy because it was not necessary to obtain all the weapons that may have been called for by U.S. policy. Conversely, as nuclear parity solidified, policymakers sought to gain the nuclear capabilities called for by the selective targeting options that had developed over the years. It was external factors (the advent of nuclear parity) that caused internal domestic politics to become important for the evolution of U.S. nuclear policy in the 1970s. Thus, the domestic political controversies of the 1970s and 1980s concerning the acquisition of U.S. nuclear weapons did not come about earlier.

Bureaucratic Politics and the Statist Approach

What differentiates the bureaucratic approach from the statist approach that I utilize in this study? Overall, the argument in this study is that strategy, not bureaucratic interests, was the driving factor in the development of U.S. nuclear policy.

There are important similarities and differences between these approaches to the study of state action. The bureaucratic approach does not recognize the important role that Congress can play in the development of nuclear strategy. The development of the bureaucratic approach took place when Congress did not have a particularly important role in the formulation of U.S. foreign policy. Furthermore, it is this shortcoming in the bureaucratic approach that also leads it to exclude a role for society in these issues. If we view Congress as the entrance point for society—as the gatekeeper of the state—then the lack of attention to Congress leads to a concomitant lack of emphasis on society. Also, most utilizing the statist approach do so with the assertion that society is kept out of the policymaking process. And because this assertion is so central to nearly all statist approaches, it does accord society a prominent place in statist approaches. Statist approaches, though often positing or finding that the public (society) has little impact on policy, do measure the degree to which society matters. From the statist perspective the role of society is a variable worthy of investigation, unlike the bureaucratic approach, which usually assumes this issue away.

The difference between the statist and bureaucratic approach is analogous to the levels of analysis problem in international relations, though applied to domestic political structures. That is, to find the sources of state behavior some argue that we need to look at the systemic level, some argue that we need to look at the state level, and others argue that we need to look at the individual level. The bureaucratic approach may be seen as analogous to the nation-state level approach, while the systemic approach, in that it emphasizes structural characteristics, is analogous to the statist approach utilized here. The bureaucratic approach looks to a lower level of analysis and chooses to focus on the disagreements that exist among bureaucrats and bureaucracies. From this perspective, it is the disagreements among these actors that are of particular interest. The statist approach looks to a higher level of analysis. It does not deny that there are disagreements among the various actors that make up the state. The view of the state as an entity worthy of analysis is predicated on the notion that there is one long-term consistent view that emerges from the state. A statist perspective can still acknowledge the internal bargaining and negotiation that take place in the various parts of the state and that this may lead to suboptimal or subrational outcomes. However, while bureaucratic politics sees this as the very essence of policymaking, the statist perspective that I develop in this study acknowledges the internal bargaining and negotiation but looks one step further to see where the state stands in relation to society.

This approach makes particular sense for this study given the conflict that often exists within the executive branch. The existence of conflict between state actors does not invalidate a statist approach. The dominance of the bureaucratic approach to the study of defense policy has overemphasized the competition that exists between various parts of the government at the expense of investigating the state and its relationship to society. By focusing on the atomistic nature of the state and the bureaucratic in-fighting that has ensued in this policy area, scholars have focused on the conflict within the government rather than on the conflict that exists between state and society.

Guidelines for Case Studies

In order to clarify these differences, the following questions will be applied to each case study.

1. What is the relationship between the three levels of policy? Does a disjunction exist, and if so what does it look like?
    declaratory policy: by the very nature of the way I chose the cases, this will change within each period;
    force development policy: what weapons are procured for each period, what are U.S. capabilities for this period, and what are the most salient political debates concerning these procurements;
    action policy: what was the SIOP for these periods?
2. Was the public, either mass or elite, interested in the announced changes?
3. What was the nature of congressional-executive relations for each period? Could the executive proceed with relative autonomy, or was there congressional interference, particularly at the force development level?

Was this congressional involvement related to societal input? What were the major nuclear weapons debates in Congress (re: the force development level)? How were these debates affected by the disjunction between the levels of policy?

4. Can certain executive branch actions within each case study be viewed as an active attempt to shape the political environment as it concerned U.S. nuclear policy?

5. What was the nuclear balance for each period? What has the role of external factors been in this? Does the nuclear balance correlate with the degree of state autonomy?

6. Finally, are the policy process and results better explained by a bureaucratic or statist perspective?

The last question is most important for this study. Thus, the following table illustrates hypotheses and observations that will indicate the relative usefulness of the bureaucratic vs. statist perspective.

It should be noted that the bureaucratic and statist perspectives are not used here as a way of predicting different outcomes for the dependent variable. Instead, this study is formulated in such a way as to measure the utility of each of these perspectives for explaining the relationship between the three levels of policy.

What type of evidence would add credence to my argument developed thus far that the statist lens offers the best way to bring into

	Bureaucratic	Statist
Role of the president	Lack of control Problem of civilian control	Presidential control Civilian control
Role of military	Pursues own policy	Civilian control
Policy results	Parochial interests; Bureaucratic interests	State interests Strategy
Consistency of policy	Lack of consistency	Same policy across bureaucracies
Role of public	Marginal	State-society relations important
Role of congress	Marginal	All parts of state important
Role of external variables	Not focused on	Relates to state autonomy

focus the various dimensions of the historical evolution of U.S. nuclear weapons policy? There are two important strands of evidence that will make this clear. The first revolves around the relationship between the three levels of U.S. nuclear weapons policy outlined in chapter 1. The second relates to the role of domestic political forces in the strategic nuclear weapons debate.

For the first strand, the case studies will detail the development of all three levels of policy. The statist lens will show that although there were sometimes gaps between declaratory and action policy, these gaps did not develop as a result of a lack of presidential control. Instead, and this relates to the second point, the lack of congruence between the levels will be shown to arise from the exigencies of the domestic political environment. To put this another way, political leaders did not clearly enunciate the real nature of U.S. nuclear targeting not because they did not know it or could not control it but instead because domestic political forces constrained what they said. Evidence in the case studies will support this, and the following will be noted:

- high state officials will speak in terms of MAD, when in fact they know MAD is not targeting;
- civilians will set the broad outlines of strategic policy at all three levels;
- continuity rather than change best describes U.S. nuclear policy over the course of this study;
- strategy, rather than bureaucratic interests, guides policy;
- the nature of the nuclear balance between the United States and Soviet Union correlated with the degree of state autonomy.

The statist lens thus offers us two things. First an understanding of the way the three levels of nuclear weapons policy move together, and second, a role for domestic political forces in the development of strategic nuclear weapons policy. It will show that during the first two case studies, declaratory policy was fashioned in a way that illustrates that state defense policymakers were indeed sensitive to societal opposition. Societal opposition did not emerge precisely because of this keen sensitivity. This changed by the late 1970s.

One of the most frustrating features of the statist debate is its lack of attention to the crucial question of when the state is autonomous from society. After all, few serious analysts would maintain that the question of state autonomy is one of absolute autonomy across time and issue area. Instead, the real key to the statist debate focuses on when the state is autonomous. This question has both temporal and issue variables associated with it, that is, the relative autonomy of the state depends on both the nature of the issue and the historical period under investigation. Furthermore, these two variables are not logically independent. Different historical periods may find state autonomy for one issue but not for others.

To illustrate the above discussion, the level of state autonomy is usually seen to vary across issues areas. The common wisdom holds that the state can achieve more autonomy in the issues of security than in issues of foreign economic policy. The logic here is that society usually defers on issues of security, particularly nuclear weapons policy. Issues of foreign economic policy are more contentious, since numerous societal actors perceive the costs or benefits from, for example, changes in trade policy.

Of course, it is the premise of this study that we cannot presume state autonomy for high politics. It is also the goal of this study to show that in fact the degree of autonomy varies with the strength of the United States in the international system. For the issue of nuclear weapons policy, then, the level of autonomy from society varied with the level of nuclear superiority. It was relatively simple for the state to maintain autonomy when nuclear superiority made nuclear weapons a noncontroversial issue. This was true in the 1960s. This window began to close in the 1970s as parity emerged, and closed even further in the 1980s as the growth of the U.S. nuclear arsenal became one of the most salient issues on the political agenda.

Conclusions

This chapter has outlined the statist approach and refined the ideas associated with it in order to apply it to the evolution of U.S. nuclear weapons policy. The focus on the coherence of the state affords a view of the development of the U.S. nuclear weapons policy from a unique vantage point. It is my hope that this perspective will add depth and insight into both the evolution of U.S. nuclear weapons policy and the nature of policymaking within the U.S. state. The assumption of autonomy for this policy area has lasted too long. Taken as a whole, the application of this perspective makes this a crucial case study. If it can be shown that the state does not enjoy a wide degree of autonomy in the formulation of the high politics of U.S. nuclear weapons policy, we may come to doubt claims of autonomy for issue areas that are more often considered salient. Such an approach can also contribute much to our thinking about the responsibility that the state has for this policy area. Because of the dominance of the bureaucratic perspective in the study of foreign policy and nuclear weapon policy, central state officials sometimes have not been held responsible for policy outcomes because they could always say "the bureaucracy made me do it." However, if we view the state and its relationship to society in the way proposed here, a different view of state responsibility may emerge. We turn now to the case studies.

4

The McNamara Years: The Shift to MAD?

Surely the SIOPs in the 60's did not fully reflect the declaratory policy of the Kennedy Administration; they were very heavily oriented toward counterforce whereas the declaratory policy of MAD did not procure weapons for counterforce.[1]

The period 1961–65 saw the rise to official prominence of an explicit American doctrine of counterforce targeting, married to a city-avoidance principle for intrawar deterrence and to aspirations for a large civil defense program, and then a very marked decline in official enthusiasm for this doctrine. Neither counterforce nor assured destruction was endorsed without qualification, but the shift in declaratory emphasis between the two targeting poles was striking in the years 1962-65. In 1962 the fairly tentative counterforce preference expressed in the civilian strategic literature of the late 1950s was superseded by a strongly worded official dedication.[2]

This case illustrates one of the largest gaps in U.S. strategic nuclear weapons policy between declaratory and action policy. Though many believed that McNamara and those around him in the Pentagon had abandoned counterforce targeting shortly after the policy was made public, the SIOP remained heavily oriented toward counterforce targeting despite the public rhetoric to the contrary. This emphasis on counterforce targeting coincided with a declaratory policy of MAD. This gap, or disjunction, or "little white lie,"[3] as one top McNamara aid termed it, will be the focus of this chapter.

This historical episode is crucial for understanding the utility of the statist approach. Many have used bureaucratic politics to illuminate the disjunctions between the various levels of nuclear policy. However, I will show that in fact the state pursued nuclear policy with the strategic goal of enhancing counterforce and flexibility, and that MAD was merely for public consumption. Furthermore, McNamara instituted civilian control over defense policy that allowed for strategic coherence in policy formation.

Historical Background

From the time of the use of the atomic bombs on Hiroshima and Nagasaki in August 1945 through at least the tenure of Robert McNamara, the United States enjoyed superiority over the Soviet Union in nuclear forces. The U.S. monopoly and subsequent preponderance of strategic nuclear forces made the questions associated with how to plan to use nuclear weapons far less complex than they would become in the decades to follow.

The United States avoided the targeting of Soviet military installations in favor of the targeting of cities from 1945 to 1950.[4] For example, in 1946 the U.S. war plan Pincher called for the targeting of 20 Soviet cities with 50 bombs.[5] In 1947, the first significant target list was drawn up and incorporated into the Joint Outline Emergency War Plan called Broiler. In this, 100 urban centers were identified for attack. In the next year, the Frolic and Half-Moon war plans emphasized the dropping of bombs on cities. The Joint War Plan Trojan, approved in December 1948, called for attacks on 70 Soviet cities with 133 atomic bombs.[6] SAC chose targets where the destruction of populations was the primary goal. As David Rosenberg has concluded, "[T]he only retardation targets were petroleum refineries, electric power plants, submarine building yards, and synthetic ammonia plants, including some in Eastern Europe."[7]

These nuclear plans aimed to kill the will, but not the ability, of the opposition to fight. The Soviet Union did not have nuclear weapons until 1949, though the primary goal of these plans did not seem to be the destruction of the Soviet conventional capability. This is due in part to the small number of nuclear weapons that the United States had. Such nuclear scarcity, coupled with a lack of accuracy, made the pursuit of full counterforce capabilities difficult. The U.S. arsenal contained only 2 bombs in 1945, 9 in 1946, 13 in 1947, and 15 by July 1948.[8]

Despite technological obstacles, however, even during this early period counterforce targeting began to play a role in U.S. nuclear war planning. The expansion of the strategic nuclear arsenal of the United States allowed for the incorporation of counterforce goals. By the end of the 1940s, the targeting of populations began to give way to counterforce targeting. For example, in 1950 the war plan Dropshot emphasized counterforce targeting for a hypothetical war. The target list included stockpiles of nuclear weapons, government and control centers, communication and military supply lines as well as troop concentrations. Dropshot envisioned 300 atomic bombs and 20,000 tons of high-explosive conventional bombs striking approximately 700 Soviet targets.[9] By 1950, the Delta category (for disruption/destruction of war-making capacity) was officially added to the categories of targets for U.S. nuclear forces. Bravo targets indicated a blunting mission, and Romeo retardation.

Counterforce targeting and pre-emption played a larger role as the years went on, for three reasons. First is the development of Soviet nuclear capability. Nuclear counterforce targeting makes sense when there are nuclear weapons to target. Second is the increased production of nuclear weapons by the United States. Though the beginning of the decade was a time of nuclear weapons scarcity, by the end of the 1950s strategic and tactical nuclear weapons were plentiful. Finally, U.S. targeting and intelligence capabilities improved to the point where counterforce targeting options were considered feasible. Without the ability to locate nuclear weapons and the accuracy to hit them, counterforce targeting could not become a major part of U.S. nuclear strategy.

Civilian control over nuclear weapons policy was lacking during this early period. SAC was reluctant to give up control over the targeting and control of the instruments of the American military. The new National Security Council (NSC) was not providing significant guidance. With its own computer facilities and the like, SAC could target nuclear weapons without interference from the civilian sector. This lack of civilian input and control during this period should not be particularly surprising. Civilian input into the specifics of targeting policy had not been common before the advent of nuclear weapons, and this proved a difficult pattern to break. SAC, under the strong and dynamic leadership of General Curtis LeMay, was responsible for drawing up the targeting plans for nuclear weapons, which the JCS was to approve. However, from 1951 until 1955 the JCS never received a copy of those plans. LeMay believed that this belonged within the purview of SAC.[10]

Massive Retaliation: The First Declaratory Policy

Nuclear war plans were not discussed in public or in Congress until the now-famous speech by Dwight Eisenhower's secretary of state, John Foster Dulles, in January 1954. This speech led to much of the confusion that ensued over the following decades on the relationship between U.S. declaratory and action policy. In January 1954 Secretary

Dulles, in a speech delivered to the Council on Foreign Relations, announced that the nuclear policy of the United States would be "massive retaliation." This policy called for the all-out destruction of the Soviet Union in the case of aggression. Though this announcement met with much skepticism, particularly regarding the credibility of such a threat, it was believed to form the foundation of U.S. nuclear policy. Subsequently, it has become clear that although this was the declaratory policy of the United States, it was not the only response planned.[11]

The rhetoric of massive retaliation called for the United States to threaten asymmetrical response: for the United States to respond to Soviet or Communist aggression not at the point of attack but instead at a time and place chosen by the United States.[12] According to Dulles, the United States would "depend primarily upon a capacity to retaliate, instantly, by means and at a place of our choosing." Implicit here was that the United States was threatening to respond with nuclear weapons against the enemy's homeland to aggression waged against the United States or its allies. One of the primary justifications for this policy was that it allowed the United States to spend less on conventional arms and would facilitate economic savings. This must be seen in the broader context of the "New Look" policy proposed by Eisenhower, which called for significant reductions in U.S. defense spending while expanding U.S. commitments abroad.

Criticism of the announcement focused on the notion that Dulles had not done enough to establish the credibility of massive retaliation. Dulles attempted to clarify the policy and backed away from massive retaliation with the publication of an article in *Foreign Affairs*.[13] Though still somewhat vague, Dulles made a plea for flexibility. This was responsive to the criticism of the original policy of massive retaliation. He wrote:

> To deter aggression, it is important to have the flexibility and the facilities which make various responses available. In many cases, any open assault by Communist forces could only result in starting a general war. But the free world must have the means for responding effectively on a selective basis when it chooses. It must not be put in the position where the only response open to it is general war.[14]

Despite this attempt at clarification, the rhetoric of massive retaliation stuck. The disjunction between the declaratory and action policy was that under the doctrine of massive retaliation, more refined nuclear war plans did exist. It is now clear that the operational plans for war were far more refined than John Foster Dulles's rhetoric implied. As Wells summarizes:

> The policy of massive retaliation thus is by itself inadequate, even as a convenient catch phrase, to sum up the nuclear strategy of the Eisenhower administration. The term massive retaliation now evokes images of SAC on the rampage that are probably indelible, and the administration played the most important part in the creation of these images. But the administration's strategy was more subtle than its spokesmen were willing to admit. Analysts of the period should no longer, twenty five years after the fact, continue to be seduced by the rhetoric of the Eisenhower administration.[15]

Targeting of the time confirms Wells's observations. By the mid-1950s the target set included 5,000–6,000 identified targets, which included big cities, small industries, and river crossings. SAC had planned to cover 1,700 of the targets, of which 409 were airfields, thus showing the counterforce emphasis of the SIOP.[16]

The rhetoric of massive retaliation laid the groundwork for the myth of MAD. This legacy has been difficult to end.

The Move Toward the First SIOP

As the U.S. nuclear arsenal grew, the military services fought to get a piece of the action. It soon became apparent that a new mechanism was needed to coordinate nuclear targeting.[17] No longer was the Air Force the sole possessor of nuclear weapons. By the early 1950s, commanders in the Pacific and Mediterranean had nuclear weapons, and tactical air units in the Mediterranean and Asia also had a nuclear capability.

Some attempts had been made to coordinate the use of the growing U.S. nuclear arsenal. In March 1952 an ad hoc committee of the JCS examined the control and coordination of atomic operations. They agreed to form Joint Coordination Centers in Europe and Asia, which would have allowed for wartime operational control. However, this did not facilitate the coordination of targeting.

By 1954 the JCS had asked all commanders to submit their target lists to CINCSAC and theater commanders to coordinate nuclear targeting. These Worldwide Coordination conferences took place yearly beginning in 1955. There had also been joint service studies looking into the targets for a major war. Despite the convening of the Worldwide Coordination Conference, duplication and triplication of targeting still existed. The separate commands may have been aware of this duplication as a result of these coordination efforts, but the overlap was not eliminated.[18] It was time for the institutional structures of the armed forces to catch up with the growth of the nuclear arsenal.

The Air Force had advocated the creation of a unified strategic command. Other services, particularly the Navy, objected to this. Admiral Arleigh Burke, chief of Naval Operations, felt that further coordination was not necessary. This conflict went on for some time. The new secretary of defense, Thomas Gates, offered a compromise that sought to bridge the differences between the branches on how to coordinate nuclear targeting policy.

New avenues for coordination had been opened up by the Defense Reorganization Act passed by Congress on July 23, 1958. Concerns over this issue went to the highest levels of the executive branch. President Eisenhower met with Secretary Thomas Gates, General N. F. Twining, Admiral Arleigh Burke, and General Andrew Goodpaster to discuss the coordination and integration of U.S. strategic targeting. At this meeting, Secretary Gates stated that while he did not advocate establishing a single command over nuclear weapons policy, he did favor establishing a director of strategic nuclear targeting. He also said that this director should be the same as the CINCSAC. Such a setup would not only ensure the coordination of policy, but also would give SAC a good deal of control over the policy outcomes. Arleigh Burke objected to this plan because he feared SAC dominance over nuclear targeting. The Navy had consistently resisted reporting to any unified command. Eisenhower expressed displeasure at this display of parochial interests and said he had hoped that an issue as important as nuclear weapons could unify the branches and move them to act in the national interest. After receiving numerous proposals on how to add coherence to targeting, Gates decided to establish the Joint Strategic Target Planning Staff in August 1960.[19]

The final decision established the JSTPS as a separate agency of the JCS. And though this was to have representation of all branches of the armed forces, the JSTPS was co-located with SAC in Omaha, Nebraska. This was difficult to implement, as the branches of the armed forces fought for representation on the JSTPS. Gates appointed the commander in chief of SAC, Bruce Holloway, as director of the JSTPS. He also appointed Navy Vice Admiral Edward Parker as vice director. He hoped that this would ensure the cooperation of the Navy. By tradition, the director of the JSTPS is the CINCSAC and the vice director has always been a vice admiral of the Navy. As late as 1972 the staff was 65 percent Air Force and 25 percent Navy, with the remainder made up of Marine Corps and Army representatives. Though one of the purposes of the creation of the SIOP and the JSTPS was to decrease the dominance of SAC and the Air Force, they have still been able to dominate planning.

The Kennedy Administration

The Communist threat and the American defense posture were among the most important issues in the campaign that pitted then-Vice President Richard Nixon against then Senator John F. Kennedy (D-MA). Kennedy accused the Eisenhower administration, and by association Nixon, of neglecting American defense. Kennedy charged that Eisenhower had allowed a missile gap to develop that gave the USSR significant strategic superiority over the United States. Though the "missile gap" turned out to be false, it set the tone for the first years of the Kennedy administration.

To assert civilian control over the Defense Department, President Kennedy appointed Robert McNamara, then Chief Executive Officer of the Ford Motor Company, as secretary of defense. McNamara brought with him the "the best and the brightest" and the "whiz kids," considered to be the top minds in the country on defense matters. Many from the Rand Corporation, the Air Force–related think tank, joined the new administration. The emphasis was not only on the substantive nature of nuclear weapons policy but also on gaining civilian control over the policy.

Accordingly, one of McNamara's primary goals was to bring civilian control to U.S. nuclear weapons policy. Several innovations were instituted, including systems analysis and cost-benefit analysis. Both were attempts to rationalize and centralize the defense policy-making process. One of the most important innovations of the McNamara period was the Draft Presidential Memorandums (DPMs). These were used from 1961 to 1969 as the mechanism for the secretary of defense to structure the decision making process within the Department of Defense. Drafted originally in the Office of the Secretary of Defense for Systems Analysis, the memorandum would go back and forth from the secretary's office to the military services and the JCS. As former head of Systems Analysis Alain Enthoven wrote:

By 1965, the DPMs had become the principal program decision-making documents in the Defense Department. As the DPMs evolved, a workable system for processing the various drafts in DoD was developed and formalized. The resulting DPM system became a unique and highly effective management tool for dealing with controversial issues of military strategy and force planning.[20]

The goal was to coordinate input for all levels of nuclear weapons policy, including targeting.[21]

The creation of the first SIOP took place during Eisenhower's final years. SIOP-62 (for FY 1962), had been completed in December 1960 and came into effect on July 1, 1961.[22] The NSTL had over 1,050 designated ground zeros. Only 151 of these were industrial targets. Though the emphasis may have been on counterforce targets rather than counter-value targets, it is difficult to call this first SIOP a refined war plan. It did increase coordination of nuclear targeting, but did not contain many different options. However, the first SIOP appeared to be a first-strike war plan, at least to the extent that it emphasized pre-emption rather than retaliation. SIOP 62 allowed for a massive first strike against the USSR, Eastern Europe, and China, with 3,500 nuclear weapons aimed at 1,042 targets in the Sino-Soviet bloc.[23] Though there were a range of options within the SIOP, each called for the full execution of the strategic arsenal against industrial and military targets. There does not appear to have been the option of hitting military targets while withholding attacks on populations, or vise versa. The only withhold was the option of putting 1,400 of the weapons on alert or short warning, enabling them to be launched immediately in the case of war. The remaining approximately 2,000 weapons could be launched within twenty-four hours.[24] In addition, among the 14 options was the ability to withhold strikes from certain satellite countries.[25] There were no provisions made here for maintenance of command and control. Potential fatalities were estimated to be between 300 and 525 million people.[26]

This was the SIOP that Robert McNamara found when he took office in 1961. McNamara immediately delved into the details of U.S. nuclear weapons policy. He was so concerned that high officials be current on nuclear strategy and tactics that he suggested that the president, secretary of defense, and other responsible officials have a one hundred-hour course on nuclear weapons.[27] On February 3, 1961, only two weeks after assuming his new responsibilities, McNamara went to SAC in Omaha to get a briefing on the SIOP. According to Fred Kaplan:

What SAC labeled "Plan 1-A" of SIOP-62—suggesting that it was the basic plan, called for an all out pre-emptive first strike against the USSR, Eastern Europe and Red China, in response to an actual or merely impending Soviet invasion of Western Europe that involved no nuclear weapons at all....As much as anyone else who had witnessed this spectacle, if not more so, Robert McNamara was horrified.[28]

McNamara wanted more limited options.

Later that year, on September 13, 1961, President Kennedy, in the company of McNamara, General Maxwell Taylor, and National Security Adviser Walt Rostow was given a full briefing on SIOP-62 by Lyman Lemnitzer, chairman of the JCS.[29] McNamara reacted with horror to the plan's lack of flexibility and options. Lemnitzer made many arguments *against* adding limited options to the SIOP. His concerns focused on two themes. First, he was concerned that options of withholding were dangerous because they could result in the destruction of U.S. nuclear weapons if not used quickly enough. Second, he considered the difference between aiming at military targets and civilian targets somewhat meaningless in the nuclear age, because of radioactive fallout and the relatively nondiscriminating nature of nuclear weapons. Military targets were so dispersed in the Soviet Union that aiming only at military targets was not likely to decrease significantly civilian casualties.

In his first DPM, written at about the same time of this briefing, McNamara stressed the need for U.S. strategic retaliatory forces to withstand a first strike by the Soviet Union and to "strike back against Soviet bomber bases, missile sites and other installations associated with long-range nuclear forces."[30] Rejecting options for "minimum deterrence" and a "full first-strike capability," McNamara opted for a posture between these two extremes. The goal was to acquire forces to move beyond the policy of massive retaliation. The chart on page 64 from the DPM summarizes the projected targeting. Note the counterforce emphasis of these plans and the projected increase in counterforce emphasis. The DPM also stated that the 200 urban industrial targets and 150 bomber bases were of the utmost importance, thus emphasizing both counterforce and countervalue targeting. McNamara used this target identification to justify his lower weapons requests. Of course, this increased emphasis on counterforce also reflected the expansion of the Soviet target base.

Of the ninety-six major projects that McNamara initiated upon taking office, the nuclear weapons issue was number two of the original

	End FY	
	65	67
Urban industrial aim points	200	200
Bomber bases	150	150
Support airfields	50	50
Defense suppression	300	300
Nuclear storage and production	50	50
Naval and sub bases	50	50
Soft IRBM sites (4 missiles per)	100	100
Soft ICBM sites (2 missiles per)	100–300	50–200
Hard ICBM sites(1 missile per)	200–500	400–1,100
Total	1,200–1,700	1,350–2,200

ninety-six. This assignment was given to Henry Rowen of the Defense Department (DoD), who then passed this onto Daniel Ellsberg. Ellsberg was struck by the singular nature of the plan and its ability to blow up all of the Soviet Union, China, and Eastern Europe.[31] McNamara's civilian apparatus made attempts through 1961 to gain control over the targeting process. This desire stemmed from both procedural and substantive concerns. Procedurally, there was the belief that civilians should have control over nuclear targeting. Substantively, the desire was to take U.S. nuclear weapons policy away from the one spasm mentality that was perceived to have dominated U.S. nuclear weapons policy in the decade before.

After Ellsberg went to Omaha, he submitted guidance to Alain Enthoven and Frank Trinkle in the Department of Defense elaborating five distinct targeting categories: 1) strategic forces; 2) air-defense sites away from cities; 3) air-defense sites close to cities; 4) command and control centers; and 5) Soviet cities. Flexibility, discrimination, and multiple options were the goals. Among some of the other features of this plan that set it apart from existing policy was that China and satellite countries were separated from the USSR for targeting purposes, Soviet strategic forces were separated from Soviet citizens on U.S. target lists, strategic forces were to be held in reserve by the U.S. in accordance with the concept of intrawar deterrence, and U.S. and Soviet command and control would be preserved so that limited exchanges could be conducted.[32] In addition, Moscow was taken off the initial target list.[33] This also called for changes in command and control and options for the targeting of nuclear weapons.[34]

The planning process was completed in the summer of 1961, formalized by Henry Rowen and General Maxwell Taylor in the fall 1961, approved by the JCS later in 1961, and officially adopted in January 1962.[35] Thus, after less than a year in office, the Kennedy administration had created a new SIOP. SIOP-63 had five targeting options: 1) Soviet strategic nuclear delivery forces; 2) other elements of Soviet military forces away from cities; 3) Soviet military forces and military resources near cities; 4) Soviet command and control; 5) and all-out industrial attack. Options 1 and 2, a pure counterforce attack, could be launched in a pre-emptive fashion in case of warning of Sino-Soviet attack.[36]

The DPMs reflected this shift in strategy. In the 1962 DPM written for FY 1963–67, McNamara justified his proposed force levels that could hit Soviet counterforce targets even after withstanding a first strike and have enough in reserve to threaten Soviet society.[37] The DPM mentioned and had a long discussion of the damage-limiting aspects of U.S. nuclear weapons policy.[38] By 1962, McNamara was ready to move these changes to the declaratory level. Officials decided to move this out of the inner sanctum of the defense and national security establishment and into the public.

The first mention of the new strategy appeared in the FY 1963 Budget Statement, issued in January 1962. McNamara wrote that "a major mission of strategic retaliatory forces is to deter war by their capability to destroy the enemy's war making capabilities." The next month, on February 17, 1962, McNamara hinted at the new strategy in a speech before the Fellows of the American Bar Foundation Dinner when he said:

With this protected command and control system, our forces can be used in several different ways. We may have to retaliate with a single massive attack. Or, we may be able to use our retaliatory forces to limit damage done to ourselves, and our allies, by knocking out the enemy's bases before he has had time to launch his second salvos. We may seek to terminate a war on favorable terms by using our forces as a bargaining weapon—by threatening further attack.[39]

The next major discussion of the new strategy came in a restricted session of the NATO Ministerial Meetings in Athens on May 5, 1962. This speech was not truly declaratory policy, but instead a move to present the shift in strategy to the allies. In a clear statement of the "no-cities" or "city-avoidance" strategy, McNamara told the ministers that:

The U.S. has come to the conclusion that to the extent feasible basic military strategy in general nuclear war should be approached in much the same way that more conventional military operations have been regarded in the past. That is to say, our principal military objective, in the event of a nuclear war stemming from a major attack on the Alliance, should be the destruction of the enemy's military forces while attempting to preserve the fabric as well as the integrity of allied society. Specifically, our studies indicate that a strategy which targets nuclear forces only against cities or a mixture of civil and military targets has serious limitations for the purpose of deterrence and for the conduct of general war.[40]

McNamara went to great lengths to justify these changes. He stated that by aiming at military rather than urban targets, both sides could hope to decrease the damage that would occur in a nuclear war. The city-avoidance program was presented as a way to save lives in the event of a nuclear war.

It was unprecedented for the secretary of defense to come before the allies and explain the force posture and strategic doctrine. According to one of McNamara's close advisers, this speech had three goals. First, it was to reassure the allies of the U.S. nuclear commitment. Second, it was an attempt to get the French and the British to forsake the development of their own independent nuclear forces. Finally, it was an attempt to convince the allies of the need for a build-up of conventional forces.[41]

After some controversy, McNamara decided to go public with the no-cities doctrine in a commencement address at the University of Michigan in the summer of 1962. The speech was different in tone from the one delivered in Athens, more appropriate for a commencement address than a detailed explication of U.S. nuclear strategy aimed at establishing allied support. Though using nearly the same language as the excerpt above in terms of the emphasis on military rather than civilian targets, McNamara did not detail how many might die under the different types of targeting scenarios. This rhetoric was expunged for the public speech, laying the groundwork for politicians not to talk about the intricacies of the effects of nuclear war. Policymakers judged that they should not go into detail publicly about the goals of a war-fighting strategy.

The administration was not insensitive to the potential negative reactions to this speech. The Ann Arbor speech was an unprecedented public explication of the details of U.S. nuclear weapons policy. According to the memo written by National Security Adviser McGeorge Bundy to President Kennedy on June 1, 1962, Kennedy had expressed concern over the Michigan commencement address.[42] Bundy had spoken with McNamara about the president's concerns on two issues. One was concern over how the French would react to the new policy; the other was a concern over offering the Soviet Union "a hand-hold for charges of missile rattling." This gave the Soviet Union reason to charge that the United States was adopting a first-strike nuclear strategy, a charge that could be used by domestic political forces who were against this new strategy. Bundy gave the president two options in this regard: cancel the speech or reorient it with an eye toward French and Soviet reactions. Obviously, the first option was not accepted.

Allied reaction to this new doctrine was mixed. On the one hand, for those countries that wanted to develop their own nuclear forces, population targeting was the only targeting of which these limited forces would be capable.[43] Counterforce targeting does not really make sense with a scarcity of weapons. Thus, the new American theory of deterrence undercut the development of these forces. French President Charles DeGaulle did not take kindly to the new policy.[44] Also, it was hoped that limited options and the avoidance of populations would be seen by other Europeans as enhancing deterrence by making more credible the extension of the American nuclear guarantee to Europe. If the United States developed a policy that was to offer the United States survival in the case of nuclear war in Europe, the credibility of extended deterrence could be enhanced.

The Fallout

Until this point, congressional involvement in U.S. nuclear weapons policy had been limited. Congress had been involved in military policy, though not through the expression of broad strategic concerns. Instead, Congress had influenced force levels and budget requests. Congress was willing to support the increases in defense funding requested by Kennedy and McNamara. The congressional reaction to the defense cuts of the Eisenhower administration and the reliance on massive retaliation and the New Look was a call for more conventional and tactical requirements. Thus, because the thrust of the new Democratic administration was in this direction, Congress did not withhold its support.[45]

The McNamara announcement came at a time of heightened sensitivity over the nuclear weapons issue. Paul Boyer called the period from 1954 to 1963 a period of "nuclear preoccupation, which was generally reflected in the culture, politics and social movements of the time."[46] Much of this was a reaction to the above-ground testing that was banned by the 1963 Limited Test Ban Treaty.

Some in Congress reacted unfavorably to McNamara's city-avoidance initiative. Senators Richard Russell (D-GA) and Margaret Chase Smith (R-ME) attacked the new policy as one of weakness, a policy that indicated U.S. unwillingness to use nuclear weapons. Chase was not an advocate of MAD. Her view was that if two people were left in the world after a nuclear exchange, they should be Americans. Conversely, some on the left saw city-avoidance as a form of legitimizing the use of nuclear weapons.[47] It was unclear to some members of Congress whether the new city-avoidance doctrine was a statement that indicated that McNamara was moving away from the U.S. commitment to use nuclear weapons or whether it was a reckless embrace of the use of nuclear weapons.[48]

This congressional activity was in part a reaction to the heightened public attention to the nuclear issue from 1961 to 1963. Public attention to the issue was at an all-time high because of the talk of limits and the strategy of actually fighting a nuclear war. Crisis and conflict between the United States and Soviet Union was at high pitch, including the Bay of Pigs, the Berlin Wall Crisis, and the Cuban missile crisis. There was also a great deal of discussion of civilian defense and bomb shelters. Such talk, though premised on the notion that populations can survive a nuclear war, reminded people of the horrors of nuclear war. Overall, Kennedy administration attempts to rationalize U.S. strategic doctrine did not sit well with the public.[49]

These concerns reflect the differences between MAD and NUTs. Talk of limits, of control or flexibility made nuclear war seem more likely. This is the paradox of talking about the limits of nuclear war. Though MAD assumes mutual suicide in the event of a nuclear war, it is less opposed by the public because its basic premise makes nuclear war seem unlikely. Such is not the case with the rhetoric of NUTs. It comes down to the visibility to the public of the nuclear weapons debate. When left alone and invisible to the public, the nuclear weapons issue can proceed relatively autonomously from public attention.

One notable example of this is the active debate that culminated in the Limited Test Ban Treaty of 1963. Before this treaty, the United States and the Soviet Union were testing nuclear weapons in the atmosphere. This made the effects of the nuclear arms race real to the public. There was widespread public fear about the level of radiation found in milk and other farm products. The Limited Test Ban Treaty pushed the nuclear weapons issue underground and thus eliminated some of the saliency of the nuclear weapons issue.

Retreat to MAD?

A great deal of confusion still surrounds the evolution of U.S. nuclear weapons policy during the remaining McNamara years. After the initial flurry of public statements on city-avoidance in 1962, the Kennedy administration and the Defense Department made it a point not to talk about this policy. After 1962 it is difficult to find any references to city-avoidance per se. Declaratory policy after 1962 embraced MAD. Talk of counterforce was not totally abandoned, but the relative emphasis given to this mission in declaratory policy decreased over the course of the decade.

This section traces the emphasis put on the damage limitation relative to that of MAD.[50] Damage limitation refers to limiting the destructiveness of a nuclear war should such a war occur. One way of limiting damage was counterforce pre-emptive targeting, to destroy Soviet forces before they could be used. For the United States, this rests on the assumption that it could knock out most Soviet forces before they were launched. Civil defense is one way to pursue damage-limitation strategies. ABM systems are another way to limit damage, and they were pursued with vigor during this period.

Though talk of counterforce, city-avoidance, and damage limitation took a backseat to MAD, this change in declaratory policy did not have any impact on the SIOP. The city-avoidance, counterforce emphasis of the SIOP continued throughout the decade, though the nuclear policy of the time was assumed to be MAD. As an assistant secretary of defense in the Johnson administration wrote in 1971:

The SIOP remains essentially unchanged since then [McNamara's Ann Arbor Speech of June 15, 1962]. There have been two developments, however: 1) it has become more difficult to execute the pure counterforce options, and its value is considered to be diminishing and, 2) *all public officials have learned to talk in public only about deterrence and city attacks. No war-fighting, no city-sparing. Too many critics can make too much trouble (no-cities talk weakens deterrence, the argument goes), so public officials have run for cover* . That included me when I was one of them. But the targeting philosophy, the options and the order of choice remain unchanged from the McNamara speech.[51]

Within the DPM, McNamara was moving away from an emphasis on city-avoidance and damage limitation.[52] In the DPM drafted in

December 1963, McNamara reported that the Joint Chiefs of Staff had recommended forces that identified assured destruction as a "vital first objective." After this objective was met, it advocated "counterforce efforts up to the point at which further weight of effort ceases to be remunerative or produce significant added damage limiting results." All this was prefaced by input from the Joint Chiefs that they would be unable in the time frame considered to limit damage with the criteria identified by the secretary of defense.[53]

Within this DPM, McNamara identified three objectives that the United States could hope to achieve with its nuclear forces. The first was assured destruction of the USSR, the second damage limitation, and the third a full first-strike capability. Assured destruction is identified as the major goal, though here McNamara does acknowledge that "*this calculation of the effectiveness of the U.S. forces is not a reflection of our actual targeting doctrine in the event deterrence fails.*"[54] Though procurement was motivated by criteria associated with MAD, the targeting remained counterforce. Assured destruction would be used to calculate the adequacy of the U.S. strategic arsenal, but it would not reflect targeting. This was never introduced to the public debate. That MAD was not targeting doctrine is clear when one looks at the target list from this DPM, entitled "Soviet Bloc Targets End-FY 1969." Of 1,790 targets identified, only 215 were urban industrial targets.[55] Despite its move away from damage limitation, this DPM detailed the desirability of limited nuclear options. Among the major goals was the ability to execute limited strategic attacks as a symbol that the United States was willing to escalate to strategic nuclear war. Another reason given for the development of U.S. counterforce capabilities was that it could force the Soviet Union to harden its silos or accept greater vulnerability.[56]

In describing the strategic forces in the FY 1965 Annual Report, McNamara referred to both "damage limitation" and "assured destruction." He stated there were two purposes for U.S. strategic forces. The first was to be able to inflict unacceptable damage on the opponent, and the second was to limit damage to U.S. population and industry. The DPM contained analysis of the degree to which U.S. policy adhered to assured destruction and damage limitation. McNamara assessed how much a damage limitation capability would cost and whether it would significantly limit damage. This analysis was done for both a U.S. and a Soviet first strike. The analysis had concluded that the damage-limitation program would cost $5–6 billion by 1970. McNamara concluded that the United States could limit damage with an additional cost above what was required for assured destruction, and that even such an investment could not guarantee limiting damage below 40 million dead. Further, an efficient damage-limitation program also would require an extensive civil defense program. MIRVs and accuracy were also advocated.[57]

By 1966 there is no mention of the desire to achieve a damage-limitation capability. The only role stressed is the ability to destroy any attacker even after withstanding an initial attack by the other side. This is more consistent with MAD than with damage limitation. In the FY 1967 Annual Report, McNamara paid lip service to the roles of assured destruction and damage limitation. He said U.S. forces would need to inflict unacceptable damage on an attacker even after withstanding a first strike from the other side. Whether this meant any kind of significant counterforce capability is unclear from this document.[58]

In the annual report that was delivered to Congress, counterforce took a backseat to the criteria associated with MAD. McNamara seems to have embraced MAD fully at the declaratory level with the following statement:

[E]ach side has achieved, and will most likely maintain over the foreseeable future, an actual and credible second strike capability against the other. It is precisely this mutual capability to destroy one another, and conversely, our respective inability to prevent such destruction, that provided us both with the strongest possible motive to avoid strategic nuclear war.[59]

Reflective during the presentation of this last budget, McNamara told the committee, "[H]aving wrestled with this problem for the last seven years, I am convinced that our forces must be sufficiently large to possess an 'Assured Destruction capability.'"[60]

McNamara went on to say:

As long as deterrence of a deliberate Soviet (or Red Chinese) nuclear attack upon the United States or its allies is the vital first objective of our strategic forces, the capability for "Assured Destruction" must receive the first call on all of our resources and must be provided regardless of the cost and difficulties involved. That imperative, it seems to me, is well understood and accepted by all informed Americans. What is not so well understood, apparently, is the basis upon which our force requirements must logically be determined—in other words, how much "Assured Destruction" capability do we need and what is the proper way to measure that need....In the case of the Soviet Union, I would judge that a capability on our part to destroy say, one-fifth to one-fourth of her population and one-half of her industrial capacity would serve as an effective deterrent. Such a level of punishment would certainly represent intolerable punishment to any 20th Century industrial nation.[61]

It would have been reasonable to conclude at this time that U.S. nuclear weapons policy had embraced MAD. It did not.

In April 1968, the Senate Armed Services Committee questioned General Earle Wheeler, the chairman of the Joint Chiefs of Staff, on U.S. nuclear policy. Referring to the difference between the words McNamara used in his 1962 Ann Arbor speech and his statement before the committee in January 1967, Chief Counsel James T. Kendall inquired about the apparent discrepancies.[62] His line of questioning arose from differences he found in statements by McNamara, which advocated MAD, and those by the JCS, which gave more emphasis to damage limitation. On the conflict between the two, General Wheeler said that it was only a difference of degree:

Now, I said that perhaps there was a difference in degree, and I mean it in this sense: Secretary McNamara, I believe, has stressed the assured destruction as a deterrent perhaps more than the Joint Chiefs have. We have stressed both, the assured destruction and the damage limiting aspects in our strategic concept and we give them both very heavy weight.[63]

Wheeler said that the acquisition of weapons systems had been based on criteria for assured destruction, not damage limitation. When Kendall inquired about the actual guidance received by the JCS from McNamara, Wheeler said the first priority was assured destruction and the second was damage limitation. Differences existed on how much officials felt that damage to both sides could actually be limited. When he was asked what was specifically targeted, the testimony was deleted from the public record. Kendall pursued this same line of questioning with John Foster, then director of research and engineering at the Defense Department. Asking Foster about whether it was damage limitation or assured destruction that determined the criteria for weapons acquisition, Foster responded that while assured destruction was the primary criteria,

we do, however, as you know, pay serious attention to the possibility of providing damage limitation....Recently...we found ways of improving accuracy of the Minuteman and Poseidon so as to be able to get much greater kill capabilities even though the warhead yields were reduced and so in fact we are beginning to get a rather effective damage limiting capability.[64]

Changes made to weapons systems were propelled by the desire to limit damage.

While this testimony indicated that there should be some emphasis on the damage-limitation role for determining force development, Alain Enthoven, assistant secretary of defense for systems analysis, testified that the United States should not invest large sums of money in limiting damage.[65] Kendall pushed Enthoven, too, on the declaratory policy put forward by McNamara in 1962. Enthoven responded that there was a change in policy, made necessary by growth in the Soviet nuclear arsenal. Enthoven was straightforward about the nature of U.S. nuclear targeting and its consistency over the years:

Dr. Enthoven: First, I would like to emphasize that our targeting policy, as reflected in the guidance for the preparation of the targeting plan, has not changed. From 1961–62 on, the targeting plan has been based on the principle that we should have different options that target the strategic forces and cities. As U.S. and Soviet forces have changed, naturally the targets have changed.

What has changed is our appreciation of how much damage we can do by targeting strategic forces. When the Soviets depended mainly on bombers and soft missiles, their forces were quite vulnerable, and we thought we could inflict considerable damage to them. Now that they are defended mainly by ICBMs in hardened silos, and submarines, we do not believe we can accomplish as much any more.[66]

Kendall followed up by stating that it was his impression that the urban-industrial complex had gone from number three priority to number one priority. Enthoven disagreed.[67] Kendall went on to talk about the relationship between the purpose behind force procurement and their use in a nuclear war. Enthoven responded that there is a "significant difference" between what determines the size of forces and principles used for the potential application of forces.

It is important to elaborate on this point.[68] Enthoven was asked why the United States had such a large nuclear arsenal if policy was

MAD. The explanation here is that the United States always needs to procure nuclear forces based on worst-case scenarios. Since these worst-case scenarios never materialized, the United States was left with excess weapons. The excess weapons, the argument goes, were used for counterforce purposes. A telling exchange between Kendall and Enthoven ensued:

> Mr. Kendall: Under the assured destruction concept, is provision made or allowed for the type of weapon needed to kill hard targets such as ICBM's and control centers, and so forth?

> Dr. Enthoven: We have been buying improved accuracy in our ICBM's in order to have that capability. The problem is that when you face an antiballistic missile defense, to some extent you are pulled in opposing directions. If you want to be able to overwhelm and penetrate the defense, there are strong pressures on you to choose the options of multiple warheads, which means smaller warheads, whereas if you did not face the defense, you could depend on large warheads. So we have been trying to offset the lower yield of small warheads by improving their accuracy, and I think are doing so.[69]

One of the results of a disjunction between action and declaratory policy is that it becomes difficult to justify counterforce weapons and improvements in accuracy if declaratory policy is MAD. In this exchange, between Senator Jack Miller (R-IA) and Secretary of the Air Force Harold Brown that difficulty becomes clear:

> Senator Miller:...why would it be desirable or necessary for us to improve the CEP [circular error probable] down to less than [deleted]. It seems to me that if we have a CEP that we now have sufficient damage could be done without worrying about it getting down to less than that.

> Secretary Brown: For assured destruction, there is not really very much gained, Senator Miller. There is some, because if you are going against a good ABM defense, it helps to be able to put each of your warheads quite accurately on a given place. The principal value for a very accurate ICBM, or very accurate MIRV, is actually in the destruction of hard military targets which, of course, is connected with damage limitation. And, so, to the extent that we

work on very small CEP's, if we do, it is a sign that we have not abandoned completely damage limitation as a role for our forces.[70]

Pushed to identify which criteria were being used for determining the force structure of the U.S. nuclear arsenal, Brown responded, "The forces are derived principally on assured destruction....[B]ut the derivation of the force remains fundamentally what is required to assure destruction. Not entirely though, for example, we put good CEP's on our weapons, although that doesn't greatly improve our assured destruction capability."[71] In a subsequent exchange, Kendall pressed Brown:

Mr. Kendall: Sometime over the past few years we have moved from a damage-limiting strategy to one in which damage limiting is sort of a fallout from assured destruction, as far as the purchase of equipment or hardware is concerned. Can you tell us when this change occurred, and what was the reasoning for it, or the facts of life which made it necessary?

Secretary Brown: I don't think that there was-that is quite so clear a change from black to white, Mr. Kendall. I think that back in the late 1950's and early 1960's, assured destruction was also the principal criterion. There was a change in emphasis that occurred between, say, 1962 and 1965 or 1966....All of these things made their forces more survivable and, therefore, reduced our capability to limit damage, just as our previous actions had greatly reduced their ability to limit damage to them. So if an evolution did take place it became clearer that assured destruction was feasible providing you planned well—and the Soviets did plan well after we began to plan well—and to the extent that assured destruction was feasible, damage limiting was much less feasible, and more chancy.[72]

This testimony is illustrative of the confusion surrounding U.S. nuclear weapons policy by the end of the 1960s. This leads us to look at the actual force development policy of the Kennedy administration to see which nuclear weapons systems were sought.

Force Development Policy

To summarize, while U.S. declaratory policy shifted from embracing city-avoidance to embracing MAD, the SIOP remained very heavily oriented toward counterforce targets. It will now be useful to examine the third level of nuclear policy, the force development or procurement level, to see what capabilities the U.S. arsenal had at this time and what the justifications were for changes in weapons systems and characteristics.

The 1960s was the most important decade for the development of the U.S. nuclear arsenal and establishing the shape of the strategic triad. Though numerous refinements and developments took place after this period, the basic structure of the triad had already been established. Some of the most important innovations—such as SLBMs and MIRVs—began in the 1960s. The move away from manned bombers and toward ballistic missiles allowed for the shift from countervalue to counterforce targeting. The emerging characteristics of ballistic missiles, including accuracy and speed, favored counterforce.[73] Despite protests to the contrary by policymakers who said that MAD governed procurement decisions, damage-limitation criteria and counterforce were very influential for the most important nuclear weapons developments during this period. Further, it is also clear that the move toward accuracy and limited options did not come from those creating weapons but from civilian decision-makers at the Pentagon.

We must look beyond the specific characteristics of particular weapons systems and to the composition of the entire nuclear arsenal. A strategy of MAD caps the number of weapons in the arsenal. After the numerical criteria defining MAD are met, the force level can be held steady, remaining sensitive to changes in the Soviet nuclear arsenal. Conversely, damage-limiting or counterforce strategies leave room for build-up because as the Soviet arsenal increases, the number of targets continues to grow. In addition, to achieve counterforce in an age of limited accuracy, many warheads needed to be targeted at each nuclear weapon.

The beginning of the decade saw the U.S. arsenal relying primarily on long-range heavy bombers, with only 54 ICBMs and 80 SLBMs in 1961. This mix began to change over the course of the decade as the *Minutemen* and *Poseidon* systems came into production and the number of ICBMs and SLBMs rose. Old, inaccurate, and high-payload *Titan* and *Atlas* missiles were retired in favor of the newer generation *Minuteman* ICBMs. By 1968, the United States strategic triad was established at 1,054 ICBMs, 656 SLBMs, and 456 bombers.[74]

Earlier, there had been pressure from the Air Force to set ICBM levels higher than the 1,000 that McNamara agreed to. Some in SAC were proposing a force of 10,000 *Minutemen*, others 3,000. These large requests materialized after McNamara announced the no-cities doctrine in 1962. This call for a counterforce damage-limiting capability gave many in the Air Force who desired a first-strike capability the window that they were looking for to build up the arsenal. It gave others who truly wanted to implement the no-cities doctrine an argument that they needed additional weapons to accomplish this new strategy.

The administration took seriously the types of procurement changes necessary for the new city-avoidance doctrine. The Net-Evaluation Sub-Committee (NESC) of the NSC began to investigate this issue in the spring of 1961 to determine the forces needed for a city-avoidance strategy. They suggested that the United States would need to build 2,000–2,150 *Minuteman* missiles, achieve lower CEP–higher yield weapons, and renew attention to the issue of command and control. The 1961 Partridge Report also suggested changes in the *Minuteman* system that would add flexibility to the U.S. arsenal. Such changes for ICBMs included an increased target selection to eight, from one, that would each be able to be launched individually instead of in squadrons of fifty, and that the range of each missile would be enhanced.[75]

The emphasis on damage limitation led McNamara to procure forces for that purpose. For example, in the 1964 DPM McNamara noted that by 1970 only about half of the projected U.S. ICBM and *Polaris* force of 1,710 missiles, and none of the bombers, would be needed to fulfill the assured destruction criteria for the USSR and Communist China. The remaining forces, McNamara went on to say, "must be justified on the degree to which they assist the U.S. defensive forces (interceptor aircraft, fallout shelters, etc.) in limiting damage to our population."[76] And though McNamara did limit the build-up of the land-based leg of the triad to 1,000, the development of MIRVs allowed the counterforce options to remain viable. Without MIRVs, the hard target kill capability of the strategic arsenal would have probably been limited to 1,000 warheads (the number of warheads deployed on ICBMs). The development of MIRVs allowed this capability to grow.

McNamara stated further in the 1964 DPM, "[A]t each budget level above $5.2 billion, about $3 billion would be allocated for strategic missiles targeted against Soviet offensive forces."[77] He said that since this damage-limitation role depends on the ability of U.S. forces to arrive before Soviet forces have left, missiles were much more desirable than manned bombers. In the 1965 DPM, McNamara stated, "feasible improvements in missile accuracy, and the use of MIRVs where applicable, can greatly increase the efficiency of our offensive forces against hard Soviet targets. However, the effectiveness of offensive forces in Damage Limiting is sensitive to the timing of nuclear exchange."[78]

In the 1964 DPM McNamara mentioned MIRVs as an important part of the damage-limitation strategy of the time. The 1966 DPM also emphasized MIRVs. The development of the MIRV took place primarily in the 1960s, though it was not deployed on the *Minuteman III* until 1970.[79] Many of the most salient debates about the MIRV, particularly those within Congress, took place in the late 1960s and early 1970s, and will be covered in the next case study. It is clear, however, that from the beginning MIRVs were justified (at the declaratory level) on the basis of their ability to overcome Soviet ABMs, not as way to increase the counterforce capability of the U.S. strategic arsenal. As Alton Frye summarized, "from the beginning of the U.S. MIRV effort, counterforce implications were muted and relegated to the background."[80] But as John Foster, director of research and engineering for the Department of Defense, testified, "The MIRV concept was originally generated to increase our targeting capability rather than to penetrate ABM defenses."[81] And in the early 1960s, when the MIRV technology was developed, there was not a great fear of Soviet ABMs. What did exist was the need to be able to hit more hard-target sites in the Soviet Union without building more ballistic missiles. This justification of MIRVs is indicative of the gap between action and declaratory policies.

In the 1964 DPM, McNamara sold the MIRV as something that could destroy hardened Soviet missile targets. In 1965, the *Minuteman III* was heralded for having much greater accuracy than the older ICBMs. In the 1965 DPM, McNamara stated that the number of *Minuteman IIs* to be deployed was to be determined by looking at the Soviet target system in the absence of ABMs.[82]

As the 1960s came to a close, evidence that the Soviet Union was researching ABM systems propelled the development of MIRVs. It was both the accuracy of MIRVed warheads and the increase in the number of warheads they would provide that attracted those who feared the development of Soviet ABMs. On January 16, 1968, a Pentagon press release announced that "each new MIRV missile warhead will be far more accurate than any previous or existing warheads. They will be far better suited for destruction of hardened enemy missiles than any existing warhead."[83]

In congressional testimony, Senator Mike Mansfield questioned Foster about the relationship between the MIRV and the ABM:

> Senator Mike Mansfield (D-MT): Is it not true that the U.S. response to the discovery that the Soviets had made an initial deployment of an ABM system around Moscow and probably

elsewhere was to develop the MIRV system for Minuteman and Polaris?

Dr. John Foster: Not entirely. The MIRV concept was originally generated to increase our targeting capability rather than to penetrate ABM defenses. In 1961–62 planning for targeting the Minuteman forces it was found that the total number of aim points exceeded the number of Minuteman missiles. By splitting up the payload of a single missile [deleted] each [deleted] could be programmed [deleted] allowing us to cover the targets with [deleted] fewer missiles [deleted]. MIRV was originally born to implement the payload split-up [deleted]. It was found that the previously generated MIRV concept could equally be used against ABM.[84]

In looking at the improvement to the *Minuteman* forces that took place over this time, McNamara supported an Air Force proposal for an *Improved Minuteman* that would become operational by FY 1966. The goal of the *Improved Minuteman* program was to double the yield of the warheads and cut the CEP in half. These provisions made the *Minuteman* more valuable for counterforce purposes. McNamara recommended 800 *Minutemen* and 50 *Improved Minutemen* by the end of FY 1968.[85]

Similar questions arise when we look at the *Poseidon* program. Harvey Sapolsky's study of the *Poseidon* makes it clear that though at times the counterforce targeting emphasis of the new submarine was one of the major goals, "apparently only a few persons involved in the FBM [Fleet Ballistic Missile] Program, and even fewer in the public were fully aware of the possible alteration of the original B-3 mission."[86] The *Poseidon* was given a second strategic mission because the hard target counterforce capability was added to the B-3 proposals in secrecy. Very few were aware of the new mission for the missiles.[87] In addition, the *Poseidon* was retargetable, a flexibility that McNamara added so more limited options would be available to the president.

In the DPM for 1964, McNamara said:

I recommend the inclusion in the FY 1966 budget $35 million to begin deployment of a new Polaris B-3. We intend to initiate a project definition for the missile during FY 1964. The B-3 would incorporate improved accuracy and payload flexibility permitting it to attack single, heavily defended urban industrial targets, or a single hardened point target, or several undefended targets, which might be separated by as much as 76 miles.[88]

The move toward accuracy for the new submarine did not come from parochial bureaucratic interests but instead from the Office of the Secretary of Defense.[89]

The existing *Polaris* was limited to soft targets. The Navy had resisted accuracy improvements to their arsenal, partly because it had never had a role in the counterforce strategy. In internal debates, the Navy had opted for finite or limited deterrence. The Navy resisted these changes because it would have been forced to take money out of its regular budget to fund new nuclear systems.[90] Later, David Packard, deputy secretary of defense under Melvin Laird, told a congressional subcommittee that the *Poseidon* SLBM was 6 percent more effective than the *Polaris* A-3 against hard targets, whether or not it was MIRVed. And a display at the Naval Museum in Washington contained a description that read: "[P]oseidon will have double the payload of the Polaris A-3. It will be twice as accurate. As a result, its effectiveness against a hardened target will be some eight times greater than the latest version of Polaris."[91] By 1969, research to make the SLBM more accurate began. As Melvin Laird told Congress:

> The increase of $12.4 million for the development of an improved guidance system for the Poseidon missile will advance the initial operating capability (IOC) of that system by about six months.... This is an important program since it promises to improve significantly the accuracy of the Poseidon missile, thus enhancing its effectiveness against hard targets.[92]

Civil defense was also an important part of the procurement strategy linked to damage limitation. The roots of this go back to the Eisenhower administration. The Gaither Committee Report, issued in 1957, proposed that $32.4 billion be spent on civil defense.[93] Pressure for this continued into the early 1960s as well, when Nelson Rockefeller and others pushed for civil defense. In addition, Robert Kennedy, the president's brother, attorney general and close adviser, also pushed for civil defense. In 1961, plans were under way to publish and distribute a pamphlet to the nation outlining the importance of civil defense. There was some hesitation on the part of officials in the White House to go public with this issue. Kaplan notes, "[S]ome White House officials felt that release of the pamphlet would create a public panic."[94] In November of that same year, Kennedy adviser Theodore Sorenson warned, "Civil Defense is rapidly blossoming into our number one political headache."[95]

Civil defense is an integral part of a damage-limitation strategy. In July 1961, President Kennedy estimated that 50 million shelters could save 10–15 million lives. McNamara stated in the 1964 DPM, "an effective nation-wide fallout shelter system would provide the greatest return for the money expended."[96] By 1965, the extensive plans had been abandoned though all efforts at civil defense were not.[97] And though the Kennedy administration had requested $695 million for civil defense, Congress cut this to $80 million the next year without much interference from the administration.[98] This issue represents everything about damage limiting or counterforce strategies that state officials cannot talk about in public. And here it became all too clear that the state was risking autonomy by bringing the issue to the declaratory level.

At the same time, one official of the McNamara period and later an observer of U.S. nuclear weapons policy said, "it [MAD] never even for McNamara was targeting policy, it never was for him a policy under which you decided to procure, it was a measure which enabled you to show that you didn't need to procure any more. That is all it was, it was invented for that purpose."[99]

One very high defense department official during the McNamara years said that the excess capabilities of this period were the result of trying to project Soviet capabilities seven or eight years into the future. According to this logic, the McNamara Defense Department only procured for MAD, but when Soviet capabilities did not go up as much as some had estimated, the excess forces were used for damage limitation.[100] Though these explanations may give part of the picture, they really fail to account for the development of an increased hard-target kill capability that was, as is shown above, associated with the development of the *Minuteman*, the *Poseidon*, and MIRVs.

Conclusions

This chapter illustrates three factors that help us to identify the myth of MAD. First, during this period declaratory policy embraced MAD. The type of rhetoric that came in McNamara's Ann Arbor city-avoidance speech was not heard again during these years. Second, the SIOP was heavily oriented toward counterforce. Third, in the middle of these two levels of policy is a force development policy oriented toward the forces appropriate for counterforce, city-avoidance, and damage limitation. From the development of MIRVs to the procurement of new submarines and an emphasis on civil defense, high state officials acted with coherence in establishing the basic foundations of U.S. nuclear weapons policy.

It is the degree of coherence during this period that is of critical importance. At one level, due largely to the myth of MAD, the nuclear weapons policy of the 1960s seemed incoherent and propelled by parochial, bureaucratic interests. In fact, as illustrated in chapter 2, much of the literature on bureaucratic politics was developed by looking at this period. However, with full knowledge of the dynamics of the three different levels of nuclear weapons policy, coherence rather than inconsistency is the best way to describe the nuclear weapons policy of the time. Central state decision-makers controlled all three levels of policy and pushed action and development policy in the direction of NUTs.

Of course, the period covered by this case study is a unique one for U.S. nuclear weapons policy because of the great U.S. strategic superiority. As will be seen in the next two case studies, waning U.S. superiority would close the gap between declaratory and action policy as the state perceived that the procurement of a significant counterforce capability was necessary for deterrence.

The literature has used variants of the bureaucratic politics perspective to explain the evolution of the three levels of U.S. nuclear weapons policy during this period. Changes in declaratory, force development, and action policy have all been explained based on the notion that there was no central control over the formulation of U.S. nuclear weapons policy. One of the main points of this chapter illustrates that we gain some explanatory power by seeing the state as unified in the developments of these various levels of policy. There were surely debates within the state, but the commitment to counterforce prevailed.

McNamara did have to fight significant bureaucratic battles over these years. But the disjunction between declaratory and action policy is not best explained through the bureaucratic lens. Civilian policymakers brought the counterforce strategies to the forefront. And though McNamara backed away from this at the declaratory level, the weapons he sought to procure were consistent with a NUTs strategy. The ABMs, MIRVs, and increased accuracy for ICBMs did not come from the military—and they were all consistent with the counterforce emphasis of the veiled SIOP.[101]

One of the perennial questions surrounding the evolution of U.S. nuclear weapons policy concerns the relationship between technology and strategy. My statist approach, unlike the bureaucratic approach, gives strategy causal primacy. The strategy of city-avoidance and counterforce targeting was developed by top level defense policymakers. The interaction between this and the technological capability to accomplish strategic goals is important, but there is little evidence that technology was driving policy.

The statist approach also demands that we pay explicit attention to the domestic political structure. For this period we see important changes in the process involved in making U.S. nuclear weapons policy. First, for action policy, targeting was coordinated in the SIOP. This took the targeting out of the hands of the military and allowed for civilian control over the process. Second, McNamara took seriously the importance of civilian control over the Department of Defense. The implementation of the Draft Presidential Memorandum significantly aided this process. Though civilians take control over nuclear weapons policy during this period, society is not yet very involved.

Finally, an assessment of the role of society is of crucial importance for the statist perspective. We see during this period a heightened awareness on the part of the general public about the nature of U.S. nuclear weapons policy. This results from the city-avoidance announcement and from the discussion surrounding civil defense programs. This limited the declaratory-level rhetoric about these programs. As the story continues, the utility of the statist lens will become clearer.

5

Shifting Sands?

Shifting sands seems the best was to characterize the strategic rationale of recent years. In 1961 the suicidal implications of massive retaliation were underscored: the United States would be faced with a choice between humiliation or holocaust. Interest then developed in damage-limiting and coercion. But there has been little willingness to invest money in either. Since 1965 the merits of Assured Destruction have been emphasized—with little attention paid to the suicidal implications found so distressing in prior years.[1]

This case study begins with the Nixon administration in January 1969 and follows developments in nuclear weapons policy through the Ford administration. During this period, the United States was preoccupied with its involvement in Vietnam. The preoccupation of the American foreign policy establishment with Vietnam may partly explain the length of time it took to implement changes in nuclear policy long in the planning stage.

In addition, there are important links between the Vietnam War and U.S. policymakers' beliefs about the potential utility of nuclear weapons. Despite U.S. predominance in nuclear weapons during the 1960s, policymakers found themselves unable to utilize U.S. power to gain victory in Vietnam. Though the U.S. predominance in nuclear weapons left it unable to dominate the Korean Peninsula only a decade earlier, the use of nuclear weapons was contemplated numerous times.[2]

The lack of utility of nuclear weapons in Vietnam led paradoxically to renewed efforts to thinking about using nuclear weapons in a limited way. This is not to say that plans for the limited use of nuclear weapons were motivated solely by concerns for use in the third world. Extending deterrence to Europe has always dominated such considerations. Nevertheless, U.S. intervention in Vietnam and Korea seemed to be unaffected by the existence of a nuclear arsenal. Policymakers could either accept this lack of utility or attempt to overcome it. They chose the latter.

Related to this last point is the Watergate scandal and its command of the administration's and the public's attention. The major shift in declaratory policy as articulated in Secretary of Defense James Schlesinger's January 1974 speech took place at the zenith of the Watergate scandal. Also important is the change and continuity of personnel in charge of security affairs during this period. Henry Kissinger's dominance over U.S. foreign policy is well known. National Security adviser to President Richard Nixon and later President Gerald Ford's secretary of state, Kissinger left an indelible mark on U.S. foreign policy. Kissinger came to office with impressive credentials, having written about the role of nuclear weapons and the possibility of the limited use of nuclear weapons.[3] Though Kissinger initiated considerations of building more limited nuclear options into the SIOP, it was not his primary concern, nor was he the sole mover of this policy.

Also important is the turnover that took place in the position of secretary of defense. Melvin Laird, Elliot Richardson, James Schlesinger, and Donald Rumsfeld each held the post during the period covered by this case study. Though we will look at these secretaries and the impact that they had on U.S. nuclear weapons policy, the most important was James Schlesinger. Schlesinger was the first U.S. secretary of defense to come into office with expertise on defense issues, having led strategic studies at the Rand Corporation in the 1960s. In addition, this period saw some important holdovers from the McNamara years, including Ivan Selin, one of the "whiz kids" who would later become acting assistant secretary of defense for systems analysis and instrumental in the changes made to nuclear weapons policy during these years.[4] At the staff level, across executive branch agencies, there was continuity in personnel. Many of the same people who were influential in the McNamara Pentagon played important roles in the 1970s as well.

The Changing Strategic Balance

There are various ways of measuring the nuclear strategic balance between the United States and the USSR. However, by virtually any measure the period 1969–75 saw the emergence and consolidation of parity. This contrasts sharply with the nature of the military balance in the previous decade, where by most measures the United States enjoyed substantial superiority. During this latter period, policymakers perceived a closing gap between the two sides. One standard measure of the nuclear balance is the number of nuclear launchers. The following table offers a comparison over ten years for the balance of launchers between the two sides:[5]

	1965	1970	1975
US			
ICBMs	854	1,054	1,054
SLBMs	496	656	656
Long-range bombers	630	550	397
Total	1,980	2,260	2,107
USSR			
ICBMs	270	1,300	1,527
SLBMs	120	280	784
Long-range bombers	190	150	135
Total	580	1,730	2,446

The USSR went from being outnumbered 3 to 1 in strategic weapons launchers to gaining an advantage by the same measure a decade later.

Perhaps more important than a count of strategic delivery vehicles is the number of strategic nuclear warheads that each side could deliver to the other. The United States maintained an advantage on this measure.[6] Though the U.S. advantage in warheads was significant during this time, these measures are only static indices of forces. A large part of the U.S. advantage in warheads comes from the MIRVing of ballistic missile systems, particularly the land-based leg of the triad. Though this gives the United States an advantage in the number of warheads that could be launched against the Soviet Union, it also made U.S. forces more vulnerable to a Soviet strike. While the perceived U.S. advantage does not disappear by the mid-1970s, the U.S. predominance in strategic nuclear weapons was beginning to wane.

These measures of the nuclear balance are only one factor decision-makers consider when assessing the adequacy of U.S. nuclear forces. Studies of the nuclear age make one point clear: policymakers consistently overestimated Soviet capabilities, relying on worst-case scenarios to determine U.S. policy. The Soviet acquisition of a significant hard-target kill capability in the land-based SS-18 was seen as a symbol of the Soviet drive for superiority. While the measures above indicated that the United States still had a clear though waning advantage, policymakers anticipated the worst.

The Long Road to Change the SIOP

Efforts to change the SIOP took a long time to come to fruition. The process began early in 1969, when National Security Adviser Henry

Kissinger issued NSSM-3 entitled "Military Posture."[7] The result of an interagency study, NSSM-3 read in part that nuclear war

> may develop as a series of steps in an escalating crisis in which both sides want to avoid attacking cities, neither side can afford unilaterally to stop the exchange, and the situation is dominated by uncertainty...war termination, avoiding attacks on cities, and selective response capabilities might provide ways of limiting damage if deterrence fails.[8]

This grew out of Kissinger's concern that the existing SIOP did not have sufficient limited options. Kissinger became frustrated by the lack of ability to use nuclear weapons in a limited way. During the Jordan crisis of 1970, when Palestinian guerrillas hijacked 4 planes to Amman, the United States was unable to threaten the Soviet Union with the use of nuclear weapons because there were no credible limited options contained in the SIOP. Kissinger was disappointed in 1974 when he asked the JCS for nuclear plans in the case of a Soviet invasion of Iran and he received what he perceived as massive options for a mission that had only limited goals.[9]

Kissinger's memorandum made the NSC the focal point for the activities to revise the SIOP. Though the Kissinger initiative had begun as an interagency project, Ivan Selin of DoD Systems Analysis was instrumental in putting the plan together. Selin had been an advocate of limited options during the McNamara years. The NSC paid less attention to this, as Kissinger and other NSC staffers took on SALT, the Vietnam War, and other pressing issues. The planning of this broad general guidance was left to others.[10] During 1970 the Systems Analysis office of the Pentagon continued to look into the issue of limited nuclear war, though by this time Selin had left the office.[11] However, the JCS, who would ultimately be confronted with the task of transforming this new civilian input into a new SIOP, were skeptical of the work the Systems Analysis staff had done during the McNamara years.

The scope of involvement widened in 1971, after it was perceived that NSSM-3 had stalled. This led the DoD to take over the consideration of revisions to the SIOP under the Foster Panel, headed by John Foster, the Deputy Secretary for Research and Development. Initially, the study was conducted without the formal participation of the Department of State, Arms Control and Disarmament Agency (ACDA), the Central Intelligence Agency (CIA), and other central actors. In January 1972 Foster issued the National Nuclear Strategic Targeting and Attack

Plan (NSTAP), an eighteen-page document outlining new flexible options for the SIOP.[12] After a year of work, the results were given to the White House, where the NSC then directed a full interagency review.[13]

Work continued on revisions to the SIOP, and a year later the Foster Panel was widened to include the State Department. Seymour Weiss, who had been the head of political/military affairs for State during the 1960s, had become deeply involved in the process. Weiss had been supportive of these efforts and had also been keeping Schlesinger informed of the work while he held various positions around Washington. By the end of 1973, after starting this process four years earlier, Kissinger wanted to regain control over these policy initiatives by bringing it back to the NSC. At this point, the NSC hesitated to move forward, as David Aaron, Kissinger's assistant on the NSC, feared what the Air Force might do with the implications of the new plans. Similar to the previous case study, some civilian decision-makers were concerned that the new policy would generate an increased demand for new weapons.

NSDM-242 and SIOP 5

This work led to NSSM-169, approved by President Nixon in late 1973. NSSM-169 called for an interagency review of all U.S. nuclear forces. Later, National Security Decision Memorandum 242 (NSDM-242) was issued by the president and signed in 1974, only a week after Schlesinger went public with the new doctrine. NSDM-242 called for limited employment options to be added to the SIOP. It also called for the targeting of Soviet recovery resources and escalation control.

There were other important aspects to NSDM-242. First, it separated Sino-Soviet-Eastern bloc targets. The goal was to treat all Communist areas as separate targeting areas. The major contribution of NSDM-242 in this regard was the establishing of regional nuclear options. In addition, there was some thought given to isolating Soviet republics for targeting purposes, though this was not implemented.[14]

NSDM-242 was a decision memorandum that authorized the secretary of defense to put forward guidance for revising the SIOP. It read in part that "[P]lans should be developed for limited employment options which enable the United States to conduct selected nuclear operations, which protect vital U.S. interests and limit enemy capabilities to continue aggression."[15] This Nuclear Weapons Employment Policy (NUWEP-1) was signed by James Schlesinger on April 4, 1974.[16] The NUWEP is the guidance issued by the Department of Defense to the

JSTPS in Omaha. SIOP 5 was formally approved in December 1975 and took effect in January 1976.

The NUWEP had four principal components. The first was the re-emphasis on the targeting of Soviet military forces, "from hardened command and control facilities and ICBM silos to airfields and army camps."[17] The second was a desire for escalation control. Third was the desire to spare certain targets and withhold strikes.[18] Finally, the new guidance emphasized the targeting of economic recovery targets. This divided possible options into limited nuclear options, military attack options, regional attack options, and intermediate attack options.

The goal of these changes was to add flexibility to targeting plans that had seemed inflexible—to add utility to plans that seemed to lack the utility that policymakers had desired since the 1960s. And though counterforce was an important part of this new plan, it was not simply a counterforce doctrine. The new doctrine also emphasized flexibility, the capability to do many things with the strategic arsenal, and to control escalation and prevent an all-out nuclear war. Of course, counterforce must be seen as an important part of this—it would not make much sense to build flexible options into the SIOP without having counterforce options. The degree to which this new doctrine relied on the acquisition of new counterforce capabilities is controversial and will be discussed below when we look at the public proclamations and weapons procurement efforts that ensued.

The military reaction to this was mixed, and the degree to which any of this guidance was incorporated into the SIOP is unclear. After a briefing on these new plans for limited options and flexibility, the JCS said that they could not make sense out of the guidance. This is not an atypical response on the part of the military to civilian desires for limited nuclear options. For example, the military had a hard time figuring out why the United States might want to send only two or three nuclear weapons and have five thousand launched back in response. To the military mind, such plans made little sense. Of course, the civilian rationale for these plans was that U.S. restraint in the beginning of a nuclear exchange might lead to Soviet restraint. Apparently the JCS did not see it this way.[19] As a participant recounted:

> I was involved in NSDM-242, about six months after the policy directive went out, supplemented with NUWEP from SECDEF [Secretary of Defense], we had a visiting delegation from JSTPS and an Admiral and four of his officers, and they came to Washington and went around to all the people who had been participants in writing this policy directive and the essential

question was what does this policy mean. I mean, explain to us what some of these ideas mean.[20]

It was not only a lack of belief in the efficacy of such a policy that made the military skeptical. In addition, because adequate changes in force development policy were not forthcoming, some in the military were doubtful that the goals of the new plans could be realized with the existing strategic nuclear arsenal. As one influential member of various committees looking at targeting recounted:

What we discovered previously, the previous major study having been NSDM-242 in the mid-70's, back in the Nixon administration, was that a lot of that didn't get implemented in the way that policymakers envisioned. And part of that was because it couldn't —there was not a willful failure to implement. Typically, the JSTPS would try to carry out some scheme—but they would say that we don't have the resources to do it, or we don't have the right kind of weapons, we don't have the right kind of command and control.[21]

Finally, as Henry Rowen has pointed out in his review of the formulation of U.S. strategic doctrine, "flexible nuclear options was not a policy which the members of the JSTPS and JCS organization advocated. They had developed some, but by and large small options were not lobbied for by these staffs. They perceived difficult problems in carrying out controlled and discriminate strikes."[22]

It took nearly two years to carry out these changes that were to become part of SIOP 5. The SIOP was to have very small options, much smaller than the two thousand five hundred nuclear weapons that were the smallest option that had existed at the time. In addition, while the options were shrinking, the actual target list, as a result of the economic recovery criteria and the growing Soviet nuclear arsenal, increased to more than twenty-five thousand targets.[23] SIOP 5 targeted more than forty thousand potential target installations, and included targets in the following four principal target categories: 1) Soviet nuclear forces; 2) conventional military forces; 3) military and political leadership; and 4) economic and industrial targets. These were broken down into four subcategories, which included major attack options, selective attack options, limited nuclear options, and regional nuclear options.[24] The limited nuclear options were designed to hit fixed enemy military or industrial targets, and the regional nuclear operations were designed to hit the forward part of the attacking forces. These were seen as potentially useful for responding to Soviet conventional and military activity in the Middle East. Here, for example, nuclear weapons might be used to hit Soviet military capabilities close to Iran to impede Soviet military moves in the area.[25]

The SIOP was to have the ability to destroy 70 percent of Soviet industry needed for economic recovery. It is not that the SIOP did not previously try to destroy industry. Instead, the new SIOP took this criterion more seriously, and calculations were made to assess the best way to achieve this goal.[26] There is an important point here about the targeting of urban industrial targets. Sagan writes:

> Ironically, although the Nixon Administration deemphasized the rhetoric of MAD and Assured Destruction, it produced guidance that apparently resulted in a war plan that put greater emphasis on urban-industrial targets than had been the case under McNamara.[27]

Sagan finds this ironic because the Nixon administration began to de-emphasize MAD as declaratory policy. However, the type of targeting associated with economic recovery is different from that which would aim to destroy only populations. Economic recovery targets are co-located with populations, and the results of the two different types of targeting might be difficult to differentiate. There is a big difference between targeting populations per se and economic recovery, at least for the *goals* of the policy. That populations might be destroyed as a result of a nuclear exchange did not mean that the Nixon administration believed in MAD as a targeting policy. Instead, it is an example of the limits inherent in what could be done with nuclear weapons.

Also important in this SIOP were "withholds," which allowed for the execution of the SIOP, sparing certain categories of targets to achieve escalation control. It was not that the SIOP had not included the capability to target these categories of weapons, but instead that it would do so at any point in a conflict where it was deemed advantageous. The first withhold was populations. The second was the USSR's command and control. This was thought to be crucial, because if you want to control escalation and fight a nuclear war, you needed to have somebody on the other side to communicate with. The final category of withhold was particular countries.[28] Finally, Schlesinger also wanted to add sub-SIOP options to the plans available to the president: options that would not be included in the actual SIOP but would be available to the president should he want to improvise during a nuclear conflict.[29]

If we compared this guidance and the SIOP with that of the McNamara years, we would find important similarities and differences. The most important similarity was that the targeting of populations was clearly not the goal of the guidance or the design of the SIOP for both periods. While counterforce targeting was important for these considerations, there were not the great sub-options or limited options during the 1960s that existed during the 1970s. The nuclear plans of this period further extended the logic that McNamara had introduced over a decade earlier.

The Public Explication of U.S. Nuclear Weapons Policy

It is necessary to look briefly at the declaratory policy that preceded the change in targeting. Though Schlesinger's speech in January 1974 was the watershed announcement of this new policy, Nixon had publicly expressed his displeasure with existing policy near the beginning of his presidency. In his foreign policy message to Congress in 1970, he said:

Should a President, in the event of a nuclear attack, be left with the single option of ordering the mass destruction of enemy civilians, in the face of the certainty that it would be followed by the mass slaughter of Americans? Should the concept of assured destruction be narrowly defined and should it be the only measure of our ability to deter the variety of threats we may face?[30]

Similar rhetoric was expounded a year later when Nixon explained the new "Doctrine of Sufficiency":

I must not be—and my successors must not be—limited to the indiscriminate mass destruction of enemy civilians as the sole possible response to challenges. This is especially so when that response involves the likelihood of triggering nuclear attacks on our own population.[31]

This is an oft-cited quotation. It is important because it embraces the notion of counterforce limited options for U.S. nuclear weapons policy. It also misrepresents the nature of existing U.S. nuclear weapons policy.[32] Public officials, in embracing limited options at the declaratory level, attempt to walk a thin line between two extremes. On the one hand, in pushing for limited options leaders have often mischaracterized U.S. nuclear weapons policy as MAD. After public reactions to calls for limited options, policymakers often went to the other extreme in an attempt to convince those who were listening that the new proposals were not all that radical. This tension between positioning declaratory policy as a radical shift and relative continuity is seen throughout the history of U.S. declaratory policy.

The Nixon administration wanted to move away from assured destruction as policy, and its public declarations attempting to do so were plentiful. But U.S. policy during the 1960s never really did have a targeting policy that had embraced MAD, though declaratory policy did. The Nixon administration was trying to distance itself from something that did not exist, further propelling the myth of MAD. This period of change in U.S. nuclear policy would help to resurrect the myth of MAD, since many of those who justified the new counterforce flexible options would compare it to (and assert that it was replacing) MAD. This thinking prevailed for all secretaries of defense during the Nixon administration. Secretary of Defense Elliot Richardson testified in April 1973, "[W]e do not in our strategic planning target civilian populations per se."[33] James Schlesinger embraced this rhetoric when he became secretary of defense.

Schlesinger's first public statements on U.S. nuclear weapons policy came in June 1973 during his confirmation hearings for secretary of defense. He testified while high-level interagency consideration of revisions to the SIOP were taking place. Schlesinger was aware of these studies since he was director of the CIA. Because he was a known quantity in Washington politics, his confirmation hearings were not confrontational. One of the goals of the Armed Services Committee was to determine whether Schlesinger's views were in line with those of Laird and Richardson. Schlesinger agreed with the views expressed by his predecessors, including eschewing the achievement of a first strike capability. Schlesinger defended calls for obtaining hard-target kill capability and flexibility.[34]

This justification for the acquisition of limited options in the SIOP is a bit different from that offered during the McNamara period. McNamara called for more counterforce and a more refined SIOP based on the goal of damage limitation. It was the growth of the Soviet nuclear arsenal that made significant damage limitation more difficult. According to Schlesinger's testimony, the desire for flexibility was not motivated primarily by concern for damage limitation.

This became more salient when Schlesinger went fully public with the policy in January 1974. The motivations for this public explication have been alluded to above. One was to move consideration of flexible options out of the NSC, a bureaucratic maneuver aimed at pushing this policy forward. It was apparently Schlesinger's conviction upon becoming secretary that it was necessary to be as clear and accurate as possible about the planning of U.S. forces. As one close adviser to Schlesinger recounted:

> He felt that you should come out and level with people and he did not want to be saddled with this somewhat deceptive view of how the forces were being planned. Second, he also felt—and here I certainly agreed with him—you wanted to really tailor the forces very explicitly to what you were trying to hit, and unless you sort of disposed of these notions of assured destruction, and talked exclusively about targets and tailoring targets and warheads and CEPs, and so on, to explicit targets, you wouldn't really be doing your job.[35]

As Desmond Ball writes, "[O]ne senior official actually conceded that the Administration had been 'soft-pedaling' the new moves in the hope of avoiding a major debate on so explosive a subject during the campaign."[36]

Speaking only from notes, Schlesinger told the Overseas Writers Association on January 10, 1974:

> There has taken place a change in the strategies of the United States with regard to the hypothetical deployment of the central strategic forces. A change in targeting strategy [to give the United States President] an option to hit a different set of targets—military targets...beyond an all-out nuclear attack against cities.[37]

Keeping in line with the hyperbole of Nixon's message to Congress more than four years earlier, Schlesinger called this "probably the greatest change in U.S. nuclear missile strategy in a decade." He went on to say that the goal was to retarget ICBMs to hit Soviet silos. But the mischaracterization of previous U.S. nuclear weapons policy continued when Schlesinger said that the United States was aiming "some existing missiles at Soviet military targets instead of aiming all of them at cities and industrial areas."[38]

Schlesinger also sought to link these changes to a shift in the balance of nuclear forces. In response to a question that asked whether these changes were necessary because the Soviet Union had achieved a second-strike capability, Schlesinger responded:

Yes, I think it is necessary now. I think that it might well have been desirable before. You will all recall that in the 1960s, in 1962 in fact, Secretary McNamara discussed this type of issue at Athens and later in his Ann Arbor address in which the emphasis was put on something called city avoidance.

Now, this is quite parallel. That was in a period of time in which the United States did retain close to a disarming capability against the Soviet Union and recognized it. Therefore, I think the subject lapsed. But it is now, I think, incumbent upon us to emphasize a variety of options in this area available to the United States. As you know, this subject has been discussed in the President's foreign policy reports since 1970.[39]

Some senators were alarmed at this announcement and communicated their displeasure to Schlesinger. Senator Edward Brooke (R-MA), who was active in opposing the development of the MIRV, contacted Schlesinger immediately after the speech. Through letters and meetings, Brooke sought an on the record explanation for these proposed changes. Schlesinger suggested that such discussions take place in a broader forum. Brooke moved to have Schlesinger publicly testify on this policy and Schlesinger agreed. In his letter to Schlesinger on the subject, Brooke wrote that

It is self evident that the issues involved here are far too important for the continued security of the American people to be decided by the Administration alone on narrow technical grounds. Therefore, I am heartened by your commitment to a "serious debate" on the strategic questions.[40]

Senator Edmund Muskie (D-ME) was also disturbed by these proposed changes. He held a meeting of his Senate Arms Control Subcommittee and invited CIA Director William Colby to testify. Colby approved of the proposed changes to nuclear strategy, citing in part the Soviet build-up of ICBMs. Later, Muskie invited Schlesinger to the committee to testify on this policy.

The new policy was explored in the Schlesinger annual report that was issued in March 1974.[41] Unlike in his public comment months earlier, Schlesinger here acknowledges that U.S. war plans had always included military targets.[42] Further explanations by Schlesinger within this annual report said that the difference with the new doctrine was not so much in the type of targets but in the magnitude of the various options that would be available to the president. Schlesinger said, "[R]ather than massive options, we now want to provide the President with a wider set of much more selective targeting options."[43] Later he said, "we have had some large scale preplanned options other than attacking cities for many years, despite the rhetoric of assured destruction."[44] This acknowledged the disjunction between declaratory and action policy that had existed over the years. In fact, it is this very disjunction that made the proposed Schlesinger changes seem more radical than they really were. Within this annual report, Schlesinger traces the history of changes in U.S. policy, reviewing the debates of the previous decade on damage limitation and counterforce. Schlesinger noted that the goal of damage limitation had to be abandoned after the ABM Treaty eliminated the possibility of deploying a meaningful defense against nuclear weapons.

As in 1962, these plans were controversial with the allies, the public, and Congress. Special measures were taken to explain the policy to the allies to ensure that it was understood that one of the motivating goals of the new policy was to enhance the credibility of extended deterrence for Europe.[45] William Kauffman (who had been an influential adviser to McNamara during the 1960s) was brought in by Schlesinger to help explain this policy on Capitol Hill. The most telling interchange on this came before the Subcommittee on Arms Control, International Law and Organization of the Committee on Foreign Relations, on March 4, 1974. Schlesinger repeatedly emphasized that the new targeting did not require any changes in the U.S. force structure. Senator Muskie pushed Schlesinger on what the actual differences were between this policy and previous U.S. nuclear weapons policy. Muskie pointed out that U.S. targeting had always included military targets as well as cities. Schlesinger agreed with this. The difference, according to Schlesinger, was the new emphasis on flexibility and selectivity. The need for these changes was linked to the changing nature of the strategic balance between the U.S. and USSR. Schlesinger noted that while the threat of massive strikes might have been credible in the 1950s and 1960s because of the overwhelming U.S. preponderance of nuclear weapons, the growth of the Soviet arsenal made such threats incredible.[46]

Muskie asked:

Are you saying that the President does not now have the option of a limited strike against missile silos?

Secretary Schlesinger: He does hypothetically in that he could ask SAC to construct such a strike in an emergency. [Deleted]

But in order to have that kind of capacity one has to do the indoctrination and the planning in anticipation of the difficulties involved. It is ill-advised to attempt to do that under the press of circumstances. Rather one should think through the problem in advance and put together relevant, small packages which a President could choose under the circumstances in which they might be required—which I stress I do not think will arise.[47]

Other members of the committee were also concerned with the new doctrine. Senator Stuart Symington (D-MO) asked "[H]as the type of selective and flexible targeting capability that you are now proposing ever been proposed in the past; and if so, why was it not adopted?"[48] Schlesinger noted that though various secretaries from 1961 to 1974 had paid lip service to the desire for flexibility, the will had been absent to develop the plans and capabilities to fulfill such desires. Schlesinger then submitted for the record paragraphs from the Posture Statements of McNamara, Clark Clifford, Laird, and Richardson that all to some extent advocated the need for flexibility and limited options.[49]

The overall tone of this unprecedented hearing was not hostility toward this new policy but instead a general inquisitiveness into what it meant, how different it was from previous policy, and what the relationship was between this and the nuclear policy of earlier administrations. Only a month after selling these changes as representing a major departure from previous policy, Schlesinger was forced to emphasize continuity rather than change. In testimony before Congress the following year, Schlesinger commented:

I should like to emphasize that the alterations in our targeting strategy, which we believe make sense, are not so novel as perhaps has been advertised, because this has been discussed at least from the days of Secretary McNamara's Athens statement in 1962.[50]

Furthermore, it is unclear how much the new flexible strategy of the 1970s relied on counterforce targeting. It clearly was not only a counterforce doctrine, but this does not mean that counterforce was not important for its design and implementation.

The press took Schlesinger's original comments at face value. *The New York Times* reported that the "United States had begun retargeting some of its strategic missiles so they could strike at Soviet military installations as well as cities."[51] The article referred to the Schlesinger doctrine as a "new counterforce concept." The implication here is that previous U.S. war plans had called only for countervalue targeting: "For 20 years United States strategic missiles have been targeted so that they could strike retaliatory blows at Soviet cities and other population centers in the event of any Soviet nuclear attack." A similar assessment of this policy was offered by the *Washington Post* the day after Schlesinger responded to questions from the Overseas Writers Association.[52] This piece stressed the accuracy improvements that Schlesinger sought and the need to fund research and deployment of new weapons for this strategy. The article again alluded to the notion that previously the United States did not aim at military targets in the Soviet Union, and that Schlesinger was going to seek increased accuracy to hit military targets in the Soviet Union.

These issues would linger after Schlesinger's tenure. Secretary of Defense Donald Rumsfeld wrote in his first Posture Statement:

Since there has been so little public discussion of options and more flexible response, there is a tendency to assume that the targets for strategic delivery systems fall into two categories: cities and enemy strategic forces. Until recently, at least, cities have been regarded as "good" targets, and hard point targets as "bad" targets. Anything that could hit a city was "good," anything that could destroy a hard point target as "bad." The list of targets has never been that limited. But, in any event, we have now acquired the combination of yield and accuracy that permit long-range delivery systems to strike at a wider range of targets and to do so with relatively low collateral damage.[53]

The Force Development Level

We turn now to the force development level. The investigation of this level is crucial because of the controversial nature of Schlesinger's 1974 remarks indicating a lack of need for the acquisition of new capabilities. One participant commented:

Schlesinger insisted, in a way which was understandable but totally illogical, that it be written into the report that this guidance is for employment policy and not for acquisition policy. That's totally illogical, if you are going to have an employment policy that is totally divorced from acquisition policy.[54]

It is possible that NSSM-169, which led up to NSDM-242, suggested that the interagency task force look not only at employment policy but at acquisition policy as well.[55] Others who were members of the Foster panel noted that they were to examine U.S. strategic nuclear targeting and did not discuss acquisition policy. Instead, beginning in 1972, the panel forecasted what forces the United States would have by 1974 and used only those forces in the new targeting plans. Thus, the specific task of the Foster panel was not to design a targeting policy and then request the additional forces to implement that targeting, but instead to target available forces to achieve as much flexibility as possible.

Despite this separation, there was an important bureaucratic link between targeting and force development. Foster, the head of the interagency task force that was looking at the targeting policy, was also (by virtue of his position at the Pentagon as director of research and engineering) in charge of procurement policy. Thus, though the task force was not mandated specifically to examine acquisition and procurement, there was an important connection because of the two hats that Foster wore. There was a clear tension between trying to make this guidance implementable without the allocation of additional weapons and getting the necessary changes in forces and command and control that would make possible the implementation of these doctrinal changes.[56] Many weapons development programs were in progress at the time that seem to have been related to the new doctrine. It was McNamara's declaratory embrace of city-avoidance that led him to face an onslaught of weapons requests from both Congress and the armed forces. The Schlesinger doctrine could have invited the same response, and Schlesinger was clearly sensitive to this.[57] This is not an either-or proposition. As one high-ranking member of the Department of Defense said, the new doctrine put forward by Schlesinger could have proceeded with or without major changes in the U.S. force structure. At the same time, "it is also true that certain force structures are better for either conveying that to the other side or alternatively for putting one's self in a better position to execute such a strike."[58] Eventually, Schlesinger estimated that the implementation of this new doctrine would require the expenditure of about $300 million.[59] It is thus quite clear that though the acquistion of new capabilities was not part of the official doctrine, all those associated with it knew that additional capabilities would in fact be needed.

Do flexible options in the SIOP require a significant counterforce capability? Theoretically, one does not need accuracy to have flexibility. One could have small options that are primarily countervalue. The argument can be made that some degree of escalation control could be provided with such a strategy. However, the desire for flexible options calls for significant escalation control capability, wherein nuclear strikes could be controlled and pinpointed to hit a wide variety of targets other than populations. Thus, while countervalue could form part of flexible options, such a policy is not optimal.

The possible changes in force structure that might enhance Schlesinger's limited options were of three kinds. The first was an actual expansion of the forces of the United States, which might include new launchers and warheads. This is primarily a quantitative improvement. Second is the question of target choice. This issue focuses on the qualitative changes that the arsenal might require. The most important qualitative characteristic was the improvement of accuracy for missile warheads. The issue of accuracy and its association with the changes that took place in nuclear policy at this time are crucial. Note that accuracy is not the only way to achieve a counterforce capability—the Soviet Union had done so with high megatonnage in their warheads. However, high megatonnage for counterforce also could result in high collateral damage and is not consistent with the goals of limits and flexibility. Part of the idea for limited options is to control escalation and limit the amount of damage sustained by civilian populations. As Donald Rumsfeld was to note years later, "[T]his degree of flexibility, which is strengthening and broadening deterrence, necessarily includes the options and the capability to strike accurately at military targets, including some hardened sites."[60] Third, when trying to implement a strategy of limits and flexibility, changes may be required for command and control. A policy of MAD does not require extensive survivable command and control. The one-spasm mentality that governed MAD does not require much communication on either side. However, a strategy based on gradual escalation presumes the existence of a highly capable and survivable command and control structure. Schlesinger publicly acknowledged command and control as crucial to this new strategy.

The two Defense Department posture statements circulated at the beginning of this period highlight the schizophrenia that results when trying to separate targeting from the size and nature of the nuclear arsenal. Thus, Schlesinger wrote in the FY75 report, "[T]he evolution in targeting doctrine is quite separable from, and need not affect the sizing of the strategic forces."[61] But only three pages later Schlesinger stated:

In the meantime, I would be remiss if I did not recommend further research and development of both better accuracy and improved yield to weight ratios in our warheads. *Both are essential whether we decide primarily on high accuracy and low yields or whether we move toward an improved accuracy-yield combination for a more efficient hard target kill capability than we now deploy.*[62]

Schlesinger continued to walk a fine line between leaving himself vulnerable to a barrage of requests for new weapons and not being able to implement his new strategy. For example, he wrote in the FY76 defense posture statement, "[A]s I pointed out last year, the flexibility that we are now developing does not require any major changes in the strategic capability that we now deploy. Some modifications in command and control are necessary and are underway."[63] At the same time, he was calling for the acquisition of new capabilities:

In addition, I believe that our response options would be enhanced by increased accuracy and a greater flexibility in the yields of the nuclear weapons available to us. In some circumstances, we might wish to retaliate against non-collocated, small soft targets, or facilities near large population centers; high accuracy and low yield, air burst weapons would be the most appropriate combination for those targets. In other cases, we might wish to respond with attacks on limited number of hard targets such as ICBMs, IRBMs, and MRBMs. The desired combination for these latter targets, especially as long as we have to depend on an inertial guidance system, is a higher accuracy and a higher yield than we now deploy."[64]

Schlesinger tried to say that the new doctrine did not require new weapons. However, it was clear there was some need for increased accuracy. And in fact $77 million was requested for the beginning of a program for enhancing missile accuracy.[65] And the approval of this money was controversial. As Lindsay summarizes, "[C]ounterforce warheads were developed despite the controversy in Congress."[66]

The MIRV debate continued during this period. In June 1969, Senator Edward Brooke (R-MA) proposed Senate Resolution 211, which sought to suspend testing of the MIRV. Brooke expressed concern about the potential vulnerability of Soviet missile silos that might result from U.S. MIRV deployment. Brooke and a handful of other members of Congress were trying to highlight the counterforce implications of MIRV. The Senate Foreign Relations Committee reported the resolution on March 24, 1970. Approved on April 9, 1970, the amendment by this time no longer called for a ban on flight tests but instead sought a "[M]utual and immediate...suspension of the further deployment of all offensive and defensive weapons systems."[67]

Brooke's efforts did not stop here. In July 1970, he proposed an amendment to the military procurement authorization bill, amendment 798 to H.R. 17123. This sought to define hard-target kill capability and ban its acquisition. The amendment read:

No funds authorized to be appropriated pursuant to this Act may be used for operational development, testing, or procurement of any MIRV system in which an individual re-entry vehicle provided a capability to destroy a hardened target. For purposes of this section, [such capability] means that the combination of warhead yield and accuracy required to generate the equivalent of one-third the level of blast overpressures and related effects considered necessary to enable a single warhead to neutralize a hardened missile silo.[68]

Brooke eventually withdrew this amendment because of the possible impact that it might have on the SALT negotiations. He did, however, succeed in raising the issue and sensitizing officials to the first strike potential of the counterforce programs under development.

There were other attempts to stop MIRV development. In September 1971 Senator Hubert H. Humphrey (D-MN) offered an amendment to the FY 1972 Military Procurement Authorization Bill, which would have frozen all MIRV funds. The amendment was introduced on a Friday when most senators had left Washington for the day, and lost by a vote of 39–12. However, at nearly the same time the DoD decided to cancel development of the stellar inertial guidance system. Whether this was related or not is unclear.[69]

Similar to the MIRV procurement debate, there were other attempts to increase the counterforce capabilities of the U.S. arsenal before Schlesinger went public in January 1974. In 1969, the DoD requested $12.4 million to develop guidance systems for the *Poseidon* missiles. This was a supplemental request to the $33.5 million that had been in the FY 1970 defense budget.[70] Laird had requested these funds to give the *Poseidon* missile a hard-target kill capability. The request for these funds was later withdrawn, partly over budgetary concerns. In 1970, the Department of Defense requested $105 million for the Advanced Ballistic Re-Entry System (ABRES). In considering this program, the committee decided to recommend a reduction of $5 million to signal opposition to the acquisition of more counterforce capability. The Committee said that it favored efforts "pointed toward a strictly retaliatory objective which can be met with substantially less accuracy and more modest yields than needed for the counterforce mission."[71] The House and Senate concurred in this judgment.

In 1971, Senator James Buckley (R-NY) proposed an amendment to the FY 1972 military authorization bill to improve the accuracy of the *Minuteman III* and *Poseidon* systems. Buckley's amendments would have allocated $17 million for the study of the improvement of the U.S. missile force. Buckley's rhetoric in defending these changes focused on how the destruction of civilian populations was not an adequate nuclear policy. He said the U.S. needed other options besides assured destruction. Interestingly, the Department of Defense opposed these amendments because of the first-strike implications. And Senator John Stennis (D-MS), chairman of the Senate Armed Services Committee, also opposed these changes. All three amendments were defeated in October of 1971.[72]

In 1972 there were Defense Department efforts made to improve the accuracy of re-entry vehicles for the *Minuteman* and the *Poseidon*. These were announced in the summer of 1972 as plans to develop, but not deploy, warheads with increased yields and accuracy with the capability to destroy hardened targets.[73] There was opposition to this plan in the Senate. Though the funds were in fact approved by the House Armed Services Committee, Senate Armed Services did not authorize the funds. The Senate view prevailed in the conference committee. The Senate passed an amendment on September 14, 1972, stating that the United States should not acquire counterforce weapons for the purpose of gaining a unilateral first-strike advantage.[74]

As can be seen, many efforts were going on even before Schlesinger's public explication of this policy to improve the counterforce capabilities of the strategic arsenal. And though Schlesinger made a point in his speech of saying that the new policy would not require the acquisition of new capabilities, there were new programs proposed in the FY 1975 annual report. In the FY75 report, Schlesinger made it clear that new efforts would focus on the land-based leg of the triad, specifically the *Minuteman III*. Schlesinger hedges his bet a bit by commenting, "[E]ven without any additional R & D funding, we believe that the CEP of the Minuteman III will gradually improve with continued testing."[75] Nevertheless, additional funding was recommended to improve the accuracy of these missiles. Thirty-two million dollars was proposed for improving the software of the *Minuteman* guidance systems to reduce CEP. The total cost of these refinements was estimated at $100 million over the course of the program.[76] There was also a proposal to develop a higher yield warhead for the *Minuteman III*, which would be retrofitted into the existing MK-12 warhead. The Defense Department costs for the development of the MK-12A warhead would be $125 million over the course of the project, with $25 million requested for FY75.[77]

The development of a terminal-guided maneuvering re-entry vehicle (MARV) for use by both ICBMs and SLBMs was also proposed. Schlesinger wrote that "[T]his MARV could give the Minuteman III a very high accuracy, if such a capability should be needed in the future."[78] Furthermore, Schlesinger noted that Defense planned to flight test the *Minuteman III* with a larger number of lower yield re-entry vehicles. As noted in the annual report, this allowed for increased target coverage without having to increase the number of missile launchers. Nineteen million dollars would be needed to finish testing this program in FY75. Some of these funds were included in the $758 million that had been requested for FY75 for the procurement and upgrading for *Minuteman III*. Other programs included in this category were the installation of the Command Data Buffer System, which allowed *Minuteman* to be retargeted from launch control centers. It was expected that installation of the command buffer system would be completed by FY78.

There was concern among senators about the long-term force development implications of Schlesinger's new strategy. Though Schlesinger had announced that this new strategy would not require new funds, the senators worried that the FY75 counterforce initiatives might mark the beginning of an increased long-term investment for strategic nuclear forces. There was some feeling that these programs should be stopped early. The Arms Control Subcommittee decided to oppose $77 million of this new funding that was clearly related to counterforce: the $25 million for the MK-12A, the $20 million for the improved guidance system for the *Minuteman III*, and the $32 million for the MARV technology.[79] This opposition to it was not motivated by budgetary concerns but instead was clearly related to doctrinal issues. For example, the program to add more re-entry vehicles to warheads was not opposed since this was not a clear counterforce program.[80] Also at issue was the impact that these new counterforce programs would have on the pace of the ongoing SALT II negotiations. Advocates of these new programs thought that they would make the Soviet Union negotiate more seriously. Opponents thought that such programs might jeopardize the success of the negotiations.

The Arms Control Subcommittee killed the funding of the counterforce programs by a vote of 3–2. However, by the time these considerations reached the full committee, Chairman John Stennis, who had previously opposed such changes by spearheading the movement against the 1971 Buckley amendment, supported the counterforce programs. Senator Robert Byrd (D-WV), who had voted against the programs at the subcommittee level, changed his vote and supported the funding. The final vote in the entire committee was 13–2. However, Senator Thomas McIntyre (D-NH) did not want to give up, and he took the opposition to these new programs to the Senate floor. After much debate, the Senate opposition to these counterforce initiatives lost by a vote of 49–37. Virtually the same process was repeated in the next year and again was defeated on the Senate floor.[81]

Throughout this period, there had also been extensive planning and research for the development of a counterforce capability for the submarine-based leg of the triad. Previously, targeting of the *Polaris* system had been limited to soft targets because SLBMs had neither the accuracy nor the yield to make them effective against hardened targets. In 1969, Secretary of Defense Melvin Laird tried to get funds to improve the accuracy of the *Poseidon* force. However, because some believed that this would make the Soviet Union fear a first strike, the request was withdrawn. These funds were again requested for the FY71 defense budget, but were eliminated by the House Armed Services Committee. In 1973 Schlesinger asked the chief of naval operations about the possibility of accuracy improvements for SLBMs.[82] These discussions resulted in the development of the Improved Accuracy Program to increase the accuracy of SLBMs.[83] However, as Desmond Ball noted, the "substantial counterforce potential of the American SLBM system has...been acquired in quasi-secrecy."[84]

John Breem, then undersecretary for strategic systems also wanted to move toward a hard-target kill capability for SLBMs, but feared that congressional forces would oppose these developments. As a result, he decided to push the C-4 based on the need for a long range missile to have an improved navigation system. This was pushed on assured destruction rather than counterforce grounds.[85] Early in the initiative for SLBM accuracy its increased publicity made it a controversial system. Breem said, "[W]hat we really wanted was a more accurate missile....I didn't want to fly in the face of all those MAD advocates."[86] As Spinardi comments:

> Paradoxically, though, this success was to backfire on the pro-ponents of stellar-inertial guidance. As its political visibility increased, stellar-inertial guidance became openly controversial.

The Instrumentation Laboratory's doubts about whether it really was a "Sweet" technology never surfaced in the public domain. But congressional critics, assuming that stellar-inertial guidance *would* enhance accuracy, began to question whether this was actually desirable.[87]

The FY75 report included the first hint at funding for what would eventually become the MX missile. At its inception, the program was simply called research on advanced ICBM technology. During this time, technologies were considered for either a land-based or a mobile missile, but it was emphasized here that "[t]his system, plus appropriately sized MIRVs would give the new ICBM a very good capability against hard targets."[88] Though the story of the MX would carry forward and become more salient during the Carter and Reagan administrations, the beginning of the project came during Schlesinger's tenure as secretary of defense. Throughout its history, the MX was alternately justified according to either the need to build ICBMs that were invulnerable or the need to build ICBMs that had more of a hard-target kill capability. This debate parallels the debate discussed in the previous chapter over the actual purposes for MIRV—whether MIRVs were intended to overcome Soviet ABM capabilities or to increase U.S. hard-target kill capability. This history shows that the original impetus for the MX was to increase the accuracy of the U.S. ICBM force.

The first mention of the MX program in the FY75 annual report did not specify the type of basing mode. Originally, the new ICBM was to be based in fixed silos since it was assumed that ABM systems might be available to enhance the survivability of fixed-based ICBMs. However, the ABM Treaty changed this. And though research on a new system had been going since the 1960s, it was the strong push by Schlesinger and Rumsfeld that propelled MX forward.

Overall, the push was not to develop a fixed-base ICBM because of concern for survivability.[89] However, at the same time, the House Armed Services Committee had prohibited funds for studying a mobile basing mode because this would have duplicated the effect of the B-2 and the *Trident*. This put the Air Force into a difficult bind. In 1975 those responsible for the program came before the Research and Development Subcommittee of Senate Armed Services. When Senator McIntyre asked about whether the Air Force had complied with the subcommittee's request not to study a fixed-based ICBM, there was an awkward response by General Alton Slay, Air Force deputy chief of staff for research and development; John Walsh, deputy director of strategic and space systems for DoD R & D; and Walter La Berge, assistant secretary of the Air Force for R & D. Slay acknowledged that it was impossible to obey both the R & D Subcommittee and the House Armed Services Committee.[90]

The goals of the program became even clearer the following year. During the 1976 hearing, when Defense Department representatives were asked if "the concern for the increasing vulnerability of Minuteman is the primary and deciding factor pacing the MX program," they responded:

> No. While an attack on Minuteman with projected ICBM capa-
> bilities in the mid-1980s could decrease Minuteman silo surviva-
> bility, it is not the primary factor pacing MX development.
> Hardening and dispersal of Soviet economic recovery targets, the
> existing shortage of high quality weapons, and a near [deleted]
> increase in "superhard" Soviet targets between now and the mid-
> 80s have been the deciding factor in the pace of the MX develop-
> ment program....The present Minuteman III force does not satisfy
> the requirement for additional numbers of high quality re-entry
> vehicles needed to cope with both the present and projected enemy
> target structure....We believe there is a need for the MX with an
> early IOC. Initial deployment will be in silos.[91]

By 1976, the Department of Defense had called for full-scale funding of the missile by FY 1978 and an initial operating capacity by 1981. Later, the Air Force presented plans to build 300 MX missiles with twelve to fourteen warheads on each launcher, with each warhead having a 90 percent kill probability for hardened targets. The Senate was alarmed at this and the possible first-strike implications of such a build-up. Furthermore, such numbers seemed to make it clear that the real purpose of the production of this missile was increasing its hard-target kill capability, not the survivability of the land-based leg of the triad.

This alerted Senator McIntyre, who had been sensitized to counterforce issues, to push within the report to have survivability become the dominant rationale for the missile. He sought to have this language written into the law and to push for a study on the overall rationale for MX to be certified by the president. The Senate R & D Committee also recommended cutting $32.4 million out of the $84 million that had been requested for this missile. This cut was approved by the full Senate.

The House, on the other hand, had not shown as much concern with counterforce issues, except for a symbolic gesture a year earlier to cut all of Schlesinger's request for counterforce. Similarly, the House had recommended a cut of only $4 million in the MX program. The conference committee split the difference and funded the missile at $69 million.[92] In addition, the conference committee was explicit about what the rationale should be for the missile:

> The rationale behind the development of a new missile system (MX) is to provide a land based survivable strategic force. The development of an alternate basing mode as opposed to a fixed or silo base mode is the key element in insuring this survivable force. The conferees are in agreement that providing a survivable system should be the only purpose of this effort, that the design of this system should not be constrained for silo basing, that none of this program's funds shall be expended on fixed or silo basing forms.[93]

Congress was pushing for survivability, while the executive branch was pushing for accuracy and counterforce. Despite congressional misgivings about the counterforce implications of the new system, the Defense Department and the Air Force were promoting the missile because of its counterforce potential. This counterforce potential was consistent with the goals of U.S. nuclear weapons policy.

The issue of command and control is a final area of force development that is central to the implementation of a strategy including flexibility and limited options. As will be recalled from Schlesinger's statements above, improved command and control would be needed to implement the new doctrine he had outlined. Efforts at enhancing U.S. strategic command and control began even before Schlesinger's speech. Deputy Secretary of Defense David Packard, in a 1971 report, recommended to the president:

> Improved communications, to assure that all possible information is available to him, sufficient civil and military advisers to provide expert evaluation of the information and to recommend appropriate U.S. reaction. Adequate time for the President and his advisers to make a considered judgment. Because the Polaris submarine fleet, surviving Minuteman missiles and Strategic Air Command bombers themselves have relatively long post attack endurance, the President ought not to be compelled to make hurried decisions for lack of airborne command post endurance.[94]

By FY 1974 Schlesinger had requested major improvements in the command structure. These would have provided more data capabilities, more room for civilian analysts to be airborne, and more flexibility. Funding as a percentage of the total budget for command and control rose from 4 percent in 1971 to over 5.5 percent in 1975, and would continue to climb in the 1990s.[95]

After this, state officials did not believe that they had acquired adequate command and control over nuclear forces. Command and control does not fall under one particular service and does not have the high-profile appeal of big-ticket weapons systems. Funds for command and control have fallen through the cracks, even as administrations moved toward more forcefully embracing limited nuclear options. Many familiar with this period of change in U.S. policy thought that even with these changes, a survivable command and control had not been acquired to ensure the ability to keep a nuclear war limited. This question rearose later in subsequent administrations. As will be seen in the final case study, the Reagan administration would take command and control more seriously and would seek significant increases in funding for it.

Conclusions

This period is noteworthy for two reasons. First, despite the professed desire for changes in targeting policy, Schlesinger did not ask Congress for a great deal of money for the new doctrine. In fact, he originally maintained that this new policy did not require additional funds, even though many involved in nuclear planning at the time knew that additional funds would be needed. Instead, small incremental requests were made for research on accuracy improvements for the existing arsenal. And these requests for counterforce and flexibility were closely related to this doctrinal change.

Moreover, during this period opposition in Congress to these requests was on doctrinal rather than budgetary grounds. As the requests in the years to come would grow larger, opposition would widen to include a much larger set of players from both inside and outside the state. There were several high ranking officials at the Department of Defense who urged Schlesinger to ask Congress for additional money to implement this new policy. They believed that the policy could not be fully enacted without new capabilities. However, requesting these capabilities would invite unwelcome scrutiny of the new targeting policy.[96] This explains Schlesinger's initial hesitation in linking the new declaratory policy to the procurement of new capabilities. Here state sensitivity to societal concerns was acute, and the state made efforts to maintain its autonomy from society.

Second, the change in doctrine and the requests for funds for counterforce purposes pushed the issue of U.S. nuclear weapons strategy toward political salience. If the change in doctrine had not required the appropriation of additional funds, Congress would have had very little power over the course of nuclear strategy. However, because the appropriation of funds became important in the implementation of this new policy, Schlesinger was forced to explain to Congress in detail the changes he wished to make in U.S. nuclear weapons policy. It is the need for funding (either for quantitative or qualitative improvements) that forces these issues out into the open, and thus makes them politically salient.

New nuclear forces were needed to implement the new policy. Though some had pressured Schlesinger not to request these new forces so as to avoid creating a political issue, the growth of Soviet forces and the importance with which counterforce and limited options were viewed by various members of the defense establishment forced him to support the acquisition of new capabilities. This required the approval of Congress. At the very least, Congress was educated regarding strategic doctrine. The hearings held on Schlesinger's new doctrine and the procurement request for new capabilities were unprecedented. Congress was not particularly successful in stopping programs, but it was able to put the executive branch on notice that a new player had entered the game.

Most important for our consideration of the relationship between state and society, the congressional involvement here was not yet motivated by general societal concerns about the course of U.S. nuclear strategy. That is, all evidence seems to indicate that these were internal state disagreements that did not spread to the public. Senators such as Muskie, Humphrey, Brooke, and McIntyre were motivated largely by staff concerns over the course of strategy. On the whole, the state was still acting with a good deal of coherence, despite a heightened level of debate.

Political saliency is not the only result of these changes in policy. When administration officials were forced to justify increases in appropriations according to some kind of doctrine, requests for counterforce, hard-target kill capability, and flexibility did not make sense under a policy of MAD. Thus, the expanding Soviet target base and the U.S. desire to cover these targets, coupled with the need to enhance the credibility of the nuclear guarantee to Europe, forced declaratory policy to embrace more clearly the limited options that it had always encompassed. It was difficult to ask for these changes while adhering to a declaratory policy of MAD—therefore declaratory policy at the time began to embrace NUTs.

The period examined above is clearly a time of significant change in U.S. nuclear weapons policy at all three levels. For declaratory policy, we see a clear and most carefully argued justification for limited flexible and counterforce options in the SIOP. At the force development level, we see a major emphasis on the procurement of an increased counterforce capability. In targeting, we see a significant increase in the flexible and limited options for the SIOP.

While much of the action and procurement changes were going on well before the 1974 Schlesinger speech, the announcement came at a time that seemed opportune in terms of domestic politics. Before 1974 the administration was pursuing détente with the Soviet Union and the SALT process. Before 1972, Nixon was running for re-election. Some believe that an earlier announcement of a new, ambitious nuclear policy would have been counterproductive. This may be why declaratory policy embraced these changes only in 1974. And though Schlesinger wanted to announce this new policy in order to level with the American people, there are some around Schlesinger who thought that he had been too honest.[97]

Thus, this case illustrates a coherent state, continuing to pursue a counterforce strategic nuclear doctrine. Though some within the state questioned the direction of policy, bureaucratic politics does not best account for the continuing emphasis on NUTs. To be clear, this is not simply a case of the defense establishment implementing standard operating procedures. And we cannot understand why Schlesinger made the announcement when and how he did without understanding state desires to remain autonomous from society. We see here a broadening scope of conflict, one that expanded within the state to Congress, but not yet to society. And while the congressional involvement was more over doctrine than money, the coming years would see the financial and doctrinal issues move side by side as the changes in U.S. nuclear weapons policy became transparent to the public at large. This will become clearer as we consider the final case study.

These changes come at a time when U.S. nuclear superiority was declining, and essential parity existed. As a result, state policymakers began to perceive that their counterforce desires needed to be implemented with the acquisition of new capabilities. As will be seen, this issue would become more acute in the following decade.

6

A Radical Departure?
PD-59 and Forward

Senator Dennis DeConcini (D-AZ): What is our strategic policy called now, in place of mutually assured destruction?

General Bernard Davis, Commander SAC: "Counterforce," or "war fighting," the two are synonymous.[1]

Anything you say about them [nuclear weapons], people are going to run hysterical. There is always somebody out there like Roger Molander, who started Ground Zero, or Gene Laroque, who will get up and make some preposterous observations, or [Paul] Warnke will have some emotional spasm on television and in front of Congress.[2]

We turn now to the last of the case studies. This chapter focuses on changes to U.S. nuclear weapons policy that took place during the Carter and early Reagan administrations. The end of this chapter will also discuss changes in U.S. nuclear weapons policy as the Cold War came to an end. This case is another example of state policymakers searching for implementable and limited nuclear options in the SIOP. The impetus that both the Carter and Reagan administrations gave to the formulation of such options and the seriousness with which they sought weapons systems mark this case as the culmination of the evolution of U.S. nuclear weapons policy.

This period is also the most perplexing and misunderstood. President Jimmy Carter came to office skeptical about the utility of nuclear weapons.[3] He had initially ordered the Joint Chiefs of Staff to study the implications of radically reducing the U.S. strategic nuclear arsenal. Though Carter campaigned for the presidency as a dove, stressing détente, he left office having presided over another round of trying to add credible limited options to the nuclear arsenal. He also initiated a build-up in force development that the Reagan administration had completed with zeal.

However, the Carter administration did not do a total about-face in its attitude toward nuclear weapons policy. More accurately, the administration displayed a schizophrenic attitude toward U.S. nuclear weapons policy. This was partly a reflection of the conflicting advice that Carter received from his close advisers. On one side was Carter's influential national security adviser, Zbigniew Brzezinski, who advocated a hard line toward the Soviet Union. On the other side was Secretary of State Cyrus Vance, more dovish and supportive of cooperation with the Soviet Union. Somewhere between these two advisers was Secretary of Defense Harold Brown. Though Brown was originally skeptical of nuclear war fighting strategies, he came around to accept these by the end of the Carter administration.

These trends continued after Carter left office. Reagan had for his entire political career been associated with the conservative wing of the Republican Party and had been a vehement, hawkish, anti-Communist. He advocated a posture of peace through strength, and sought to implement this policy by increasing the U.S. defense budget and procuring new weapons that would give the United States a position of strength, if not superiority, vis-à-vis the Soviet Union.

The Reagan administration was serious and vocal about the importance of nuclear war fighting. After less than a year in office, it announced a five-year, $180 billion Strategic Modernization Program. It will become clear in this chapter that the Reagan administration was more honest at the declaratory level and more committed to NUTs at the force development level than other administrations had been. And though the Carter administration had begun some limited embraces of NUTs at the declaratory level, NUTs permeated nearly all public utterances by the Reagan administration in the early 1980s about nuclear weapons.

By the time covered in this last case, strategic parity existed between the United States and Soviet Union. As only one measure of this balance, in June 1979 the Soviet Union had 2,504 nuclear delivery vehicles, compared with 2,058 for the United States.[4] Many conservatives in the United States claimed that the Soviet Union had pulled ahead of the United States in the development of its nuclear weapons. Groups such as the Committee on the Present Danger warned of the growing counterforce potential of the Soviet land-based leg of the triad (particularly the hard-target kill capability of the SS-18), and feared that U.S. ICBMs were becoming vulnerable to a strike by the Soviet Union.

This supposed "window of vulnerability" became one of the most contentious issues of the period and played a prominent role in debates over the procurement of the MX missile. By any measure, the Soviet Union had closed any significant gaps that may have existed.

Carter and Changes to the SIOP

The Carter administration initiated a review of U.S. defense policy when it took office. National Security Adviser Brzezinski brought in Harvard Professor of Political Science Samuel Huntington to chair a wide-ranging study of the U.S. military posture. The study was split into two parts, with Huntington serving as the overall chair and Lynn Davis, a deputy assistant secretary for policy planning at the pentagon, chairing the section on the strategic nuclear posture.[5] The "Comprehensive Net Assessment and Military Strategy and Force Posture Review," PRM-10, was completed in June 1977.

PRM-10 concluded that nuclear weapons requirements were not high and that a nuclear war would be difficult to win. It specified strategic needs based on what was necessary to achieve an assured destruction capability.[6] Assuming the deployment of new weapons systems including cruise missiles, the MX, and the MK-12A warhead, the report said that in case of a major nuclear war, the United States would suffer 140 million fatalities and the USSR 143 million. The PRM-10 study was reviewed by the Special Coordination Committee, dominated by Brzezinski, Vance, and Brown, and led to the president's signing in August 1977 of Presidential Decision 18 (PD-18) on U.S. National Strategy.[7] Brzezinski was not happy with this report, which stressed deterrence and restraint, when he saw that the Soviet Union was embracing a war-fighting strategy.[8]

PD-18 called for further studies of targeting, reserve forces, command and control, and counterforce capabilities.[9] It reaffirmed the use of NSDM-242 and its accompanying NUWEP 1 until the Carter administration issued new guidance for the SIOP. As the Carter administration began its review of PRM-10, advisers were about to toss out the NSDM-242 guidance. However, many of those who had participated in the formulation of NSDM-242 were disturbed at its impending demise. They successfully lobbied Brzezinski and Brown to keep it in force until the Carter administration had time to develop its own guidance.[10]

The PD-18 follow-on study had three findings. First, that strategic forces should be targeted more flexibly. It asked the joint chiefs to prepare such options for the president. Second, it found that U.S.

strategic nuclear forces and the command and control for these forces should have increased endurance.[11] Finally, the directive recommended accuracy improvements to minimize collateral damage.[12] PD-18 highlighted the importance of having the United States maintain the ability to inflict unacceptable damage on the Soviet Union even after withstanding a Soviet first strike. It also stressed the importance of developing limited nuclear options and ending a nuclear war on favorable terms for the United States. PD-18 differed from NSDM-242 by deemphasizing the degree to which targeting should be determined by the desire to impede a Soviet recovery. Because, it was believed, it would be difficult to assess how recovery would actually take place after a nuclear war, targeting should not emphasize this.[13]

The Nuclear Targeting Policy Review (NTPR) mandated by PD-18 was headed by Leon Sloss, a long-time adviser on nuclear targeting to various administrations. This proceeded along two tracks. The first was completed in December 1978 and forwarded to the secretary of defense. The report identified the acquisition of an enduring system of command and control as the most important force development issue. It also called for more flexible options in the SIOP and for less emphasis on Soviet economic and industrial targets and more emphasis on achieving an effective capability to attack military targets.[14] Though completed by the end of 1978, this study was not acted upon until the summer of 1980. Action was delayed for several reasons. First, it came during the ongoing SALT II negotiations, which was perceived as an inopportune time to announce a change in U.S. doctrine. Second, there was disagreement within the administration about the future of U.S. nuclear weapons policy. Some members of the Pentagon and the State Department were unhappy with the counterforce direction that the NTPR took.[15]

Generals William Odom and Jasper Welch submitted a draft of a new presidential directive to Brzezinski, who gave it to Harold Brown for comment. In late July 1980, it was given to President Carter and approved soon thereafter.[16] This would eventually make its way to declaratory policy in the form of a leak of the contents of Presidential Directive 59 (PD-59) and a speech by Harold Brown at the Naval War College in the summer of 1980. PD-59 was further codification that MAD would not govern the action policy of the United States. The targeting of Soviet military, political, and leadership targets was a crucial aspect of PD-59. Though leadership had been targeted by the U.S. strategic nuclear arsenal, it took a more prominent role in PD-59.[17] PD-59 also called for the United States to gain the capability to fight a prolonged nuclear war. It authorized the development of NUWEP 80, guidance that was submitted to Omaha for changes in the SIOP. SIOP 5-F came into effect on October 1, 1981.[18]

According to this guidance, U.S. nuclear policy would emphasize the targeting of seven hundred underground shelters for key Soviet officials, ICBMs and command and control bunkers, other military targets including airfields and power projection forces, and key factories.[19] As a result of these changes, the National Strategic Target List grew from 25,000 to 40,000 targets. Of these, approximately half were military targets and 35 percent were industrial targets. Two thousand of the targets were leadership and control posts, including the KGB (internal security) and Communist Party headquarters.[20] These changes also continued the emphasis that NSDM-242 had put on the development of selective and regional nuclear options.[21]

PD-59 must be seen within the context of other presidential directives issued by the Carter administration. Signed before PD-59 (in November 1979), PD-53—"National Security Telecommunications Policy"—addressed the survivability of communications during and after a nuclear war. PD-57 and PD-58, signed in the spring and summer of 1980, called for studies on how to rebuild the United States in the event of a nuclear war. These directives addressed the issue of civil defense and national command authorities.[22]

In addition to changes in the SIOP, the NTPR took the issue of civilian control over nuclear weapons policy to new heights. It institutionalized the review of targeting by creating the Nuclear Targeting Policy Review Group within the Office of the Undersecretary of defense for policy.[23] There were also efforts taken to strengthen civilian review of targeting. This was incorporated into the charter of the undersecretary of defense for policy. Under the Reagan administration this responsibility was given to the assistant deputy undersecretary of defense for policy review. As one participant recounted:

In the NSDM-242 period....[T]he civilians that developed the policy were aware of all the problems, once the policy was enunciated they walked away from the job so to speak, and the services were left with the task of trying to implement it, much of which they didn't understand or much of it they disagreed with and didn't care to implement....[B]y the time PD-59 was developed, we quite understood what had happened, we looked into what the services were told and what actually had been done and we believed that in order to prevent the same thing from happening again, it was necessary to have full-time staff of civilian people who are expert in this and are constantly making certain that things were done.[24]

PD-59 made explicit guidance not only for targeting but also for U.S. force planning and systems acquisition.[25] PD-18 and PD-59 made explicit demands upon the force development level. It was recognized that to implement limited nuclear options, new weapons and command and control would be needed.[26]

This was further institutionalized under the Reagan administration. Fred Ikle, undersecretary for defense policy, undertook a review of U.S. nuclear weapons policy in the spring of 1981, as the Carter administration had done four years earlier. The Reagan administration confirmed the direction that the Carter administration was moving in by secretly approving NSDD-12 and NSDD-13, covering nuclear weapons employment policy and communications. Such changes in policy were explicitly linked to force development policy through the "Nuclear Weapons Employment and Acquisition Master Plan."[27] Though only one line of NSDD-13 has been declassified, the line reads, "[T]he President has directed that the following will be US policy governing *the deployment and employment* of our nuclear forces."[28] Secretary of Defense Caspar Weinberger noted that the nuclear guidance "clarifies and emphasizes the direct link between nuclear weapons strategy and acquisition strategy, i.e., our objectives and national security requirements if we fail to deter in a conflict will directly determine our systems acquisition and weapons requirements in peacetime."[29] This culminated with NUWEP 82. Finally, this resulted in the formation of a new SIOP-designated SIOP 6, which took effect in October 1983.[30]

The emphasis on the link between action and force development policy marks a crucial turning point in the evolution of U.S. nuclear weapons policy. Without an explicit link to force development policy, flexibility and limited nuclear options remained more a goal and aspiration than reality. Though this link existed in reality—that is, action policy could never develop wholly independent of force development policy—it never before had an institutional link like the one created here. This link brings the state to a position where it risks its autonomy in the formulation of U.S. nuclear weapons policy.

Public Explication of the Carter Doctrine

The Carter administration shifted its declaratory policy from one that did not embrace the use of nuclear weapons to one that embraced war fighting. There were parts of the Carter administration that felt that MAD was an adequate policy for deterring the Soviet Union. This became clear in the confirmation hearings of Paul Warnke as the head of the Arms Control and Disarmament Agency and chief negotiator for SALT II. A member of the McNamara Pentagon in the 1960s and later a Washington attorney, Warnke was well known in Washington circles as a dove on strategic nuclear issues. His confirmation hearings in February 1977 provided a full hearing on his views and, more broadly, the battle between MAD and NUTs.

Warnke embraced the idea of counterforce and limited nuclear options during these hearings. This troubled hawkish senators such as Jesse Helms (R-NC) and Henry Jackson (D-WA) who thought that Warnke has suddenly changed his views for the benefit of the confirmation hearings. Warnke told Senator Gary Hart (D-CO) that "having a counterforce capability improved deterrence by improving the number of options that the President would have in the event of war." Senator Jackson found this troubling because Warnke had in the past argued against counterforce and limited flexibility. Jackson quoted Warnke as having said, "flexibility in nuclear weapons just means a greater chance that nuclear weapons will be used."[31] Warnke attempted to explain this apparent discrepancy by stating that certain types of flexibility were good and others were not. The tone of his comments made it clear that he was not committed to counterforce and limited nuclear options. He embraced flexibility to the extent that it provided for a response short of an all-out attack, not in the belief that a nuclear war could actually be fought and won.[32] He responded to a further written inquiry by saying:

[O]ur forces should have, and have had for many years, the flexibility to attack some military targets. However, for us and the Soviet Union to have the type of counterforce capability which can threaten a significant portion of the other's deterrent would be destabilizing.[33]

Eugene Rostow of the Committee on the Present Danger claimed in a letter to the Senate Armed Services Committee that Warnke was a "prisoner of Robert McNamara's theory of Mutual Assured Destruction."[34]

There were other factions within the Carter administration that eschewed the limited options of the past in favor of a policy of MAD. Harold Brown, during his confirmation hearings for secretary of defense, distanced himself from Schlesinger's views on limited nuclear options. In January 1977 he said, "[I] do not think it at all likely that a limited

strategic nuclear exchange would remain limited."[35]   The subsequent
annual reports issued by Brown are, in the words of Desmond Ball,
"ambiguous" on this score.[36] They illustrate a tension between believing
that limited options might be the best deterrent and the view that under
most circumstances any use of nuclear weapons would result in mutual
suicide for both the United States and the Soviet Union. As the years
went on, Brown would begin to move toward supporting counterforce.

In the annual report for fiscal year 1979, issued in February 1978,
Brown stated the goal of U.S. nuclear weapons policy was "essential
equivalence," which called for equivalence in both forces and the
perception of the strength of these forces. It allowed for offsetting
asymmetries within the two sides' nuclear arsenals. Brown warned of
the growing counterforce strength of the Soviet strategic nuclear arsenal.
He called for the development of an increased counterforce capability for
the U.S. land-based leg of the triad. Brown also argued for flexibility in
the U.S. strategic arsenal, stating, "[T]he Department of Defense must
not be committed to a single, inflexible war plan—it must not have only
a particular set-piece battle, campaign or war in mind."[37] Furthermore,
he warned that the distinction between deterrent forces and war-fighting
forces was underspecified, stating that a U.S. response that was highly
destructive but could only threaten urban industrial targets lacked credibility.[38] Though he acknowledged that the goal of assured destruction
was indeed important, it was a necessary but not sufficient condition for
deterrence. Within the same report, Brown argued that it was not

> at all clear that an initial use of nuclear weapons—however selec-
> tively they might be targeted—could be kept from escalating to a
> full-scale thermonuclear exchange, especially if command-control
> centers were brought under attack. The odds are high, whether the
> weapons were used against tactical or strategic targets, that control
> would be lost on both sides and the exchange would become
> unconstrained. Should such an escalation occur, it is certain that
> the resulting fatalities would run into the scores of millions.[39]

An interesting exchange took place in 1979 when Brown testified
before the House Armed Services Committee. Representative Ron
Dellums (D-CA) asked Brown whether he agreed with McNamara's
statements of nearly two decades earlier that "[O]nce we are sure that in
retaliation, we can destroy the Soviet Union and other potential attackers
as modern societies, we cannot increase our security or power against
them by threatening to destroy more."[40] Brown responded:

No. I don't agree. I realize it is tempting to believe that the threat to destroy some number of cities—along with their population and industry—will serve as an all-purpose deterrent....Unfortunately, however, a strategy based on assured destruction alone no longer is wholly credible....It is little wonder, in these circumstances, that for many years we have had alternatives to counter-city retaliation in our plans, and a posture substantial enough and responsive enough to permit the exercise of these options.[41]

Brown also had conflicting views on the vulnerability of U.S. ICBMs. This is well illustrated in the annual report for fiscal year 1980. Brown wrote:

Even without MINUTEMAN, our surviving second-strike capability would remain large—in the thousands of warheads. Not only could we still destroy a wide range of targets; we could also cause catastrophic damage to the Soviet urban industrial base. It is difficult, in these circumstances, to see how the Soviets could expect to gain any meaningful advantage from starting a mortal exchange.[42]

Brown presented the other side of the argument later in the same document:

I make these points in order to correct any notion that MINUTEMAN vulnerability by itself is catastrophic. However, the capability of the Soviets to threaten the prompt destruction of a major portion of our retaliatory force, while that segment of their own force is not subject to such a threat, will be a serious matter in military terms and, if it were to continue for an extended period, would be a major political problem. I therefore believe we must act to correct it as we modernize our strategic forces.[43]

Brown dismissed assured destruction as "no longer wholly credible."[44] He pointed out that the United States had for some time had options other than assured destruction for the arsenal.

It is here that Brown refers to the changes that would later become embodied in PD-59 with the phrase that was most often associated with the new policy at the declaratory level: "countervailing strategy." To achieve such a capability, Brown asserts that:

our forces must be capable of covering, and being withheld from, a substantial list of targets. Cities cannot be excluded from such a list, not only because cities, populations and industry are closely linked, but also because it is essential at all times to retain the option to attack urban-industrial targets—both as a deterrent to attacks on our own cities and the final retaliation if that particular deterrent should fail.[45]

In the middle of presenting this countervailing strategy, the assured destruction part of the mission was emphasized.

In testimony before the Senate Committee on Armed Services in the spring of 1979, Senator Carl Levin (D-MI) asked Brown about reports that the United States was considering altering its deterrence philosophy to a strategy based on nuclear war fighting. Levin was concerned that this was inconsistent with Brown's previous testimony that he did not think a nuclear war could be kept limited. Brown hedged in his answer to this question, stating that the review going on at the Defense Department and the NSC had not yet been completed. He noted that targeting was very important from the standpoint of war fighting and deterrence and that the goal was to have employment policy enhance deterrence. Thus, he concluded, "it is possible to say that there is no suggestion that we change the basic aim of our nuclear employment policy—deterrence."[46] Such a response begs the question. The real question is not whether U.S. policy was designed for deterrence, but what it was that U.S. policymakers believed best deterred.

In the following year's annual reports, still six months before the public unveiling of the countervailing strategy, Brown began to report on the administration's examination of strategic policy. Brown explained in more detail what he hoped to accomplish with the new strategy. Among the goals enunciated in this annual report was gaining the capability to prevent the enemy from achieving meaningful victory, inflicting higher costs on it than the gain it might hope to accomplish through an attack on the United States or its allies, and leaving open the possibility of ending the exchange before complete and total damage had been inflicted on both sides.[47] Brown was ambiguous on how to present and sell the new policy:

That is what I referred to last year as the countervailing strategy. In certain respects, the name is newer than the strategy. The need for flexibility and calibrating U.S. retaliation to the provocation is not, of course, a new discovery, whatever interpretation may have been placed on general statements of counter-city options in retaliation, nor have our plans been so circumscribed. For nearly 20 years, we have explicitly included a range of employment options—against military as well as non-military targets—in our strategic nuclear employment planning. Indeed, U.S. nuclear forces have always been designated against military targets as well as those comprising war supporting industry and recovery resources. In particular, we have always considered it important, in the event of war, to be able to attack the forces that could do damage to the United States and its allies.[48]

Before the policy was made public, PD-59 was leaked to the press.[49] It was also reported that Secretary of State Muskie had not been informed of the policy shift. On August 6, 1980, Michael Getler reported in the *Washington Post* that the Carter administration was seeking to modify U.S. plans for a nuclear war. Getler correctly pointed out that the goals of the strategy were not all new. According to Getler, the difference in PD-59 was that the United States would seek the new weapons, the accuracy, and the command and control to implement fully such a policy.[50] Thus, even before going public, the Carter administration had to respond to criticisms of PD-59. The Soviet Union called the policy "nuclear adventurism," and Secretary Brown had to reassure the allies that the United States had "no desire to fight a nuclear war."[51]

The declaratory flurry related to PD-59 and the countervailing strategy culminated in a speech at the Convocation Ceremony at the Naval War College in Newport, Rhode Island, on August 20, 1980. Many attributed the timing of the summer 1980 announcement to the heat of the presidential election campaign battle.[52] Only weeks before this announcement Carter had learned that he would face the hawkish Ronald Reagan in the November general election. Whatever the motive, Brown gave a full public explanation of the new policy. Acknowledging that President Carter had recently signed PD-59 and given guidance for the acquisition of nuclear weapons, Brown noted that though the actual guidance associated with PD-59 remained classified, the United States should be clear on the nature of its deterrent policy. He went on to characterize PD-59 as an example of continuity:

At the outset, let me emphasize that PD 59 is *not* a new strategic doctrine, it is *not* a radical departure from U.S. strategic policy over the last decade or so. It *is*, in fact, a refinement, a codification of previous statements of our strategic policy. PD 59 takes the same essential strategic doctrine and restates it more clearly, more cogently, in the light of current conditions and current capabilities.[53]

Brown made a few central points regarding PD-59 and the counter-vailing strategy. First, the new strategy required that the administration give more attention to how a nuclear war might actually be fought. Second, the United States needed to understand what Soviet leaders value most. It was determined that leadership and control were most important, and that the United States should target those Soviet assets. Brown noted, "we have increasingly the means and the detailed plans to carry out this policy," and that the United States could target in a limited way political and military control targets, nuclear and conventional forces, and the Soviet industrial capacity to make war.[54] Finally, Brown stated that though this new policy represented more continuity than change, the growing Soviet strategic nuclear capability made it necessary for the United States to seek even more limited options.

Despite Brown's attempt to sell PD-59 as representing continuity in U.S. nuclear policy, some of the press and the public reacted as if the policy were a radical departure. Those who saw PD-59 as a radical departure misunderstood U.S. policy as MAD over the previous years. This misperception is well represented by the following excerpt from an article that appeared two days before Brown's address to the Naval War College:

> The new strategy calls for the United States to respond to a Soviet strike with limited strikes against Soviet military targets—such as missile silos and political command centers. Until now, the United States has relied on a Strangelovian concept in which it would respond to a "first strike" with an all-out attack that annihilated major Soviet cities and industrial areas, as well as military centers. That doctrine—known as MAD for "mutual assured destruction" —held that the threat of such devastation was so terrifying that the Soviets would not attempt a first strike.[55]

As a result of such interpretations and the general fear that talk of fighting a nuclear war invited, the administration was forced to spend the following months clarifying the policy and assuring the Soviet Union, allies, and the American public that the United States did not seek to fight a nuclear war or obtain a first-strike capability.

In responding to questions submitted by the Senate Foreign Relations Committee in September 1980, Brown had first to counter the myth that before PD-59, U.S. nuclear policy was MAD. He commented, "[I]n contrast to some pronouncements by the press, the United States had never had a doctrine based simply and solely on reflexive, massive attacks on Soviet cities."[56] Brown's efforts at damage control echoed many of his previous statements about nuclear war.[57]

Walter Slocombe, then deputy undersecretary of defense for policy planning and a key player in the formulation of PD-59, clarified the policy. Slocombe stressed that the new policy did not necessarily mean that the United States was increasing the number of military targets in the Soviet Union. Instead, he maintained that U.S. nuclear war plans would continue to have a variety of industrial, economic, and military targets as part of the arsenal. Further, though acknowledging that the United States would indeed contemplate a limited nuclear strike, Slocombe said that the United States would never initiate such a strike.[58]

In some ways, the protestations of those in the Carter administration asserting that PD-59 was not a radical departure created the impression that it was just that. And the leaks that came out of the administration reinforced the impression that the Carter administration was developing a new strategy. Hard-liners took the idea of fighting and winning a nuclear war very seriously. This faction clearly won out in pushing PD-59 and eventually making it public. Part of this was no doubt motivated by domestic pre-election politics.

Some close to the formulation of PD-59 regretted how it was sold to the public.[59] One National Security Council member recalled that "it's the kind of thing that you simply don't gain very much talking about, you simply get very simplistic, hysterical reactions."[60]

But as late as 1979, Carter inferred that he supported a policy of MAD when he commented, "just one of our relatively invulnerable Poseidon submarines—comprising less than 2 percent of our total nuclear force of submarines, aircraft, and land-based missiles—carries enough warheads to destroy every large and medium sized city in the Soviet Union."[61] The habit of MAD at the declaratory level proved difficult to break.

Reagan Declaratory Policy

The Reagan administration further pursued PD-59 and the countervailing strategy at the declaratory level. Though it was accused of adopting a new war-fighting policy, this was not new to the Reagan administration. The only significant departure taken by the Reagan administration was that declaratory and force development policy were brought into line to match the counterforce war-fighting emphasis that U.S. action policy had always had. It was honest at the declaratory level about the real nature of U.S. nuclear weapons policy, pursuing NUTs at the declaratory level much more completely than had the Carter Administration. There were, after all, members of the Reagan administration who wanted to be more honest about what U.S. nuclear war plans called for. As one high Defense Department official reported:

> [I] think policymakers in this country are, if anything, unduly aware of and concerned about public perceptions of this thing [nuclear war]. I think that [to] some extent it may prevent them from being a bit more honest to the public than they could otherwise be."[62]

When the Reagan administration took office and examined nuclear war plans, it did not have major problems with the general direction of the policy laid out by the Carter administration.[63] Though initial Reagan administration efforts called for changes in U.S. conventional forces and strategy, the nuclear policy announced at the end of the Carter administration suited the Reagan administration well. The Reagan presidential campaign did not make an issue of the Carter administration's nuclear strategy, though it did at times call for more extensive efforts to modernize U.S. nuclear forces.

Secretary of Defense Caspar Weinberger's first annual report to Congress stressed that the administration would increase spending on nonnuclear capabilities, but were limited in how much they could do because of the "severe inadequacies it inherited in the realm of strategic and other nuclear weapons."[64] The report said that the four goals in U.S. nuclear weapons policy included deterring nuclear attack on the United States and its allies, helping deter conventional attack against U.S. forces and allies, being able to terminate a major war—and to ensure the termination of the war "on terms favorable to the United States and its allies"—and negating any attempts at Soviet blackmail against the allies and the United States.[65] It was the concept of ensuring termination of a nuclear war on terms favorable to the United States and its allies that gave rise to the belief that the Reagan administration believed it could fight and win a nuclear war.

General Bernard Davis, the head of the Strategic Air Command and JSTPS, testified in 1981 before the Senate Armed Services Committee that the Reagan administration accepted PD-59. However, given current capabilities he was unsure as to whether the guidance could be implemented. In response to a question from Senator Sam Nunn (D-GA) about PD-59 and reported changes that the Reagan administration was going to make to that policy, Davis responded:

The Carter administration never forwarded PD-59 to the major air command level nor to the Joint Strategic Target Planning Staff. However, the dictates of PD-59 are reflected in both the Nuclear Weapons Employment Policy and the Joint Strategic Capabilities Plan. No changes in these documents resulting from President Reagan's review have yet reached us. The prevailing guidance, however, provided for many challenges to expand the flexibility and responsiveness of strategic forces. This is particularly true with regard to [deleted] and the requirements to develop near term capabilities for the conduct of protracted conflict. Today's overall capabilities to respond to those challenges are very limited. Our forces inherently possess some of the capabilities required, but we are constrained by shortfalls in the endurance of in-being C-3 [command, control and communications] systems. The President's strategic program is designed to correct these deficiencies in our forces and supporting C3I [command, control, communications and intelligence].[66]

One of the first major declaratory flaps came when Secretary of State Alexander Haig testified before the Senate Foreign Relations Committee that the United States would use nuclear weapons for demonstration purposes if the Soviet Union launched a conventional attack on Western Europe.[67] Though this referred to theater rather than strategic nuclear weapons, it left the general impression that the Reagan administration would not be as hesitant as other administrations had been about actually using nuclear weapons. Haig's rhetoric, coupled with the plans that the United States and NATO announced in 1979 to deploy *Pershing II* and ground-launched cruise missiles, left many in Western Europe uneasy about the use of nuclear weapons in the European theater. Weinberger attempted damage control and said there was nothing in the plans that would call for using nuclear weapons in a demonstration capacity. In testimony before the Senate Armed Services Committee, he stated that such an option did not and should not exist in U.S. plans.[68]

The disagreement between Haig and Weinberger reached the highest levels of the Reagan administration as it attempted to clarify this public dispute. Eventually, the Pentagon issued a statement that said that NATO did not rule out any options, including the use of a warning shot. As one reporter noted, "[I]n his zeal for dampening down Europe's current nuclear nervousness, the Secretary of Defense had denied more than was deniable, as the later statement indicated."[69] In trying not to say that either high-level official was wrong, the statement said that Haig was correct that demonstration shots could be used, and Weinberger was correct that such a contingency was not part of NATO war plans. President Reagan further inflamed the issue a week later when he reported at a news conference that he had been unable to determine whether the firing of a demonstration shot was part of NATO strategy. He also said that he could envision the limited use of nuclear weapons in Europe without the employment of the U.S. strategic nuclear arsenal. Such declarations did not please European allies.[70]

As the administration settled in and examined U.S. nuclear strategy, it became apparent there would be some differences in the new administration's strategy. The part of PD-59 that called for acquiring the capability to fight a prolonged nuclear war received new emphasis during the Reagan years. The administration's first complete defense guidance, leaked in May 1982, stated that the U.S. was planning to acquire the capability to fight a protracted nuclear war against the Soviet Union.[71] Part of the document read:

> Should deterrence fail and strategic nuclear war with the U.S.S.R. occur, the United States must prevail and be able to force the Soviet Union to seek earliest termination of hostilities on terms favorable to the United States. This requires...
> —Forces that will maintain, throughout a protracted conflict period and afterward, the capability to inflict very high levels of damage against the industrial/economic bases of the Soviet Union and her allies, so that they have a strong incentive to seek conflict termination short of an all-out attack on our cities and economic assets.
> —U.S. strategic nuclear forces and supporting C3I capable of supporting controlled nuclear counterattacks over a protracted period while maintaining a reserve force of nuclear forces sufficient for post-attack protection and coercion.[72]

The Defense Guidance said that nuclear war strategy would emphasize the decapitation of Soviet military leadership and communications lines.[73]

Part of the difference between this policy and the one put forward by the Carter administration is that while PD-59 called for targeting leadership and military targets, the new strategy called for rendering these targets ineffective. It took this mission more seriously and carried it to its logical extreme. However, when this document was leaked, Weinberger and others clarified their views on nuclear war so as not to inflame domestic and allied audiences further. In a speech at the Army War College, Weinberger said that the United States did not think that a nuclear war was winnable or that a nuclear war with the Soviet Union had to be protracted.[74] Instead, he justified the new strategy on the basis of better deterring the Soviet Union: "But nowhere in all of this do we mean to imply that nuclear war is winnable. This notion has no place in our strategy. We see nuclear weapons only as a way of discouraging the Soviets from thinking that they could ever resort to them."[75] (Secretary of Defense Harold Brown had made similar comments after PD-59 leaked to the press in 1980.) However, Weinberger muddled the distinctions that he was trying to make as he attempted to clarify the U.S. position on nuclear war. While maintaining that nuclear war was not in fact winnable, Weinberger also said, "we certainly are planning not to be defeated" and "we are planning to prevail if we are attacked. You show me a Secretary of Defense who is not planning to prevail and I'll show you a Secretary of Defense who ought to be impeached."[76]

In an attempt at further spin control, Weinberger took the unusual step of sending a letter to the editors of newspapers around the world to clarify the administration's position on nuclear war.[77] Despite these efforts, the damage to the administration's credibility and ability to pursue nuclear weapons policy autonomously from society had already been done. There were other attempts in 1982, and later in 1983, to move away from the war-fighting rhetoric that had dominated the discussion in the early years of the Reagan administration. In the spring of 1982, Richard Perle, assistant secretary of defense for international security policy, and T.K Jones, deputy undersecretary of defense for research and engineering, appeared before a Senate Committee to claim that the Reagan administration did not seek to minimize the damage that would come about as a result of nuclear war. However, the Reagan adminis-tration requested $4.2 billion for civil defense and Jones had commented a year earlier that the United States could recover from a nuclear war if it had enough shovels.[78]

The declaratory retreat is seen fully in the Defense Guidance for 1985–89. In contrast to the Defense Guidance of a year earlier, Wein-berger made little mention of the idea of a protracted nuclear war. In addition, the word "prevail," which caused a stir in the 1982 Defense Guidance, was dropped from the secret document.[79] Press reports indicated that the Defense Guidance did not indicate any real change in

U.S. military doctrine, but that the rhetoric had been softened in the expectation that it would be leaked to the public. An unidentified Pentagon official said, "[W]e just didn't want to get beat over the heads by our political enemies....We went through and carefully vetted out all inflammatory language. Wouldn't you have done the same?"[80]

The Public Response

The citizens' movement against U.S. nuclear weapons policy was a response to this perceived change in doctrine. The movement that grew in support of the nuclear freeze became a potent political force. Though the freeze idea was first introduced in 1979, it received most of its attention when the Reagan administration embraced the idea of fighting and winning a nuclear war. Before the nuclear weapons issue became salient in the United States, the early 1980s saw citizen protests in major European capitals. These were largely in response to the December 1979 NATO dual-track decision to deploy *Pershing II* and ground-launched cruise missiles in Western Europe. They were further propelled by the rhetoric of the Reagan administration and its talk about fighting a limited theater nuclear war. Europeans perceived that the "theater" would be limited to Europe. In late 1981 and early 1982, there were protests numbering 300,000 in Bonn, 250,000 in London, 250,000 in Paris, 200,000 in Rome, and 400,000 in Amsterdam.[81] These served as a precursor to the freeze movement in the United States.

Protests against U.S. nuclear weapons policy, as measured by media coverage of the events, blossomed during this period. From 1979 to 1981, fewer than twenty articles a year in *The New York Times* mentioned antinuclear protests. However, by the middle of 1982, there were nearly one hundred articles, and the number rose and fell through 1985 until it stabilized at the levels that had preceded the Reagan administration. These findings are confirmed by looking at the number of stories about these protests that were broadcast on the CBS evening news. Fewer than ten stories a year appeared before 1982, but nearly twenty-five were broadcast in 1982. A peak was reached in 1984, after which the number returned to pre-Reagan levels.[82] Finally, articles listed in the *Reader's Guide to Periodical Literature* that mention atomic war, atomic weapons, and disarmament rose to 540 in 1982 and 723 in 1983. This is a remarkable increase from the 129 articles listed in 1980 and 314 listed in 1981.[83]

Public opinion had never before displayed such a concern over nuclear issues. In response to the question "What do you think is the most important problem facing this country today," in November 1983, 37 percent of the respondents answered "threat of war and international tensions." (By contrast, 27 percent of the respondents identified the recession as the most important issue facing the United States.) This was up from 11 percent who gave this answer in 1982. The percentage began to decline in 1984, but well into 1987 nuclear issues continued to be identified among the most important problems facing the country.[84]

Citizens clearly feared the military policies of the Reagan administration. In August 1983, 47 percent of those surveyed believed that the Reagan administration's defense policies had brought the United States closer to war, while only 28 percent believed that these policies brought the United States closer to peace. Further, 48 percent thought that the president was not going far enough to bring about a nuclear arms control agreement with the Soviet Union, while 40 percent thought he was going too far or doing just enough for such an agreement.[85] Such concerns led to an increased fear of nuclear war. In 1981 only 5 percent of those surveyed felt that nuclear war was very likely or fairly likely in the next ten years. This percentage rose to 47 percent in 1982 and 44 percent in 1983.[86]

By 1982 the freeze had won widespread support. It was not a fringe movement. In May 1982 an AP/NBC poll showed that 83 percent of those asked supported a nuclear freeze.[87] Other polls showed similar levels of support. As summarized in one study, "in nine separate polls taken between April 1982 and April 1984, support for the Freeze stayed consistently above 70 percent and in 1984—after the Freeze movement had passed its peak—more than 80 percent of all Americans still favored a Freeze."[88] Widespread religious support was also evident, as the United Presbyterian Church, the Union of American Hebrew Congregations, the United Methodist Church, and over half the Roman Catholic bishops supported the freeze proposal.[89] Prominent personalities such as Paul Newman and Carl Sagan took a leading role. Ex-government officials Paul Warnke, George Ball, George Kennan, and Henry Cabot Lodge supported the movement. Business officials such as Thomas Watson, Jr., (of IBM) and Harold Willens championed the movement and used their financial resources to support it. Professional groups such as the Physicians for Social Responsibility, led by Dr. Helen Caldicott, also brought the movement to the mainstream. Not since the Vietnam War (and perhaps not even then) did societal forces unite to oppose the specific military policies of the U.S. national security state. These recruits to the peace movement joined long existing organizations to funnel their energy—and the peace organizations grew. The membership of SANE, for example, grew by 70 percent in 1981 to over 15,000.[90] Council for a Livable World, one of the nation's oldest and largest arms control organizations, nearly doubled its membership.[91] Approximately 10.8 million voters of a possible 18 million supported the freeze in the 1982 elections. The freeze proposal won in Massachusetts, Michigan, Montana, New Jersey, North Dakota, Oregon, Rhode Island, California, and the District of Columbia and lost in only three of thirty-nine areas where it was on the ballot.[92]

Many of the efforts of freeze proponents were symbolic. Nonbinding local and statewide referenda supporting a bilateral freeze resolution were offered throughout the country. An effort was also made to pass a resolution in Congress. Though this was also non-binding, its passage would have been a symbolic victory for freeze proponents. Senators Edward Kennedy (D-MA) and Mark Hatfield (R-OR) and Representatives Edward Markey (D-MA), Silvio Conte (R-MA) and Jonathan Bingham (D-NY) introduced legislation on the freeze on March 10, 1982.[93] One hundred ninety senators and representatives signed the freeze resolution. The groundswell in support of the freeze continued to grow, culminating in the historic march on Central Park on June 12, 1982. More than 750,000 showed their support for the freeze, making it the largest antimilitary demonstration in American history.[94]

When the freeze came up for a vote in Congress in the spring of 1983, a modified version of the freeze bill passed the House by a vote of 278–148. This resolution had an amendment that called for a revocation of the freeze if it was not quickly followed by reductions in nuclear weapons. Those who opposed the freeze and supported the Reagan administration rhetoric of reductions saw this as a victory for their side, and a defeat for the idea of a freeze. This sapped the freeze movement of much of its vitality.

As the freeze gained congressional and media attention, Congress became more interested in the issue of arms control. Senator Hart introduced STOP legislation aimed at the prevention of war, and Representative Al Gore (D-TN) introduced legislation calling for a freeze on selected weapons systems. Later, Senators Nunn and John Warner (R-VA) introduced "build-down" legislation, which called for the dismantling of older weapons systems as new ones were deployed. President Reagan supported the Nunn-Warner proposal. From the perspective of freeze supporters, the problem with these latter two proposals was that they allowed modernization, something the freeze was designed to prevent.[95]

The freeze movement was further derailed by President Reagan's dramatic announcement in March 1983 of the Strategic Defense Initiative (SDI), calling for the nation's scientific community to render nuclear weapons impotent and obsolete. With this, Reagan identified with many of the motivations of freeze supporters who feared the consequences of nuclear war. Reagan's proposal to build a 100 percent effective peace shield over the United States gave him the moral high ground for what had now become a salient political issue. More importantly, the SDI proposal became the central arms control issue in the coming years, and replaced the freeze as the focus of attention. Reagan was successful at regaining control of the political agenda by redefining the terms of debate.[96]

But the disappearance of the freeze by no means meant the demise of societal opposition to U.S. nuclear weapons policy. As the freeze movement was beginning to make inroads in Washington, some freeze supporters were focusing efforts on ways to stop or slow-down various weapons systems, primarily the MX missile. Later, SDI would become the target of arms control advocates. During this period we see a movement that began with societal opposition to the nuclear weapons policy pursued by the state. First in the form of the freeze, and later in the form of opposition to changes at the force development level, this societal opposition percolated up through Congress to the very heart of the national security state. The American public had shown that it was hesitant to accept any plans for fighting a nuclear war.

Force Development

A comparison of the initial procurement strategies of the Carter and Reagan administrations yields different pictures of the administrations' perceived need for strategic modernization. The Carter administration initially canceled the B-1 bomber and delayed the MX missile, and boosted only slightly the *Cruise* missile and *Trident* programs. Conversely, the Reagan administration was committed to propelling the development of the MX, B-1 bomber, acquiring new *Trident* submarines with the D-5 missile, and furthering efforts at command and control. The latter were part of the administration's $180 billion strategic modernization program announced in October 1981.

The period from 1976 to 1983 saw a great increase in state efforts to procure hard-target counterforce capabilities. And though efforts were made even before PD-59 and NSDD-13 to acquire weapons for these purposes, both presidential directives mandated that the acquisition of weapons be brought into line with the other levels of nuclear weapons policy. This contrasts with the public presentation of NSDM-242, in which Schlesinger maintained that the acquisition of new weapons was not necessary to implement the modifications in strategy that he had proposed. The explicit link between procurement and targeting that came with PD-59 and NSDD-13 and the institutional mechanisms that were set up in order to assure that these two levels of policy moved together represented an important structural change in U.S. nuclear weapons policy.

This link was most pronounced in the Reagan administration. Senator Nunn asked Fred Ikle, undersecretary of defense for policy, how the Reagan program differed from that of previous administrations. He responded:

The Reagan program does not represent any major shift in U.S. policy—except that, unlike our predecessors, we are now procuring the kinds of forces we need to support our policy effectively. The Reagan program will insure the continued viability of the Triad, including ICBMs in a survivable basing mode.[97]

Such a policy assured that declaratory policy would merge with action policy as policymakers sought to justify these increased requests for weapons.

Improved ballistic missile accuracy continued to be sought.[98] The MK-12A warhead, which would represent an improvement in accuracy and yield over the MK-12, was designed to be deployed in the existing *Minuteman III* ICBMs as well as in the MX. The increase in the yield for the MK-12A warhead was sought to bolster confidence in the hard-target kill capability of the new warhead.[99] By March 1981, 93 *Minuteman III* missiles were retrofitted with 279 MK-12A warheads, and by December 1982, the retrofitting of the MK-12A on 300 *Minuteman IIIs* was completed.[100]

The ABRES program continued to receive funding. This program, with the participation of all three services, was designed to enhance reentry and penetration capabilities for ballistic missiles. This developed into the MARV program, which was designed to enable warheads to defeat terminal defense while maintaining a low CEP. The goal of this program was to overcome the degradation of accuracy that seemed to be inherent in attempts to evade defenses. It was hoped that this technology could operate in an atmosphere in which defense would predominate but would still achieve the high degree of accuracy deemed necessary for the strategic nuclear arsenal. This program had been funded at $53.2 million in FY75, $52.3 million in FY76, and it was projected to require $46.2 million for FY75.[101] The latter technology was to be deployed on the MX prototype and the *Trident I* missile.

Also of note was renewed interest in *Cruise* missiles. Though they lacked a prompt hard-target kill capability because of their slow speed, they could destroy Soviet military targets. William Perry, undersecretary of defense for research and engineering, testified in 1980:

> The cruise missiles which we will be adding to the force beginning in 1982 do have a substantial countermilitary potential. They have, in fact, a greater hard target kill capability than do our ICBM's, even MX ICBM's when they become operational. The difference between the two is in the timing of the response. But they do have a very substantial countermilitary potential.[102]

The MX Missile

The most controversial force development issue during these years was the MX missile. There were two public justifications for the MX, and those who supported the expensive missile did so for one of the two, or sometimes both, rationales. First was the concern over the survivability of the land-based leg of the triad. This became popularized as the "window of vulnerability." To address these concerns, proponents of the MX favored a basing mode that would enhance the survivability of the system. The second overriding motivation for the MX was to enhance the prompt hard-target kill capability of the land-based leg of the triad. This was originally to be accomplished by deploying the MX with the MK-12A warhead. The accuracy goals appear to have been paramount since eventually the missile was deployed in fixed silos, which did not satisfy the goal of deploying the MX in an invulnerable basing mode. In June 1973, after the initial decision to proceed with full-scale development of the MX missile, the Office of the Secretary of Defense opposed giving this new system a counterforce capability. And many in the Senate agreed. It was only later that this would become a central aspect of the MX program.[103]

Many of Carter's defense advisers, including Warnke, Vance, and Brown, were not convinced of the need for the MX. This opposition led to cuts in Air Force requests for the MX in the early years of the Carter administration.[104] However, after PD-18 and its advocacy of a new accurate missile, coupled with a deterioration of U.S.-Soviet relations, the administration began to look upon the MX more favorably. There were also some in the administration who thought that the MX was necessary to gain conservative congressional support for the SALT II treaty.

Carter officially approved the MX in June 1979. At the end of the summer Carter announced that the administration would adapt a multiple protective shelter (MPS) basing mode. Analogous to a race-track, this basing mode would have 200 missiles deployed on 200 separate oval tracks, with each track having 23 hardened shelters.[105] Missiles and dummy missiles would be shuttled around these tracks. This basing mode originally received support from the Armed Services Committees in both the House and the Senate.[106]

Though the Reagan administration fully supported funding and deployment of the MX, it immediately rejected the Carter MPS scheme. The basing mode left the missile vulnerable. Some cite the fact that the proposed location of MPS, Nevada, was the home of Reagan supporter Senator Paul Laxalt and thus was rejected on political grounds.[107] As an interim solution, the Reagan administration announced in the fall of 1981 that it would deploy 100 MX missiles in hardened *Minuteman* silos. The deployment of the MX in vulnerable silos was perceived as strange since one of the overall justifications for the missile was to decrease the vulnerability of the land-based leg of the triad. However, the Reagan administration needed to deploy the system immediately both as a bargaining chip in arms control negotiations and for the hard-target kill capability that the missile would add to the nuclear arsenal.

Congress began to express its displeasure with the course of the MX. It cut funds from the FY82 appropriations for superhardening of silos and mandated that a final decision on basing be made by July 1982. In November 1982, the administration introduced dense pack as the basing mode for MX missiles not deployed in existing *Minuteman* silos. The dense pack scheme envisioned *Minuteman* missiles deployed closely together so that incoming Soviet missiles would interfere with one another and lose their hard-target kill capability. This plan did not meet with very much approval. In December 1982, Congress agreed to allocate funds for MX procurement, but withheld expenditures for a basing mode. By the end of the year, Congress had agreed to eliminate all funds for MX procurement, to prohibit flight testing, and to fence off R & D funds for the basing mode until Congress released the money through a concurrent resolution.[108]

The next milestone for the MX was President Reagan's January 1983 appointment of a commission led by former National Security Adviser Brent Scowcroft to determine the future of the missile. Though initially the commission was to make its report within a month, it did not issue its report until April. The commission endorsed the deployment of one hundred MX missiles in existing silos and the development and deployment of a single-warhead mobile *Midgetman*. It also pushed for arms control negotiations to reduce the number of strategic warheads on both sides. Most interesting of all, the commission rejected the window of vulnerability argument saying that the potential vulnerability of ICBMs was not so dangerous as some feared. Nonetheless, it supported the procurement of the MX as a bargaining chip in the strategic arms control negotiations. The Reagan administration accepted the commission's report one week after its release.

On November 1 the House moved the MX forward by approving funds for the procurement of the first eleven missiles. The Senate did the same on November 7.[109] Thus, the first actual funds for MX production, rather than research and development, were approved in November 1983. The votes were close, as the $2.2 billion in the FY 1984 defense appropriations bill to produce the first twenty-one MX missiles won by only nine votes in the House and nine in the Senate.[110] The following year, President Reagan requested $3.2 billion for the production of an additional forty missiles. The House and Senate Armed Services Committees reduced this number to twenty-one and submitted their reports to the House and the Senate. There were important efforts in the House to scale back the program further. An amendment to cut all production funds for the MX lost by six votes. Another amendment, which called for the funds to be withheld until the spring of 1985, was approved by a narrow margin, and Congress would have to approve the release of funds.

The Senate voted 48–48 on an amendment that would have canceled the twenty-one new missiles but kept the production line open for the twenty-one missiles that had already been approved. Vice President George Bush voted against the amendment, and the committee recommendation of twenty-one missiles passed. The difference between these bills was left for the conference committee, which did not come to an agreement until September 1984. It agreed that new production funds would be withheld until March 1984 and that the president would have to certify that he was making progress on arm control. Two votes in each chamber would be necessary to release the funds.[111] Congress limited and shaped the course of the MX. And though the missile went forward, this change in the way strategic weapons are procured should not be downplayed. Lindsay captures this well: "Congress forced the most popular president of the post-war era to accept a permanent cap on the number of MX missiles that could be deployed in fixed silos."[112]

Much of this was a result of popular opposition that had grown out of the freeze movement.[113] Grass-roots and Washington lobbying around the MX was unprecedented. Local and national coordination, visits, postcards and telephone calls were extensive in many swing districts.[114]

The battle over the MX became symbolic of the battle over the direction of U.S. nuclear weapons policy. As the vulnerability issue became less important at the rhetorical level and the hard-target kill capability of the MX became obvious, the question of what the United States should do with its nuclear arsenal became paramount. And to procure funds for a hard-target killer that was going to be in a vulnerable basing mode was fully and unequivocally to endorse NUTs at the declaratory level. As Colin Gray comments:

> MX advocates have tended to be nervous of making a case for the MX missile, as opposed to "survivable ICBMs," because a focus on the missile has led to a discussion of why large payload (for U.S. ICBMs) and small CEP (high accuracy) is deemed to be desirable. Logically, this leads one into a discussion of deterrence that focuses upon Soviet fears and vulnerabilities regarding MX as a war-fighting instrument. It appears to have been judged, until very recently, to be the case that opinion leaders in the U.S. political system were not quite ready for forceful explanations of why "a good defense is a good deterrent," and of why there is no contra-diction between deterrence and defense.[115]

Gray notes that such an embrace was feared to produce negative political ramifications because of the discussion of nuclear war that would follow from defending such a strategy.

Command and Control

Though the issue of command and control was emphasized by both Carter and Reagan, it was the Reagan administration that gave this issue the highest priority at the force development level. This was made particularly clear in October 1981, when the Reagan administration issued NSDD-12, which read in part that command and control "is the highest policy element in the program. It would develop command and communications systems for our strategic forces that survive and endure before, during and after a nuclear attack." This directive mandated that funding for command and control be given at least as high a priority as strategic weapons systems.[116] The Reagan administration planned to spend over $22 billion on command and control over the following six years.[117] Fred Ikle testified before the Subcommittee on Strategic and Theater Nuclear Forces that the Reagan administration would put a renewed emphasis on the issues of command and control.

> The qualities of endurance and survivability have long been an essential part of a credible deterrent strategy. The Reagan Administration is, however, placing greater emphasis on obtaining enduring systems and support C3 to assure that we are capable of retaliating with overwhelming strength under all circumstances.[118]

Similarly, James Wade, principal deputy undersecretary of defense for research and engineering, made a case for the importance of fully funding command and control: "[P]erhaps no portion of the program is as important as the improvements we plan in command, control and communication."[119] Wade noted that it made little sense to modernize forces if those forces could not be adequately controlled. He criticized the previous ten years of funding of command and control, saying that such funding had resulted in an inadequate amount of endurance for the system. ·

The Reagan administration proposed the upgrading of the survivability of warning satellites, the creation of mobile ground sensors, and the improvement of ground-based warning satellites. To enhance the survivability and capability of command and control, the administration proposed deploying E-48 airborne command posts, hardening existing E-135 airborne command posts, establishing high-frequency satellite communications for the president, and upgrading communications for submarines.[120] At the time, Senator Warner noted that his committee had been ahead of this issue, having recommended increased funding for command and control a year earlier. Warner said that of all the aspects of the president's force modernization program, the substantial sums requested for command and control were the least controversial.

Trident II

The development of higher accuracies for SLBMs continued to be pursued. For FY 1976, $65.8 million was requested.[121] The acquisition of this system came under some sharp criticism from Representative Dellums who noted that the acquisition of the *Trident II*, air-launched cruise missiles (ALCMs), the MX, the MK-12A, and the MK-500 *Evader* re-entry vehicle might indicate that the United States was moving toward a war-fighting or even first-strike capability. Brown responded that the MK-500 ensured only that the United States would be able to penetrate Soviet ABM systems if the Soviet Union violated the ABM Treaty and that no funds were being used beyond advanced development. Brown noted that other systems would only "improve the degree of flexibility we can exercise in our response options."[122]

The *Trident II* (D-5) missile did not receive so much attention as the MX, though the plans for the D-5 in the early 1980s would have added more hard-target kill capability to the U.S. strategic nuclear arsenal than the MX. As mentioned in chapter 5, concerns about the accuracy of SLBMs began to receive some attention in the mid-1970s, after the limited nuclear options initiative was launched by Secretary of Defense Schlesinger. The program, the Improved Accuracy Program, began to receive funding in FY75 and sought to discover and correct the sources of SLBM inaccuracies.[123] This funding was completed in FY 1982.

In its planning stages, the D-5 would have cut in half the CEP of the existing C-4 *Trident I* missiles and would be fitted with two different warheads, one with a yield of 475 kilotons and the other with a yield of 1,900 kilotons. The Carter administration took a half-way stance on this by providing some money for R & D but not fully committing itself to the deployment of the D-5 at any specific future time. Carter had funded about half the amount that the Navy had requested for the new missile. In 1979, the Senate Armed Services Committee eliminated $40.6 for the *Trident II* missile because of the perception that there was no clear statement of need for the new missile and that a rival weapons system, the MX, needed to be funded.[124]

The Carter administration had decided that the modernization of the land-based leg of the triad should receive more priority than the modernization of the sea-based leg. This view was expressed by Seymour Zeiberg, deputy undersecretary of defense for research and engineering under the Carter administration. He testified in April 1980 before the House Committee on Armed Services:

> If we move out with a vigorous MPS (multiple protective shelter) program and we buy a new strategic capability which has high accuracy potential and has the capability to cope with counterforce missions, certainly the urgency to move out the Trident II for that reason diminished....If we don't have an accelerated MX program of that sort, we would endorse the very accelerated Trident II program.[125]

Instead of taking money from other strategic nuclear programs, Congress in 1980 transferred $34 million from other naval programs to research the *Trident II*.

The tying of force acquisition to employment policy provided a coherent rationale for the funding of the D-5 missile. The justifications for the system at the time focused on the addition that the new missile would make to the hard-target kill capability of the U.S. strategic arsenal. The Reagan administration took the *Trident II* missile much more seriously than did the Carter administration, asking for funding to be increased from $97 million in 1981 to $243 million in 1982 and $354 million for 1983.[126] In the spring of 1980, Vice Admiral Charles H. Griffith, deputy chief of naval operations for submarine warfare, testified that "we predict that by 1982...we will have the technology in hand to give the SLBM forces the accuracy at SLBM ranges comparable to the accuracy of long range ICBMs."[127] Similarly, Admiral William A. Williams III, director of the Navy's Strategic and Theater Nuclear Warfare Division, said that the new missile would be effective "across the entire target spectrum—from hard silos and command and control facilities to softer military and war supporting targets."[128]

The hard-target kill capability aspect of the project was undeniably crucial. For example, when Senator Warner asked James P. Wade, Jr., principal deputy undersecretary of defense for research and engineering, "[H]ow high a priority is attached to achieving a hard-target kill capability in our strategic submarine force?" Wade responded, "We attach significant importance to this capability. We must attain a capability to render ineffective the total Soviet military and political power structure, including control facilities and military forces."[129] By October 1983, the *Trident II* missile had the full approval to be deployed at the end of the decade. As Admiral James Watkins, chief of naval operations told the House Appropriations Committee at the time, "we were directed by the President to accelerate the introduction of D-5 and we are on the maximum acceleration rate right now."[130] The new missile received its approval at the same time that the MX was running into obstacles in Congress.[131]

As seen in the case of the MX missile, executive branch officials usually justified weapons systems on the basis of their hard-target kill capability. Nonetheless, by the time period covered in this case study, such justifications had become necessary to procure such systems. As Spinardi notes in his study of the development of accuracy for SLBMs:

The targeting plan, the Single Integrated Operational Plan (SIOP), remained based on the earlier counterforce doctrine, but nuclear policy came to be publicly justified, and "sold" to Congress, on the basis of retaliation against urban industrial targets. Early attempts to fund accuracy enhancements explicitly to provide hard-target kill capability—such as three Mk4 stellar inertial guidance systems for Poseidon—were not then well received.[132]

But as declaratory policy began to embrace NUTs, such systems were easier to justify. The acquisition of counterforce weapons was now clearly seen as necessary for national policy.

There were some minor attempts to kill the *Trident II* missile. In July 1982, Representative Tom Downey (D-NY) proposed an amendment to cut $366.7 million for D-5 research and development, but the amendment was defeated by a margin of 312–89.[133] In 1984, Representative Ted Weiss (D-NY) offered an amendment to delete $152 million for production funding for the missile. This was defeated by a margin of 319–93.

Why was the MX such a controversial and salient political issue while the *Trident II* remained relatively secret and unheralded? Both systems were expensive, with the cost of the *Trident II* estimated at around $40 billion; the MX was originally projected at a similar cost.[134] The major difference was that the MX seemed more like a first-strike weapon than did the *Trident II*. The sea-based leg of the triad had generally been perceived as invulnerable, and thus a hard-target kill capability was not perceived as being as dangerous. At the peak of this public concern, the *Trident* was only in the research and development stage, more insulated from societal impact than if it were in the deployment and production stage.

All this indicates the significantly changed role that Congress began to play in nuclear weapons policy in the 1980s.[135] Unlike in previous decades, much of the focus of congressional activity moved from the House and Senate Armed Services Committees to the floors of both chambers. One measure of this is the number of successful amendments both chambers offered on nuclear weapons–related defense authorizations. In the House, this rose from one in 1980 to fifteen in 1984 and to a peak of twenty-three in 1985. In the Senate, this rose from two in 1980 to a peak of sixteen in 1984.[136] And as Lindsay comments: "[S]imply put, the floor became more involved in decision making because a considerable number of members wanted to change the direction of U.S. nuclear weapons policy."[137] He adds that while the Vietnam War stimulated floor activity in the 1960s, fears of nuclear war did so in the 1980s.

Strategic Modernization in the Late 1980s

Societal opposition to the broad Reagan strategic modernization plan began to wane as the Soviet threat receded. With the rise to power of Mikhail Gorbachev in 1985 and his "new thinking" in foreign policy, the U.S. build-up that had been planned in the early 1980s continued. However, by 1991, as the Cold War ended, the United States began to cut back on the procurement of many of the most controversial aspects of its strategic modernization plan. Many of these cuts were first presented as part of sweeping unilateral cuts announced by President Bush in September 1991. They were matched by Gorbachev and later Boris Yeltsin.

The basing-mode issue for the controversial MX missile continued to pose a problem for Reagan, and later the Bush administration. After years of proposals and debates, an invulnerable basing mode could not be agreed on. As a result, the MX was deployed in existing *Minuteman* silos. The Reagan administration developed and began to fund a rail garrison basing mode to place the MX on railroad cars to be dispersed on the nation's rails in a time of crisis. The plan originally called for the development of twenty-five specially designed trains, which would each carry two MX missiles. The plans called for the deployment of fifty missiles on rail garrison and fifty in fixed silos. Congress initially resisted the rail garrison, in favor of the single-warhead, mobile *Midgetman* missile.

When the Bush administration took office in 1989, it supported both the rail garrison and single-warhead *Midgetman*. But as the Cold War began to wind down, the Bush administration cut the planned one hundred missile deployment to fifty. Though the rail garrison began testing in 1990, the system was canceled in late 1991 as part of the sweeping changes announced by President Bush. The *Midgetman* was also slowed by the end of the Cold War. In September 1991 the Bush administration announced that it was canceling the mobile part of the *Midgetman* but would continue work on the single warhead missile as a possible replacement for silo-based *Midgetmen*.

For the submarine-based leg of the triad, the new *Trident II* D-5 missile began testing in 1987 and became operational in 1990, after 247 MIRVed D-5 missiles had been procured. Congress had not strongly opposed this counterforce system with the same vigor that it mustered for the MX missile. But a cutback in deployment and procurement in this new system was announced by the Bush administration in the September unilateral cuts.

The controversy over the B-2 bomber also continued. This expensive radar-eluding bomber's cost rose to close to $1 billion per plane. Though some in the Bush administration and the Air Force began to tout the conventional virtues of the bomber, it became difficult to justify the new bomber as the Cold War came to a close. Originally, the Reagan administration planned the deployment of 132 of these bombers. Congress resisted the purchase of so many B-2s and had refused to authorize more than fifteen. The Bush administration reduced this to seventy-five, and in the unilateral cuts of September 1991 reduced its request further, to 20.

Perhaps the most controversial program during the mid-1980s was the SDI. Despite significant increases in the SDI budget, the fate of the program remained uncertain through much of the late 1980s. Political and fiscal pressures mounted. The Strategic Defense Initiative Organization (SDIO) issued a new phase I study that reduced the cost of SDI from $115 billion to $69 billion. This study called for an emphasis on sensors and communications, and de-emphasized the importance of space-based weapons. After President Bush took office, he announced his determination to proceed with SDI in a scaled-down version from the original Reagan vision.

As the program evolved further, it became clear that the vision of the 100 percent effective shield that promised to render nuclear weapons "impotent and obsolete" would give way to a more limited program. In 1989 Vice President Dan Quayle publicly acknowledged that former President Reagan's vision for SDI was little more than "political jargon." During that same year President Bush signed National Security Directive 14 which called for reorienting SDI toward "options for strengthening deterrence and stability through the deployment of strategic defense based on advanced technologies." The emphasis here is on strengthening deterrence rather than replacing it.

In the words of President Bush's 1991 State of the Union address, his plan for SDI would build defenses for "providing protection against limited ballistic missile strikes—whatever their source." Dubbed the Global Protection Against Limited Strikes (GPALS), this new configuration of SDI aimed at countering an unauthorized or accidental launch from the Soviet Union or the third world. This announcement emphasized near-term deployment. By the summer of 1991 the fate of the program was still in question. The SDI received a boost because of the perceived success of U.S. *Patriot* missiles shooting down Iraqi *Scud* missiles aimed at Saudi Arabia and Israel during the Persian Gulf War. Furthermore, the fracturing Soviet Union and the potential for nuclear proliferation were seen by SDI advocates as a reason to go ahead with the program. Congress authorized $4.1 billion for the SDI, more than $1 billion more than it had a year earlier. But the debate continued.

Changes to U.S. Nuclear Weapons Policy at the End of the Cold War

In a series of articles in the summer of 1989, Robert Toth of the *Los Angles Times*, with Desmond Ball, investigated revisions to the SIOP as the Cold War ended in an article "Revising the SIOP: Taking War-Fighting to Dangerous Extremes."[138] The overall direction of the new SIOP, SIOP 6F, which took effect in October 1989, was perfectly consistent with previous war-fighting doctrine. Most significant was the seriousness with which the Bush administration regarded the goal of destroying Soviet leadership early in a conflict.[139] The targeting and destruction of mobile targets was also taken seriously in this revision to the SIOP.[140]

The guidance that led up to SIOP 6F found that the U.S. strategic arsenal did not contain adequate counter-leadership and command and control to accomplish the goals of overall policy. The study of earth-penetrating warheads, which had begun years earlier, was given renewed emphasis. The ability of the B-2 *Stealth* bomber to locate and strike mobile ICBMs was seen as important. However, this never became the prime justification for the system.[141]

Societal sensitivity to public embraces of war-fighting theories of deterrence have been evident during periods when relations between the United States and Soviet Union were particularly strained. The state has tried to procure such capabilities when the balance had deteriorated to a point where U.S. nuclear capabilities were doubted. During these periods fears of a nuclear war were intensified. Under present circumstances, nuclear war appears highly unlikely and public sensitivity to the issue appears quite low. Perhaps we will not see the same type of societal reactions as in the past.

Even more recent revisions to U.S. strategic nuclear weapons policy are noteworthy in that despite the end of the Cold War, the counterforce emphasis of U.S. nuclear weapons policy was hard to break. Despite significant changes, which include the signing of the Strategic Arms Reduction Treaty (START) agreement and procurement and unilateral cuts, the counterforce emphasis remained.

In 1989, after the fall of the Soviet empire, the Bush administration ordered a study of U.S. strategic nuclear weapons policy. Initiated by the military and conducted by civilians in the Pentagon, one of the overall results of this study was to cut back on the number of targets the U.S. arsenal would need to cover. Thus, the resulting SIOP, which was due to take effect in October 1991, eliminated many of the former targets in the Soviet Union and Eastern Europe.[142] Many of these changes were made possible by the new openness in the Soviet Union. With the increasing ability to know what it was targeting, less overkill and redundancy were required in the SIOP.

Despite these changes the philosophy guiding nuclear strategy remained the same. The Bush administration continued to be guided by the Reagan administration's NSDD-13, which had been signed in 1981. No recommendation had been made to change the thrust of this policy, which called for the ability to destroy Soviet military targets. According to a secret 1989 Pentagon document that had been issued by Admiral William T. Crowe:

> Our forces will hold at risk those assets that the Soviet leadership would need to prevail in a nuclear conflict and dominate a post-nuclear world. These targets include the Soviet military forces, political leadership structure and war-supporting industry.[143]

With the cutbacks in the traditional targets in the Soviet Union and Eastern Europe, policymakers faced the difficult task of figuring out what to do with nuclear weapons.

A new flurry of activity at all levels of nuclear weapons policy began to surface. Much of this took place in the form of a study by an advisory group to the JSTPS headed by Thomas Reed. Reports on this study began to appear in the beginning of 1992, and the sanitized version of the results were presented to Congress in January 1992.[144] The report was rewritten from the unclassified version of the report. Overall, the study had an expansive view of U.S. nuclear weapons policy and did not break with historical views of the importance of nuclear weapons for U.S. national security policy.

The report advocated that the United States reorient its nuclear strategy toward targeting "every reasonable adversary." It urged that the United States target nuclear and nonnuclear countries in the third world and should not guarantee that it would not use nuclear weapons against nonnuclear states. Overall, the goals of U.S. nuclear weapons were quite broad. According to one report:

> The panel did not list potential target nations, but Reed's briefing said U.S. arms could deter annihilation of states such as Israel and

Taiwan, the seizure of critical raw materials, such as oil, or foreign domination of a segment of outer space.[145]

In advocating an increased reliance on the submarine-based leg of the triad, the classified version of the report also advocated replacing the Single Integrated Operational Plan with the Systems of Integrated Operational Plans, which would have five major goals and options: 1) SIOP alpha, a nonnuclear option aimed at suppressing defenses; 2) SIOP echo, which called for a "nuclear expeditionary force" for targets such as China and third world countries which required only a small number of nuclear weapons; 3) SIOP Lima and 4) SIOP Mike, which would be limited attack options on the Soviet Union, with Mike resembling the pre-existing SIOP; and finally 5) SIOP Romeo, which contemplates a nuclear reserve force for war termination and other purposes.[146]

When this became public in testimony before the Senate Armed Services Committee, the lack of real change from NUTs to MAD can be seen clearly. The report explicitly rules out more radical reductions in nuclear forces and rejects the adoption of a strategy of pure MAD (referred to here as vague threats to destroy cities) as "immoral and unwise."[147] This testimony urged many missions for U.S. nuclear forces, including those in the third world and extended deterrence. One passage reads:

Some have argued that the United States can discourage nuclear proliferation in the third world by adopting a highly visible declaratory policy (and presumably supporting implementing policies) that American nuclear weapons serve no purpose except to deter other nuclear weapons. We are not comfortable with the implications of that argument, especially the suggestion that a nation can engage in any level of chemical or biological aggression and still be shielded by an American non-nuclear pledge.[148]

In rejecting MAD outright in the beginning of 1992, the report said "[T]he U.S. should return to its policy of not deliberately targeting urban populations. This is a distinction of enormous importance in sustaining a nuclear posture."[149]

However, there were some signs during 1993 that this overall direction might change. Two actions by the Clinton administration suggest such changes. The first was the announcement in the fall of 1993 of a total review of U.S. nuclear weapons policy. As is seen in this study, this is common in all new administrations. However, during the fall of

1993 there were suggestions that the Clinton administration might consider not targeting the former Soviet Union with nuclear weapons and instead targeting nuclear weapons on the ocean. This could indeed be a major shift in policy.

Conclusions

Flexibility, hard-target kill capability, counterforce, and the like came to the fore of declaratory policy during the period covered by this case study. Though both Robert McNamara and James Schlesinger had made declaratory statements on the need for such capabilities in the U.S. nuclear arsenal, the embrace became clear, dominant, and unequivocal under both Presidents Carter and Reagan. The acquisition of the MX, *Trident II*, enhanced command and control, and so on could not be coherently justified on the basis of a declaratory nuclear strategy of MAD. The myth of MAD had to be abandoned. And it was, such that by the middle years of of the Reagan administration, public embraces of war-fighting strategy were prominent.

And the Reagan administration abandoned MAD with full force, even though its policy was not totally different from what had preceded it. As one Carter administration official observed:

And because it was stated so boldly, they did have to retract it. It's been there all the time, they carried it somewhat further to the notion of winning. And when confronted it with it they back off. At this point it does enter into domestic politics, but generally it does not, and the only reason it did then was that it was stripped of all nuance and argumentation and it came down to the question of whether these guys thought you could fight a nuclear war and win.[150]

At the same time, the state faced a catch-22 in its pursuit of NUTs. If it continued to embrace MAD at the declaratory level, it could not procure those forces that it believed were needed either to deter the Soviet Union or defeat it in a nuclear exchange. And as the nuclear gap between the United States and the Soviet Union closed, state defense decision-makers believed it was essential for them to procure counterforce weapons. Yet if they did embrace NUTs at the declaratory level, as they did during the time discussed in this chapter, they faced the loss of a national consensus on nuclear weapons policy and the interference of society.

This interference from society, or loss of autonomy for the state in its formulation of U.S. strategic nuclear weapons policy, met with mixed results. On the one hand, its impact cannot be underestimated. The degree to which society expressed its displeasure with the overall direction of U.S. nuclear weapons policy and, through Congress, specific weapons systems, represented a revolution in state-society relations in U.S. strategic nuclear weapons policy. On the other hand, this change in relations did not radically alter the course of the nuclear weapons policy of the United States. Though it is significant that the procurement of the MX missile was slowed by societal and congressional opposition, this weapon became part of the U.S. arsenal. But this opposition is best seen as just the beginning of the changing impact of societal forces in the making of U.S. nuclear weapons policy. The state's autonomy in the formulation of U.S. nuclear weapons could no longer be assumed.

The historical pattern of U.S. nuclear weapons policy proved difficult to change. Even with the end of the Cold War, state policy-makers' desire to implement counterforce targeting and to plan to use nuclear weapons as political tools continued. Though revisions to U.S. nuclear war plans did take into account the collapse of the Soviet empire, they did not represent any fundamental change in the way the officials viewed nuclear weapons.

Societal opposition to U.S. nuclear weapons policy peaked during this period. This opposition confirmed what policymakers had known all along—that a public embrace of nuclear war fighting would constrain the state. The statist lens utilized in this study highlights the important role that societal forces came to play in the evolution of U.S. nuclear weapons policy. The autonomy of the state was indeed limited, even for the high politics of strategic nuclear weapons policy.

7

Conclusions: State, Society, and U.S. Nuclear Weapons Policy

Domestic consensus has clearly eroded in most Western countries with respect to national and alliance nuclear policies. Why?

Political leaders will also need to discuss forthrightly with their publics both all the requirements and all the ambiguities of nuclear deterrence.... Nuclear plans and credible nuclear response options should be explained to Western publics in terms of their intended purposes.[1]

—Harold Brown

How did the high politics of nuclear weapons policy so penetrate society that by the summer of 1982 it would be the subject of the largest political protest in U.S. history? How did debates over the type of land-based missile the United States would deploy become subject to extensive congressional and societal debate? Why by the 1970s and 1980s did defense policymakers come to embrace war fighting publicly though they had historically been reluctant to do so? Finally, why did critics accuse the Reagan administration of radically changing U.S. nuclear weapons policy when its policy reflected continuity rather than change?

The preceding chapters have considered these questions. This final chapter will add coherence to the above by considering the three cases that make up this study in the form of answers to the questions presented in chapter 3.

Focused, Structured Comparison

The Three Levels of Nuclear Policy

The first question focuses on the substantive concerns of this study—the three levels of nuclear weapons policy and the relationship between them. The case studies illustrate a trend toward a convergence among the three levels of policy. By the final case study, declaratory policy, force development, and action policy had converged to embrace war fighting. This convergence was evolutionary and sharply contrasts with the relationship between the levels during the first case study, when Secretary of Defense Robert McNamara embraced MAD at the declaratory level, but action policy (and, to some extent, force development) remained committed to counterforce.

Between these two extremes, the relationship between the three levels of policy was in a state of flux for the second case study. The targeting was clearly moving further in the direction of war fighting while declaratory policy was slowly moving in the same direction. As I have shown, policymakers feared losing their autonomy by pursuing counterforce aggressively at the force development and declaratory levels.

In answering this first question I have focused on the case studies as the units of analysis. Another perspective on this is provided by focusing on the nature of each level of nuclear policy over the years that make up this study. Overall, there have been seven major revisions to the SIOP, six of which took place within the time period considered in this study: SIOP 62, which took effect on January 15, 1961; SIOP 63, which took effect on August 1, 1962; SIOP 5 took effect on January 1, 1976; SIOP 5F took effect in October 1981; SIOP 6 took effect on October 1, 1983; and SIOP 6F took effect on October 1, 1989.[2]

Targeting policy has shown more continuity than change. Of course, SIOP 6F does not look like the first SIOP, created by the McNamara Pentagon. The Soviet target base had expanded dramatically, and the U.S. arsenal has grown both in quality and quantity. However, the general philosophy guiding the formation of the SIOP has been constant. NSDM-242 and PD-59 provided guidance for the creation of new SIOPs that changed the emphasis put on command and control, leadership targeting, and the like. But on a continuum between MAD and NUTs, the targeting has always been much closer to NUTs than MAD.

Looking at force development policy, we see a complex historical development. The desire to acquire more accurate nuclear weapons systems pushed procurement. For ICBMs, the *Minuteman II* in 1966 had a CEP of .26, by 1979 the *Minuteman III* had a CEP of .12, and by 1985 CEP was reduced to .06 for the MX missile. For SLBMs, the changes are just as clear. In 1964 the *Polaris* A-3 had a CEP of .5 at 2,500 nautical miles. By 1979 the *Trident* C-4 had a CEP of .25 at 4,000 miles, and by

1990 the *Trident* D-5 has a CEP of .06 at 4,000 miles.[3] The move toward greater accuracy is clear.

What guided the development of weapons systems? Force development has often been explained as resulting from bureaucratic politics or technological innovation. Desmond Ball, whose work I have relied on extensively throughout this study, finds that technology drive weapons acquisition and strategy. This study shows that force development policy has been perfectly consistent with the broad doctrine developed by civilian and military decision-makers. The bureaucratic perspectives developed to explain force development policy focused on the notion that weapons were developed to target military (counterforce) targets—which did not make sense under a policy of MAD. Such explanations did not recognize that MAD was never targeting policy.

The most important evidence for this is that the move toward counterforce and war fighting came before the technological developments that made such strategies possible. This is particularly apparent during the beginning years of the shift toward city-avoidance in the early 1960s. During the development of the first SIOP, defense policymakers were consistently disappointed with the undiscriminating nature of the SIOP. Even later, military officials often found that they did not have the forces that they needed to meet civilian objectives. If the technological argument was correct, we should find the opposite. Force development policy has lagged behind strategy, not vice versa. The strategy set by central defense decision-makers drove the procurement and targeting of weapons.

Finally, and closely related to the point above, declaratory policy evolved from MAD to NUTs. Defense policymakers conducted limited probes early on, probes that brought declaratory policy into line with targeting. These probes sometimes met with opposition from other defense policymakers or the public, and retreats followed. By the end of the period studied here, declaratory policy came to embrace NUTs.

The Domestic Political Structure

The domestic political structure for U.S. strategic nuclear weapons policy is a mediating factor, or intervening variable, between the international system and domestic politics. The nature of the domestic political structure, and changes to the domestic political structure, are important for determining the capabilities of the state to withstand political pressures from society. The domestic political structure changed as civilian policymakers felt that the existing structure did not allow them adequate control over nuclear weapons policy. The first and most important change in the structure was the creation of the SIOP and the JSTPS to coordinate the targeting of nuclear weapons. This took targeting out of the sole purview of the JCS and allowed oversight by civilian decision makers. The degree of oversight to this process has varied over the years.

McNamara vigorously pursued civilian oversight of defense policy. The Draft Presidential Memorandum was a vehicle for such control. Later administrations pursued similar mechanisms to control nuclear weapons policy, particularly the development of specific guidance for the creation of the SIOP. This enhanced civilian control. In addition, the important role of the National Security Council for changes to U.S. nuclear weapons policy is crucial for understanding the domestic political decision-making that influenced the formulation of U.S. nuclear weapons policy.

As time went on, civilian decision-makers took more seriously the role of oversight to coordinate civilian control of the targeting process. This trend became apparent in my interviews with policymakers. This is also demonstrated by the fact that the Department of Defense, both during the 1970s and 1980s, created institutional positions that were specifically designed to oversee the translation of civilian guidance into targeting. The Reagan administration created new positions for this purpose.

Structural changes to Congress during the 1970s enabled it to become a major player in the formulation of defense policy by the mid-1970s. This increased the ability of Congress to conduct its own independent analysis on defense matters and gave it the resources to compete with the executive. And these changes in structure allowed societal impact as well.

The changes in the domestic political structure opened access points to the state by society. Without this, the state probably would have been able to withstand the pressures from society on nuclear weapons policy. Society cannot easily gain access to matters decided primarily by the military. Nonetheless, the state faced a paradox because those weapons needed were difficult to procure without increasing the saliency of the issue. The increased number of access points to the state, that is, the change in structure, in turn decreased the capacity of the state to formulate U.S. nuclear weapons policy autonomously from society.

Public Attention to Nuclear Weapons Policy

The public's attention to nuclear weapons issues has varied over the years. However, when declaratory policy has embraced nuclear war-fighting theories of deterrence, the public's attention to nuclear weapons matters was piqued. This can be seen in the early 1960s, when McNamara announced city-avoidance and the Kennedy administration began to discuss plans for civil defense. Public attention did not crest after Schlesinger's announcement of limited nuclear options. This is best explained by the fact that at the time of the announcement, the country was embroiled in both the Watergate scandal and the Vietnam War.

By the time of the most recent embrace of limited nuclear options and war-fighting theories of deterrence, public attention had peaked. By all measures, including public opinion, press coverage, election results, and public protests, U.S. nuclear weapons policy had become a salient political issue. Societal forces had not favorably greeted talk of limited options. Such talk reminds the public of the horror of nuclear weapons and nuclear deterrence and makes the chance of a nuclear war seem more likely. Talk of MAD, though implying suicide for both sides of a conflict, does not indicate that policymakers really think that they will use nuclear weapons. In fact, NUTs advocates have always criticized MAD advocates precisely on this score, saying that the threat of mutual suicide was never credible.

Something else is going on here as well. An embrace of MAD does not call for state policymakers to talk about nuclear weapons policy. Additional nuclear capabilities do not need to be procured for such a policy, and thus nuclear policy can remain in the background. However, in their search for limited and implementable nuclear options, in the search to implement a war-fighting theory of deterrence, state policymakers had to bring to saliency an issue that they would have preferred not to talk about at all. This is the catch-22 that policymakers have faced throughout the nuclear age.

Congressional-Executive Relations

In the definition of the state utilized throughout this study, Congress is an important part of the state. I have qualified this definition by classifying Congress as the gatekeeper of the state—that is, as the entry point for society. Congressional involvement in strategic nuclear matters in the 1960s was not particularly extensive. As noted in chapter 4, both hawks and doves reacted to McNamara's announcement of the city-avoidance policy. Hawks thought it showed a reluctance to use nuclear weapons, and doves thought it demonstrated too much desire to use nuclear weapons. But Congress was not extensively involved, except for the ABM debate in the late 1960s.

This changed in the 1970s. By this time, Congress had developed numerous mechanisms that enabled it to perform a watchdog role over nuclear weapons policy. Congress launched extensive investigations concerning general strategic nuclear doctrine and the rationale for the procurement of weapons systems. This congressional involvement grew in the following decade, when Congress conducted repeated investigations into the nature of U.S. nuclear weapons policy and the procurement of specific weapons systems. Two points should be made about this involvement. First, it was more extensive than ever before. Second, societal concerns propelled congressional involvement. Congress had become the conduit through which society expressed its concerns over U.S. nuclear weapons policy.

Debates over Force Development

Closely linked to the nature of executive-congressional relations is the nature of the substantive congressional debates concerned with the force development level. Such developments became particularly important for the last two case studies. The ABM debate heralded a role for Congress and its involvement in U.S. nuclear weapons policy. This debate focused on the purpose behind building an extensive defense for nuclear weapons. This was alternatively justified as keeping up with the Soviet Union and building defenses to limit damage in case of nuclear war. Congressional involvement in force development increased after this initial debate, focusing on modernization of the land-based leg of the triad. These controversial developments included research programs for increasing the accuracy of ICBMs, the development of MIRVs and MARVs, and eventually the development of the MX missile.

The net effect of congressional and societal involvement in weapons acquisition and accuracy improvements is mixed. On the one hand, Congress did not radically change the types of weapons that the executive procured in the pursuit of a counterforce strategy. However, the limits that Congress placed on the MX missile and the general nature of congressional opposition to that system marked a watershed in the history of U.S. nuclear weapons policy and an end to the autonomy of the state for this policy area.

Executive Attempts to Shape the Political Environment

Public opinion is not only an independent variable but can be a dependent variable as well. Public opinion influences and constrains policymakers; it is also shaped by state policymakers as they try to control the political environment. This is particularly relevant as we look at the ebbs and flows of declaratory policy over the course of this study. Though I have outlined how declaratory policy shifted from MAD to NUTs, announcements embracing war fighting were quickly followed by announcements that sought to clarify nuclear weapons policy. Though the announcements in the 1970s and 1980s often heralded a radical departure in U.S. nuclear weapons policy, they often contained arguments that were examples of continuity rather than change. This was a difficult line to toe. Policymakers sometimes created more confusion than clarity in trying to make it look like the United States was not contemplating fighting a limited nuclear war.

It is ironic that declaratory shifts that embraced NUTs often served to enhance the myth of MAD. It did so in two ways. First, announcements of the need for flexibility, limited options, and the like, were initially presented as a contrast to MAD. And MAD was used to describe existing nuclear weapons policy, though it was not. Second, the public reaction to the declaratory embraces of war-fighting theories of deterrence caused policymakers to do two things: they backed away from a wholehearted embrace of NUTs at the declaratory level—thus not accurately indicating how much U.S. nuclear weapons policy contemplated the limited use of nuclear weapons—and public officials were hesitant to talk about nuclear weapons policy. Both served to keep the myth of MAD alive.

The Role Of External Factors

The relationship between domestic political structure, domestic politics, and the nature of the international environment is of crucial importance to this study. The waning U.S. superiority in nuclear weapons over the years allows us to treat external factors as variables. When the United States enjoyed unequivocal superiority over the Soviet Union in nuclear weapons, state autonomy on this issue was most pronounced. Defense policymakers proceeded as they wished in developing strategic nuclear weapons policy. Of course, analytically there are two possibilities. First, that the public did not have views on this issue, in which case, the state was undoubtedly autonomous from society.

Another possibility is that society fully agreed with the state in its pursuit of nuclear weapons policy; in this case, can it still be said that the state enjoyed autonomy? I think that the answer is yes, particularly for security policy. As Eric Nordlinger notes, "[W]here society defers or is indifferent to state preferences, the latter enjoy at least some explanatory priority."[4] This is particularly the case in security policy, where the state can prevent or forestall the emergence of divergent societal pressures through its power to shape the political environment. The lack of societal divergence is regarded as a given, but should be seen instead as a result of state actions. Of course, a pluralist model might posit that a lack of divergence indicated that societal wishes have been translated into public policy. But there is no evidence of societal input during the early years.

Though defense policymakers wanted to obtain the ability to fight a controlled nuclear war since the early 1960s, they were often disappointed with the resulting SIOPs. In the early days, however, the vast superiority that the United States enjoyed in strategic nuclear weapons seemed to satisfy policymakers. By the mid-1970s, as U.S. superiority began to wane, defense policymakers took more seriously the need to gain the capability to add limited nuclear options to the SIOP. Though they stopped short of formally and institutionally linking action and force development policy, serious efforts were made to acquire the weapons needed to implement such options. But even during this time defense policymakers recalled this period with frustration, perceiving that they had failed to procure the weapons and capabilities needed to acquire the options desired.

As the gap in the nuclear balance between the United States and Soviet Union closed even more, policymakers linked the action and force development levels so appropriate weapons could be procured. This was supposed to enable SIOP planners to institute limited nuclear options. Changes in institutional structure allowed the procurement of a variety of systems, from enhanced accuracy to survivable command and control. These made the attainment of limited nuclear options seem possible.[5]

This is where we find the ultimate catch-22 state policymakers faced as the nuclear balance changed. As the United States lost its strategic nuclear superiority, state policymakers took more seriously the need to procure those weapons needed to obtain the types of limited nuclear options that they had always desired. However, to procure such systems, they needed to embrace war fighting at the declaratory level. And it is exactly this embrace that led to the loss of state autonomy. It was U.S. involvement in world affairs, particularly the extension of the nuclear umbrella to Western Europe, that propelled the loss of autonomy. It is possible that if the United States had not needed to implement flexible and limited options for extended deterrence, it could have pursued U.S. nuclear weapons policy more autonomously.

Statist vs. Bureaucratic Perspectives

One of the main contributions of this work is to show the superiority of the statist over the bureaucratic lens for understanding the evolution of U.S. nuclear weapons policy. My contention is not that bureaucratic politics has nothing to add to our understanding of U.S. nuclear weapons policy, but rather that the statist perspective is superior when we recognize the three levels of strategic nuclear weapons policy. Unlike the bureaucratic perspective, it offers a holistic approach to U.S. nuclear weapons policy. As such, my aim here is to offer the statist perspective to sharpen and bring into focus the evolution of U.S. nuclear weapons policy. The bureaucratic lens, which has been dominant for viewing this policy area, has obscured the vision of analysts.

Second, though I utilize a statist perspective for the three case studies above, I am not attempting to resurrect a view of the state as a unitary, rational actor. Many who draw on statist approaches try to do so, but any realistic appraisal of all the views of defense policymakers would find such a view wide of the mark. State officials had important differences of opinion, particularly during the Carter administration. However, even with these differences, policy emerged with some coherence. The adaptation of the lens provided here allows for insights that could not have been gained by using the bureaucratic approach.

Despite my use of a statist lens, I am not a "statist." To the contrary, my argument here is that the state was unable to pursue the nuclear weapons policy it desired without interference from society. To clarify this latter point, I will explicitly compare the bureaucratic and statist approaches according to several criteria.

1) The Role of the President (and other Central Decision-Makers): One of the central claims of the bureaucratic perspective is that the president does not control the formulation of U.S. foreign policy. As Halperin and Kanter note:

> But complete and faithful implementation of a Presidential decision remains the exception rather than the rule. More often than not, governmental outputs noticeably diverge from the President's expectations regarding the implementation of this decision. The gap between decision and follow-through results in part from the fact that compliance is not routinely forthcoming, particularly in cases where subordinates feel strongly about their positions and have a reasonable expectation of escaping detention and/or punishment.[6]

Conversely, most working from the statist perspective posit central control by the president. In nuclear weapons policy, the reality lies somewhere in the middle. Two points need to be made in this regard.

First, that the SIOP sometimes diverged from the preferences of central decision-makers, including the president, has often been misinterpreted as evidence of bureaucratic politics. This lack of congruence results instead from the nature of nuclear weapons.

Second, central state decision-makers, including the president, have been involved in the formulation of U.S. nuclear weapons policy. Though it has most often been secretaries of defense who have pushed and announced supposed changes to U.S. nuclear weapons policy, presidents have been centrally involved in these policy initiatives. The history of this policy shows Kennedy closely involved in the initial changes to the SIOP during his first years in office, as is shown by the SIOP briefing he received soon after taking office. Nixon's involvement is a little less clear, though his public rhetoric indicated at least some desire to add implementable nuclear options to the SIOP. It is well known that Carter took an interest in the details of U.S. nuclear weapons policy and had approved all the changes leading to SIOP 6. Finally, though Ronald Reagan was not a president who became familiar with the details of most policy areas, he saw nuclear weapons as political instruments. The move during his tenure to more implementable options was perfectly consistent with his views.

If we examine the role of the various secretaries of defense, the developments associated with changes to U.S. strategic nuclear weapon policy were in line with their desires. Nuclear policy did not come about as a result of bureaucratic maneuvering taking place below the central policymaking level. Policy was not taken over by the military or pursued by lower-level bureaucrats who believed in the efficacy of limited nuclear options despite their superiors' desires for a policy of MAD. The overall direction of U.S. nuclear weapons policy, from declaratory to targeting, was directed and controlled by central state defense policymakers.

2) Relationship between Government Bureaucracies: The bureaucratic politics perspective views government bureaucracies in an atomistic fashion, analogous to the way in which the pluralist model views societal groups. According to this perspective, competition among various government bureaucracies takes place because they are not guided by one conception of the national interest. Instead, they are guided by many different conceptions based on the particular role of the bureaucratic participant. As Allison and Halperin comment in their seminal piece, "Players choose in terms of no consistent set of strategic objectives, but rather according to various conceptions of national security, organizational, domestic, and personal interests."[7] My point here is that the entire history of U.S. nuclear weapons policy indicates just the opposite of this. There was a single overriding strategic objective that consistently dominated this policy area: the desire to make a nuclear war fightable and winnable, and to procure more accurate weapons and survivable command and control to accomplish that goal.

3) The Role of Congress: As Dan Caldwell notes, "Bureaucratic politics analysts give inadequate attention to the role of public interest groups and Congress in the formation and implementation of foreign policy."[8] The statist perspective adopted in this study gives Congress a very important role. It is part of the state, but located at the juncture of state and society. Therefore, the statist approach used here offers an improvement over the bureaucratic approach.

Of course, it has never been deemed as troubling by analysts that foreign policy scholars did not conceptualize a role for Congress in the formulation of U.S. foreign policy. There have been significant historical periods when Congress was not a particularly important actor in the foreign policy process. However, Congress has begun to act as the conduit for society, as a connection between the state and the people. The statist lens utilized here allows a fuller view of the domestic political structure that comprises the national security state.

Morton Halperin acknowledges that the bureaucratic perspective views only a small part of the policymaking picture:

> There is no question that the reality is different. The actions of the American government related to foreign policy result from the interests and behavior of many different groups and individuals in American society. Domestic politics in the United States, public attitudes and the international environment all help to shape decisions and actions. Senators, congressmen, and interest groups are involved to varying degrees, depending on the issue. Here we focus on only one part of this process—that involving the bureaucracy and the president as he deals with the bureaucracy.[9]

Allison and Halperin at times acknowledge that Congress and society are players in the foreign policymaking arena. Nonetheless, their focus on bureaucratic actors to the exclusion of these other actors has led analysts astray.

One final point. Does the relationship and occasional battle between Congress and the executive invalidate my statist approach to this policy area? The answer to this question is no for two reasons. First, for much of the history of U.S. nuclear weapons policy, Congress acted in concert with the executive in formulating nuclear weapons policy. Second, my statist approach is an approach that seeks to assess the role that society has played for nuclear weapons policy, not to posit a unified state. This assessment of the role of Congress allows us to do just that.

4) The Importance of Domestic Politics: The bureaucratic politics model is inconsistent in its view of the importance of domestic political structures for understanding the policymaking process. The bureaucratic politics literature was a response to two different sets of literature. The first, by the likes of Walter Lippman and Gabriel Almond, emphasized that American foreign policy was subject to variations in American public opinion. None of these works explicitly referred to security policy, but the tradition of the literature was well established.

The bureaucratic politics literature was also a response to the dominance of external explanations, which ignored the importance of domestic political structures for understanding security policy. As Evangelista writes, "the traditional understanding has been that while economic policy demands analysis of the domestic structure, military policy can be adequately explained at the international level of analysis."[10] Furthermore, he comments, "[E]ven proponents of domestic structural approaches who seek to demonstrate the relative autonomy of the state (defined as the central decision-makers and bureaucratic apparatus), do not view security policy as germane to their concerns."[11] He also expresses some surprise that those who have emphasized bureaucratic politics have not talked about domestic political structures. While Evangelista makes a good point, in that the bureaucratic theorists have not adequately developed the concept, it has not been ignored. For example, Halperin and Kanter state:

> Accordingly, we argue that a focus on the international objectives of a state is essentially misleading, in that the participants' attention is primarily focused on domestic objectives. Events in international affairs, according to this perspective, are most often the reflection of those internal concerns; scholars require an understanding of a nation's domestic political structure and of its national security bureaucracy in order to explain or predict the foreign policy actions it will take.[12]

Thus, we clearly have a case of proponents of the bureaucratic perspective advocating some attention to the importance of domestic political structure. However, the bureaucratic perspective does not really pay attention to domestic political structures. It instead focuses on a much narrower set of issues, circumscribing its concerns to include only the competition among bureaucracies. As such, it has ignored the importance of the structure of the relationship between bureaucracies and Congress, the president, society, and the international system. The statist perspective on domestic political structure is more inclusive and thus is of greater value in studying nuclear weapons policy.

The statist perspective examines the importance of domestic political structures in order to see how easily they are permeated by society. In my use of the statist paradigm, the role of society is a variable worthy of study, and the results of this study consider it crucial for understanding the development of U.S. nuclear weapons policy.

"Bringing the state back in" was the call of the seminal work by Theda Skocpol and associates, a call to bring back the importance of the state for a literature on domestic politics that had, according to the authors, overemphasized the societal sources of public policy. Similarly, my rallying call here may be "Bring society back in" to the study of security policy, an issue area that has not considered the importance of society.[13]

5) The Source of State Interests: Another important difference between the two approaches is the source of state interests. The bureaucratic perspective, in nearly all its various guises, does not look to state interests as a whole. Instead it looks to the interests of bureaucracies. From this perspective, individuals develop their interests out of their bureaucratic roles. In fact, government positions are often seen as the most important determinant of policy positions. Halperin and Kanter write, "[W]e believe that membership in the bureaucracy substantially determines the participants' perceptions and goals and directs their attention away from international arenas."[14] However, as I have shown above, members of the state decision-making apparatus seem to have common interests that cannot be best described as emanating from bureaucratic interests. Some have incorrectly concluded that the counterforce emphasis of the SIOP came largely from the military. However, as the case studies above show, the first serious move toward counterforce came from the civilian strategists of the Rand Corporation. Further moves in this direction also came from civilian policymakers, and were sometimes resisted by the military. This clearly contradicts the bureaucratic perspective.

The statist perspective posits a different source for state interests. In pure statist works such as Krasner's *Defending the National Interest*, the state derives its interests from the international system. Such a view is perfectly consistent with the Realist view of international relations. And though I have argued that the nature of the nuclear balance clearly affected policymakers' perceptions of the need for developing real nuclear options, the origins of counterforce doctrine is not adequately explained, or is left undetermined, by such a perspective.

One area that needs to be explored further in order to understand state interests is the impact of ideas as a source of state interests, and the privileged nature of some ideas for policymakers.[15] As Ikenberry notes:

> An avenue of investigation that has increasingly occupied the attention of social scientists is the role of political ideas or ideology that, in complex interaction with societal and political structures, occasionally provides openings for policy innovation and institutional change....Their attention to the role of ideas in policy innovation is consistent with the broad outlines of the institutional approach. Ideas are never completely disembodied from the complex of professional and governmental institutions within which they emerge. Indeed, the institutional setting of policymaking is likely to be crucial to the location and shape that the ideas themselves are likely to take.[16]

Though the perspective offered here is relevant to Ikenberry's concerns in that it focuses on the importance and power of ideas, I am not here concerned with ideas as a source of innovation. Instead, I am more concerned with ideas as a source of consistency in policy.

The roots of such an explanation lie in the notions associated with the conventionalization of the nuclear weapons policy. This conventionalization led policymakers to think about nuclear weapons as if they were conventional weapons. As a result, counterforce has dominated nuclear targeting. This is consistent with previous thinking on military targeting, targeting that preceded the advent of nuclear weapons. Thinking of nuclear weapons as rational political instruments was thus perfectly consistent with how military and civilian leaders had always thought about using weapons. The privileged place of this idea, in the minds of both civilian and military leaders, is a partial explanation for the staying power of counterforce targeting in the nuclear age. The deep historical roots of this type of thinking made counterforce targeting a privileged idea adhered to by the state throughout the history of nuclear weapons policy. Those roots also made such targeting a difficult habit to break.

Finally, my use of the statist perspective yields findings that are not consistent with all statist approaches. Put another way, I find that the state is not autonomous in the formulation of U.S. nuclear weapons policy, for three reasons. First, as I indicated in chapters 2 and 3, the statist paradigm draws our attention to issues that have been neglected by scholars in security studies. This has been documented throughout this study. Second, the statist perspective looks for the autonomy of the state, and I have indeed found that the state has enjoyed a great deal of autonomy during some periods. Finally, the state's loss of autonomy in the latter period examined in this study demands that scholars utilize a new analytic lens for studying security policy. In this sense, I have shown that the statist perspective, with its assumption of state autonomy for security policy, is of limited analytic value.

The question then becomes, which is the best analytic perspective for viewing the evolution of U.S. nuclear weapons policy in the current era? Perhaps one that draws on the pluralist tradition once dominant in the study of American politics would yield interesting results. Group activity became significant during the latter period of this study, and a focus on groups might yield important observations on the formulation of nuclear weapons policy. This notion makes it clear that I have left the concept of society underdetermined. A more explicit discussion of the nature of societal involvement in this policy area is called for by the results of this study.

The findings discussed above are summarized in the table on page 166.

The Wider Context

The loss of autonomy in the sphere of nuclear weapons policy did not take place in isolation. Of course, much has been made of the loss of consensus that the state experienced in its pursuit of the Vietnam War.[17] By the late 1960s and early 1970s, societal opposition in the form of public protests and then congressional activity impinged on the state's ability to pursue the war autonomously from society. Some have said that the state's failures to raise taxes to pay for the war led to inflation and a weakened economy, which made the war a more salient political issue. Nevertheless, just as in the case of nuclear weapons policy, opposition to the war did not rest solely on fiscal grounds. Instead, the fiscal aspects served as an entry point for society to examine the overall nature of the policy.

There are other similarities between these issues. As long as the real nature of the Vietnam War, in terms of both its economic and human costs, stayed out of the limelight, society was not an important player in

	Case 1 (1960–68)	Case 2 (1969–75)	Case 3 (1976–85)
Declaratory Policy	MAD (except city-avoidance in 1962)	MAD and limited nuclear options	MAD to NUTs; countervailing, prevailing
Major Declaratory Address	McNamara, June 1962 "city-avoidance"	Schlesinger, January 1974 "limited nuclear options"	Brown, August 1980 "countervailing strategy"
Major Force Development Issues	Establishment of triad; ICBMs and SLBMs; civil defense	Attainment of increased accuracy; MIRVs	MX; Trident; SDI
Action Policy	First SIOP; counter-force targeting	Increased Flexibility; Limited Nuclear Options	War fighting; more counter-force
SIOP(s)	SIOP-62; SIOP-63	SIOP-5	SIOP-6
Major Classified Studies	Presidential Decision Memorandums	NSDM-242 NSDD-13	PD-59
Nuclear Balance	U.S. superiority	Parity emerging	Parity with asymmetries
Congressional Role	Acquiescent	Sensitized	Contentious
Public	Not active after 1963	Not active	Sensitized and Active
State-Society Relations	State is autonomous from society	State is largely autonomous	State loses autonomy

determining the policy. However, as the costs mounted, a broad-based social movement rose to oppose the state's pursuit of the war. The state can use secrecy and deception to pursue an autonomous foreign policy. As alluded to above, the existence of consensus at the beginning of the war can still be framed in terms of state autonomy because of the steps states take to achieve and enhance autonomy. Focusing on the state helps us understand the basis for this consensus. Of course, a pluralist model says that the consensus was an indication of society determining policy; the statist paradigm turns this around to give analytic primacy to the state to see why the public may simply acquiesce in policy.

Both cases indicate the paradox for the state of bringing publicly declared policy in line with actual policy. To obtain the funds and support, the policy must become public. But then the policy can be opposed. From the perspective of those who object to this societal constraint, societal interference leads to military failure, which in turn leads to a lack of domestic support. Colin Gray writes:

> However, as President Johnson demonstrated in Vietnam, if a theory of and doctrine of war are selected with regard to their likely domestic accountability, in disregard of their fit with the objective needs of the conflict in question, then the result is going to be a military failure in the field which must erode, and eventually destroy, the willingness of society to stay the unsuccessful course.[18]

The state confronts this in numerous issues, particularly those dealing with military matters. The pursuit of the Strategic Defense Initiative makes this point clearly. The declaratory goal of the SDI, as announced by Ronald Reagan in March 1983, was to build a defense against nuclear weapons that would "render nuclear weapons impotent and obsolete." That is, the avowed goal was to build a 100 percent effective shield that would protect the United States from nuclear weapons. I see this as analogous to a declaratory policy of MAD, for it in many of the same ways made nuclear war unthinkable and nondangerous. Though Reagan actually proposed SDI as the antidote for MAD as a condition, it was, at least at the declaratory level, a policy that did not contemplate the possibility of fighting a nuclear war.

However, as the SDI evolved over the years, it became clear that advocates of strategic defense did not envision the building of a 100 percent defensive shield. They had more limited goals for the program. By the end of 1984, scientists in charge of research for the SDI argued that the president's goal for a defensive shield would have to be scaled down to a system that would protect land based ICBMs. In December 1984, Dr. George Keyworth, Reagan's science adviser, one of the most enthusiastic supporters of the SDI, said that while the ultimate goals remained the president's vision of a 100 percent shield, "now we're addressing more and more what I call the transition, from the first deployment to the second and so on."[19] This shift was also reflected in the budget requests. These limited goals were entirely consistent with the existing war-fighting theories of deterrence because they foresaw the use of defenses to enhance the survivability of ICBMs. As is shown in the previous chapter, by the time of the Bush administration, the limited view of the SDI had taken root

Because this is a critical case study, we should look beyond the issue of security policy. As has been shown in the introduction to this study, though some have posited the autonomy of the democratic state in many areas, few if any have investigated the autonomy of the state in security policy. The fact that I have shown limits to the state's autonomy in this sphere should give credence to other claims of a lack of autonomy. That is, I have found a lack of autonomy in the policy area where we would least expect to find it. Thus, we may wish to investigate other issue areas where scholars have assumed autonomy for the state.

After the Cold War

What implications do the findings here have for the post–Cold War world? This question can be addressed at many different levels. The first is to look at the implications that these findings have for the future of strategic nuclear weapons policy. We need first to keep in mind that societal forces are indeed sensitive to the threat of nuclear war. It seems clear that the threat of a strategic nuclear war between the United States and the former Soviet Union has greatly receded. In fact, in the post–Cold War world the entire question of strategic nuclear weapons policy has taken on a different quality. We no longer think of it in terms of threats, or even what best deters. Public utterances about nuclear weapons policy are kept to a minimum, and debates over targeting seem to be of secondary importance. There is even talk (at the end of 1993) of targeting strategic nuclear weapons at the ocean.

The strategic nuclear balance has thus given way to questions of nuclear proliferation as the primary nuclear issue considered by both policymakers and the general public. As the fear of an intentional nuclear strike from the Soviet Union receded, new fears arose about the control of nuclear weapons in the former Soviet Union and the proliferation of nuclear weapons in the third world. At this point it is difficult to tell how the nature of state-society relations will affect these issues. Nonetheless, if these proliferation issues begin to make nuclear war seem more likely, societal forces would probably become agitated. But the proliferation issue may not agitate societal forces since the all-out destruction threatened by strategic nuclear war between the superpowers is not usually an issue in proliferation.

The nuclear arms race between the United States and Soviet Union is a unique historical phenomenon. Because of the destruction threatened by it, an analogous issue is difficult to conjure. But there are broader issues that may also be instructive for the future of U.S. nuclear weapons policy. The most important of these is that it is difficult for the government to pursue a secret foreign policy in a democratic society. Though policymakers can clearly attempt to keep society out, this is ultimately difficult to do, especially when Congress in involved.

Another important aspect of the post–Cold War implications of this study relates to the external position of the United States in the international system. As has already been noted, U.S. nuclear weapons policy became more politically salient and contentious as the United States moved from nuclear superiority to nuclear parity. This may also be true for other issues in the post–Cold War world. That is, as the United States spends less on defense, cuts its nuclear arsenal, and withdraws forces from various parts of the globe, its military capabilities may be matched by those of other countries. Overall, this could lead to a situation in which many defense and foreign policy decisions are seen as contentious, and where societal involvement may increase. The course that the United States will take in the post–Cold War world is far from clear, and waning military superiority may make for great societal involvement for issues of war and peace. During the Cold War, many of the choices that the United States had to make in the international system were supported by what was considered to be a broad consensus. As new issues arise, and the choices become more complicated, this consensus may indeed give way to political battles. It will be difficult for the state to act autonomously from society in the high politics of security policy in the post–Cold War world.

As discussed toward the end of chapter 6, the United States does not seem to be moving away from a reliance on nuclear weapons. The country may be moving toward a period analogous to the early 1950s, when in the aftermath of World War II pressures existed to take men out of uniform and to decrease the defense budget. At that time, the United States increased its reliance on nuclear weapons. The early 1990s are similar in some respects. Namely, that there seem to be great popular pressures to demobilize and to cash in on the peace dividend. As some of the current official thinking on nuclear weapons indicates, the United States may attempt to save money by increasing reliance on nuclear weapons, which might allow global reach with a smaller defense budget.

The State, Society, and Limited Nuclear War

This study has examined the relationship between state and society in the formulation of nuclear weapons policy. Much has been written about the state and war making, and there is a well-developed literature on the close and symbiotic relationship between the formation of the nation-state system and the capability to wage war. However, there has not yet been an adequate discussion of how the advent of nuclear weapons has affected the nature of the relationship between state and society.

Though this is not the place to summarize all that has been written about the nature of state-society relations for war preparation, a few general points should be noted here. First we are confronted with the extraction issue. Society has been intimately related to the state's war-waging capacity because the resources for fighting wars have, at least since the end of the seventeenth century, came from society.[20] First in the form of capricious extraction and later in the form of taxation, societies have funded the state's desires to acquire the means of war. This has provided a crucial link between state and society, and a potential source of restraint for societal forces for the state's war preparations. Societal forces may refuse to pay the cost of further militarization. Some have concluded that such a refusal was at least partially responsible for the end of the Vietnam War: a broad range of societal forces opposed the war as President Johnson's reluctance to raise taxes (in part because of the potential domestic political consequences) to pay for the war began to have a significant negative impact on the national economy.[21]

Second, societies have been able to affect the state's ability to wage war through serving in the armed forces of the state. Once conscription became the norm, various parts of society enhanced their relationship with the state and its ability to wage war. In the United States, the shift from conscription to an all-volunteer force has changed the nature of this relationship. Conscription during the Vietnam War and the death of young men from a wide strata of society may have also acted as a source of constraint by society on the state.

There is one last phenomenon that speaks to the relationship between state and society on the conduct of war: societal vulnerability in the case of war. Particularly relevant here is the issue of noncombatants' involvement in hostilities. This was not a particularly important issue for the United States until the advent of nuclear weapons.

How did the advent of nuclear weapons in the United States affect the nature of state-society relations? Let us explore this question by examining how nuclear weapons affected each of the three areas above. Regarding the extraction issue, there are a few noteworthy points. First is the idea that nuclear weapons have been seen as *relatively* inexpensive, which took hold early in the nuclear age as President Eisenhower implemented the New Look policy. During this period, the United States defined its foreign interests broadly and at the same time tried to constrain the growth of the defense budget. Because of the long-standing U.S. bias against the establishment of a standing army during peacetime, there was considerable pressure to bring the boys home. Nuclear weapons provided part of the solution. Though expensive, they cost less than keeping men and women in uniform and procuring more conventional weapons.

This issue was particularly relevant for efforts to defend Western Europe. The Red Army remained a formidable force after World War II, and fear in the United States and NATO of Soviet expansionism demanded that the Soviet threat be met. Because of efforts to cut the defense budget, the deployment of tactical nuclear weapons in Europe allowed for the defense of Western Europe on the cheap.

The defense of Western Europe remained one of the central goals of U.S. strategic and tactical nuclear weapons. And throughout the nuclear age, the need to protect Western Europe would mitigate against decreases in strategic weapons or the declaration of no-first-use of nuclear weapons. Those who were against such cuts or declarations said that the cost of protecting Western Europe without nuclear weapons would be prohibitive.

What is the overall lesson from this first point? It is possible that society would not have acquiesced in the state's broad conception of U.S. national security interests after World War II had the state sought to extract even more resources from society. There is little doubt that had the state tried to pursue these strategies without nuclear weapons, more would have been spent on defense. Thus, it is hard to tell how much the advent of nuclear weapons served to sever the relationship between society and the state for war preparation.

Similar conclusions can be drawn from the second point as well. Without the need to keep as many Americans in uniform, the link between state and society was also severed in this area. This point, however, should not be taken too far. The United States, even with nuclear weapons, had a large proportion of its population in uniform, but without nuclear weapons U.S. policymakers perceived that they would have to put even more soldiers in uniform in Europe.

Significant changes also resulted from the switch from a draft to an all-volunteer force. In some senses, the all-volunteer force may have severed the tie between state and society a bit. With conscription, societal forces could question the legitimacy of armed conflict by objecting to the unwitting participation of society. This debate manifested itself again during the gulf war.

Finally, we have the question of society as noncombatants. Overall, the advent of nuclear weapons involved society in the state's preparation for war more than ever before. The dividing line between combatants and noncombatants became increasingly blurred, more so than at any time since the introduction of air power. Whether one believed in the possibility of limited nuclear war or the apocalyptic vision of those who maintained that any use of nuclear weapons would lead to the end of the planet, the advent of the nuclear age inspired societal fear and interest. It gave the issue of war preparation a great deal of salience.

This gets to the heart of the questions considered in this study and the type of targeting that the state pursues to deter nuclear war. For MAD targeting, populations are the primary targets. For NUTs, the opposition's means of waging war are the primary targets. The connection between state and society may be counterintuitive for examining these two different targeting policies.

On the face of it, a policy of MAD might seem to threaten society and thus involve society in the state's preparations for war. Some who have opposed MAD targeting have done so on moral grounds, that is, that it is immoral to target noncombatants. However, MAD policies had the opposite effect. Because declaratory policies of MAD did not talk about fighting a nuclear war, they made the issue more remote. Because declaratory policies of MAD masked actual targeting policy, the state did not need to talk about fighting a nuclear war.

Conversely, NUTs serves to agitate and thus involve societal forces in state deliberations on war preparation. Because those who believe in NUTs talk about actually using nuclear weapons in a limited way, they make the likelihood of nuclear war seem higher. Those who support NUTs as the best policy to deter war in fact want to make nuclear war seem more likely in order to make it less likely. It is this paradox that served to involve societal forces in consideration for war preparation.

Democratic Control and Normative Concerns

I close this study with reflections on the issue that forms the backdrop for this study: democratic control over nuclear weapons policy. Some of these were addressed in the introduction. Perhaps before the normative question is the descriptive one that has been discussed throughout this study. How much has society controlled the evolution of U.S. nuclear weapons policy?

There is some controversy regarding how a statist paradigm views the issue of democratic control. Krasner claims that the statist perspective is perfectly consistent with models positing democratic control.[22] I disagree with this characterization. If the state's interests are derived independently of societal inputs, if domestic politics are black-boxed, than it is difficult to see how such policies are derived from a democratic process. In fact, those who fear democratic control over foreign policy fear it because societal involvement does not allow the state to pursue its interests based on the objective needs created by the international system.

Thus, in the 1960s, societal input and thus democratic control over nuclear weapons policy had been limited. The state pursued a policy largely in secret, without much input from society. This changed over the years to a point where policy became responsive to democratic control. Debates over this question have sometimes focused on the degree to which civilians have controlled nuclear weapons policy. For those what have asserted that the military and/or bureaucracies have controlled nuclear weapons policy, democratic control was lacking because of the lack of central civilian control. However, because a central part of my findings shows that civilians have controlled the evolution of U.S. nuclear weapons policy, democratic control has at least been possible during this time.

One of the most important changes that helps to explain the source of this democratic control is the increased knowledge that society gathered regarding nuclear weapons matters. This increased knowledge and capability came from the state's increased interactions with society, which allowed societal forces to become more familiar with the nature of nuclear policy and the possible options that the state can pursue.

A full discussion of the normative aspects of this question would entail another study. Overall, state policymakers have been committed to NUTs and war-fighting theories of deterrence. Societal interests seem committed to MAD, skeptical that a nuclear war can, in fact, be kept limited. Thus, a determination regarding the normative aspects of democratic control over nuclear weapons policy comes down to a view of the best way to deter a nuclear war.

The history of nuclear weapons policy demonstrates that policymakers have consistently been frustrated in their search for implementable options. This is not because bureaucrats have interfered with presidential guidance or even because the military has failed to abide by civilian guidance. It is because nuclear weapons are not ordinary weapons. In contemplating a conflict between the United States and the Soviet Union, no one was able to chart a rational use of nuclear weapons. This failure has resulted in a loss of autonomy for the state—a loss of autonomy brought on by societal interference. There are important lessons to be learned from this failure. Policymakers have not been able to plan the use of nuclear weapons in a way that makes the chance of limited nuclear war acceptable. As such, society's recognition of MAD as a condition has withstood the test of time.

Strategic nuclear weapons policy may be complex, and the technologies associated with it are difficult to understand. Yet an argument can be made that the public has been the most responsible player in the policymaking game. From this, we may draw great hope for the future. As Albert Einstein once said, "the facts of nuclear energy should be taken to the village square and from there the decision made about its future."

Notes

Chapter 1. Introduction: An Overview of U.S. Nuclear Weapons Policy

1. No consensus exists on the terms for these various levels of policy. The terminology that I have adopted is used by Desmond Ball, "Developments in U.S. Strategic Policy under the Carter Administration," CISA Working Paper No. 21, Center for International and Strategic Affairs, UCLA, February 1980.

2. I will not cover the period before the creation of the SIOP in 1960. For a treatment of these issues for that period, see David Alan Rosenberg, "The Origins of Overkill: Nuclear Weapons and American Strategy," *International Security* 7, no. 4 (spring 1983): 3–69, and Samuel Williamson, Jr., and Steven L. Reardon, *The Origins of U.S. Nuclear Strategy, 1945–1953* (New York: St. Martin's Press, 1993).

3. For a discussion of this topic, see Paul Joseph, "Making Threats: Minimal Deterrence, Extended Deterrence and Nuclear Warfighting," *The Sociological Quarterly*, 26, no. 3 (1985): 293–310; and Philip L. Lawrence, *Preparing for Armageddon: A Critique of Western Strategy* (New York: St. Martin's Press, 1988).

4. Aaron L. Friedberg, "A History of the U.S. Strategic Doctrine," *Journal of Strategic Studies* 3, no. 3, (March 1980): 49.

5. Robert Jervis, "Security Regimes," *International Organization* 36, no.2 (spring 1982): 374–375.

6. Paul Nitze, "Atoms, Strategy and Foreign Policy," *Foreign Affairs* 34, no. 2 (January 1956) 190.

7. See Henry S. Rowen, *Formulating Strategic Doctrine*, from the Commission on the Organization of the Government for the Conduct of Foreign Policy (The Murphy Commission), Vol. 4, Part III, Appendix K (Washington, DC: GPO, 1975).

8. Harold Brown, "Domestic Consensus and Nuclear Deterrence," in *Defense and Consensus: The Domestic Politics of Western Security*, (London: International Institute for Strategic Studies, Adelphi Paper 183), 26.

9. Though this will be documented below, I will clarify some basic issues here. Many former government officials within the nuclear policymaking

community have told me that although targeting policy has never embraced MAD, very few people ever thought that it did. Policymakers have told me in interviews that anybody who has paid attention realizes that MAD has not been targeting policy and has not been our "real" strategy. This belief is indicative of the gap between the public and state policymakers. I will show that nuclear weapons policy has often been misunderstood by society and parts of the state and will evaluate the extent to which the state has encouraged this misunderstanding.

10. There are many works that have evaluated the claims of these schools of thought. See Edward Rhodes, *Power and MADness* (New York: Columbia University Press, 1989). Other explorations of this debate include Robert Jervis, *The Illogic of American Nuclear Strategy* (Ithaca: Cornell University Press, 1984). Also see Spurgeon Keeny and Wolgang Panofsky, "From MAD to NUTS," *Foreign Affairs* 60, no. 4 (winter 1981–1982): 287–304. For a piece that classifies these into three schools of thought, see Charles L. Glaser, "Why Do Strategists Disagree about the Requirements of Strategic Nuclear Deterrence," in Lynn Eden and Steven E. Miller, eds., *Nuclear Arguments: Understanding the Strategic Nuclear Arms and Arms Control Debates* (Ithaca: Cornell University Press, 1989), 114. Glaser classifies these schools as punitive retaliation, military denial, and damage limitation.

11. Robert Jervis, *The Meaning of the Nuclear Revolution* (Ithaca: Cornell University Press, 1989), 74.

12. There are some who acknowledge that though MAD may be the true condition of the nuclear age, the United States needs to have counterforce weapons and strategies to threaten limited nuclear war because of Soviet skepticism concerning MAD as a condition. This will be further explored in chapter 6 on PD-59 and the countervailing strategy.

13. The best-known advocate of such postures within the academic literature is Colin Gray. See his "Nuclear Strategy: A Case for a Theory of Victory," *International Security* 1, no. 4 (summer 1979): 66–90; Colin S. Gray and Keith Payne, "Victory Is Possible," *Foreign Policy* 39 (summer 1980), 14–27; and Colin S. Gray, "Targeting Problems for Central War," *Naval War College Review* (January–February 1980), 3–21.

14. Central to this debate has been the notion of extending deterrence to Western Europe. The goal of deterring a Soviet conventional invasion of Western Europe was a major factor in the search for these implementable nuclear options. And though the fear of a Soviet invasion of Western Europe is now virtually nonexistent, the United States may still be concerned with extended deterrence to stem the spread of nuclear weapons in Europe. See Edward Rhodes, "Hawks, Doves, Owls and Loons: Extended Deterrence without Flexible Response," *Millenium: The Journal of International Studies* 19, no. 1 (1990): 37–57.

15. See Ron Paarlberg, "Forgetting About the Unthinkable," *Foreign Policy* 10 (spring 1973): 135.

16. For an example see Desmond Ball, "U.S. Strategic Forces: How Would They be Used?" *International Security* 7, no. 3 (winter 1982/1983): 59.

17. See Philip Lawrence, "Strategy, the State and the Weberian Legacy," *Review of International Studies* 13, no. 4 (October 1987): 310.

18. Steven Kull has put forward this type of explanation in *Minds at War: Nuclear Reality and the Inner Conflicts of Defense Policymakers* (New York: Basic Books, 1988). He argues that defense policymakers experience inner conflict that manifests itself in the coexistence of traditional (warfighting—NUTs) and adaptive (MAD) thinking for nuclear weapons policy. This results in some policymakers' advocating hard target kill capability and limited nuclear options while also believing that we live in a MAD world.

19. It is not my argument that action policy does not change. The SIOP has evolved over the course of the nuclear age. The point instead is that it often develops according to a logic separate from that of declaratory policy. This logic has remained constant throughout the nuclear age.

20. Graham T. Allison and Frederic A. Morris, "The Determinants of Military Weapons," in Daniel J. Kaufman, Jeffrey S. Mikitrick, and Thomas J. Levy, eds. *U.S. National Security: A Framework for Analysis* (Boston: Lexington Press, 1983), 317.

21. Ibid., 313.

22. Stephen Van Evera, "The Cult of the Offensive and the Origins of the First World War," *International Security* 9, no. 1 (summer 1984): 107.

23. Edward A Luttwak, *The Grand Strategy of the Soviet Union* (New York: St. Martin's Press, 1983), 51.

24. Carl Builder, "Why Not First Strike Counterforce Capabilities?" *Strategic Review* (spring 1979): 32.

25. Richard Betts, "Nuclear Peace: Mythology and Futurology," *Journal of Strategic Studies* 2, no. 1 (May 1979): 92.

26. Richard B. Foster, "From Assured Destruction to Assured Survival," *Comparative Strategy* 2, no. 1 (1980): 54.

27. Scott D. Sagan, *Moving Targets: Nuclear Strategy and National Security* (Princeton: Princeton University Press, 1989), 11.

28. Ibid., 12.

29. See Burton Pines, "Rethinking the Unthinkable: Carter Revises the New Game Plan for Fighting a Nuclear War," *Time*, August 25, 1980, p. 30.

30. Ibid., 30–31.

31. There are other examples that will be further explored in the case studies. The first quotation in this paragraph is from *U.S. News and World Report*, August 25, 1980, and the second is from *Newsweek*, August 18, 1980. They are both cited in Fred Kaplan, "Going Native Without a Field Map: The Press Plunges into Limited Nuclear War," *Columbia Journalism Review* (January–February): 28.

32. Congress, House, Committee on Armed Services, *Military Posture*, Hearings Before the House Armed Services Committee, 96th Cong., 1st sess., part 1, p. 547, cited in Friedberg, "A History," 66.

33. From Congress, Senate, Committee on Foreign Relations, *The SALT II Treaty*, 96th Cong., 1st sess., part 1, 1979, p. 381, cited in Friedberg, "A History," 66.

34. Malcolm Wallop, "Opportunities and Imperatives of Ballistic Missile Defense," *Strategic Review* 7, no. 4 (fall 1979): 13, cited in Sagan, *Moving Targets*, 188.

35. Henry Kissinger, "NATO: The Next Thirty Years," *Survival*, 21, no. 6 (November–December 1979): 267, cited by Friedberg, "A History," 66–67, note 1.

36. President Reagan, interview with *New York Times* correspondents, February 11, 1985, cited in Arms Control Association, *Star Wars Quotes* (July 1986).

37. Congress, Senate, 1979, cited by Friedberg, "A History," 67, note 1.

38. Peter C. Wagstaff, "An Analysis of the Cities-Avoidance Theory," *Stanford Journal of International Studies* 7, no. 1 (1972): 169.

39. For a discussion of these changes, see Lynn Etheridge Davis, *Limited Nuclear Options: Deterrence and the New American Doctrine*, (London: International Institute for Strategic Studies, Adelphi Paper 191, 1974).

40. Ibid., 4.

41. For a discussion of this, see Jeffrey Richelson, "PD-59, NSDD-13, and the Reagan Strategic Modernization Program," *Journal of Strategic Studies* 6, no. 2 (June 1983).

42. Cited in Leon Sloss and Marc Dean Millot, "U.S. Nuclear Strategy in Evolution," *Strategic Review* 12, no. 1 (winter 1984): 20–21.

43. These works include, Alexander L. George and Richard Smoke, *Deterrence in American Foreign Policy: Theory and Practice* (New York: Columbia University Press, 1974), 88–103; Harry Eckstein, "Case Study in Theory and Political Science," in Fred L. Greenstein, ed., *Handbook of Political Science:*

Strategies of Inquiry (Reading, MA: Addison Wesley Publishing Company, 1975), 80–137; Alexander L. George, "Case Studies and Theory Development," in P. Lauren, ed., *Diplomacy: New Approaches in History, Theory and Policy* (New York: Free Press, 1979), 43–68; Alexander L. George and Timothy McKeown, "Case Studies and Theories of Organizational Decision Making," in R. Coulam and R. Smith, eds. , *Advances in Information Processing in Organizations, Research On Public Organizations* (Greenwich, CT: JAI Press, 1985), II: 21–58.

44. See George and McKeown, "Case Studies," 24.

45. See Alexander George, "The Causal Nexus Between Cognitive Beliefs and Decision-making Behavior: The 'Operational Code' Belief System," in Lawrence Falkowski, ed., *Psychological Models and International Politics* (Boulder: Westview, 1979); and ibid., 35.

46. George and McKeown, "Case Studies," 36.

47. George and Smoke, *Deterrence.*

48. Bruce Russett, "The Democratic Governance of Nuclear Weapons," unpublished manuscript, January 1, 1987, 10.

49. Robert Dahl, *Controlling Nuclear Weapons: Democracy Versus Guardianship* (Syracuse: Syracuse University Press, 1985), 3.

Chapter 2. U.S. Nuclear Weapons Policy and Theory Development

1. Examples include Thomas C. Schelling, *Arms and Influence* (New Haven: Yale University Press, 1966); Alexander L. George and Richard Smoke, *Deterrence and American Foreign Policy: Theory and Practice* (New York: Columbia University Press, 1974); and Glenn Snyder, *Deterrence and Defense: Toward a Theory of National Security* (Princeton: Princeton University Press, 1961).

2. For more on the field of security studies as a body of literature and the need for the integration of the study of national security and domestic politics, see Joseph S. Nye Jr., and Sean M. Lynn-Jones, "International Security Studies: A Report of a Conference on the State of the Field," *International Security*, 12, no. 4 (spring 1988): 5–27. Such calls have been made for some time, and it would be inaccurate to say that this separation has been absolute. Those whose research interests are more narrowly defined as foreign policy (as opposed to international relations) are more likely to pay attention to the domestic roots of foreign policy than those whose primary concern is international relations. For some examples of the consideration of domestic politics and foreign policy from the 1960s, see Gabriel Almond, *The American People and Foreign Policy* (New York: Praeger Publishers, 1960); and Samuel Huntington, *The Common Defense: Strategic Programs in National Politics* (New

York: Columbia University Press, 1961). In addition, the first wave of bureaucratic theorists also wrote about domestic politics.

3. For some examples, see Stephen Krasner, *Defending the National Interest* (Princeton: Princeton University Press, 1978); Peter J. Katzenstein, *Between Power and Plenty: Foreign Economic Policies of Advanced Industrial States* (Madison: University of Wisconsin Press, 1978); and G. John Ikenberry, *Reasons of State: Oil, Politics and the Capacities of American Government* (Ithaca: Cornell University Press, 1988).

4. John A. Hall and G. John Ikenberry, *The State* (Minneapolis: University of Minnesota Press, 1989), 12.

5. Graham Allison and Morton Halperin, "Bureaucratic Politics: A Paradigm and Some Policy Implications," *World Politics* 24, supplement (1972) 44.

6. Graham Allison, *Essence of Decision: Explaining the Cuban Missile Crisis* (Boston: Little Brown and Company, 1971), 67 (emphasis in original).

7. Allison and Halperin, "Bureaucratic Politics."

8. Ibid., 43.

9. Michael H. Armacost, *The Politics of Weapons Innovation: The Thor-Jupiter Controversy* (New York: Columbia University Press, 1969). This book appeared before the Allison/Halperin conceptual work on bureaucratic politics and does not refer to the approach as such, though it contains its conceptual underpinnings.

10. Ibid., 15.

11. Harvey M. Sapolsky, *The Polaris System Development: Bureaucratic and Programmatic Success in Government* (Cambridge: Harvard University Press, 1972). Sapolsky notes in this book that the idea of making SLBMs more accurate was controversial at the time, so controversial that it was kept secret. Note that this occurs when U.S. declaratory policy had embraced MAD. Such weapons developments were not considered to be consistent with the overall policy. This will be further explored in chapter 4.

12. Edmund Beard, *Developing the ICBM: A Study in Bureaucratic Politics* (New York: Columbia University Press, 1976).

13. Allison's work attracted attention because it is a critical case study. If bureaucratic politics could explain a decision for a crisis the magnitude of the Cuban missile crisis, it should add even greater insight into more routine foreign policy decisions. The logic here is that an issue as important as the Cuban missile crisis might lead policymakers to stop bureaucratic infighting and to adopt a policy that represented the national interest.

14. Beard, *Developing the ICBM*, 11.

15. Ted Greenwood, *Making the MIRV: A Study in Defense Decision Making* (Cambridge, MA: Ballinger, 1975), 52.

16. Morton H Halperin, *National Security Policy-Making: Analyses, Cases and Proposals* (Lexington, MA: D.C. Heath and Company, 1975).

17. See Lauren Holland, "Explaining Weapons Procurement: Weaving Old Conceptual Threads into New Theory," presented at the Annual Meetings of the American Political Science Association, September 3–6, 1987.

18. Ibid., 4. Although Holland does not make note of this, E. E. Schattsneider pursued the concept of the scope of conflict in *The Semi-Sovereign People* (New York: Holt, Rinehart and Winston, 1960).

19. This point has also been confirmed to me in interviews with former policymakers. Several confirm that bureaucratic politics is particularly important for explaining the beginning stages of weapons procurement.

20. Donald A. Mackenzie, *Inventing Accuracy: A Historical Sociology of Nuclear Missile Guidance* (Cambridge: MIT Press, 1990), 391.

21. Two critiques are Robert J. Art, "Bureaucratic Politics and American Foreign Policy," *Policy Sciences* 4 (1973): 467–490; and Dan Caldwell, "Bureaucratic Foreign Policy-Making," *American Behavioral Science* 21, no. 1 (September–October 1977): 87–100. Art points out that the works of Hilsman, Huntington, Neustadt, and Schilling were bureaucratic approaches (though somewhat more "political" than the Allison model in that they allowed for a role for the public in the formulation of policy). Two critiques that appeared on the twentieth anniversary of the publication of *Essence of Decision* are David A. Welch, "The Organizational Process and Bureaucratic Politics Paradigms: Retrospect and Prospect," *International Security* 17, no. 2 (fall 1992): 112–46, and Jonathen Bender and Thomas Hammond, "Rethinking Allison's Models," *American Political Science Review* 86, no. 2 (June 1992): 301–22.

22. Morton Halperin, *Bureaucratic Politics and Foreign Policy* (Washington DC: The Brookings Institution, 1974), 5.

23. Caldwell, "Bureaucratic Foreign Policy-Making," 96.

24. Francis E. Rourke, *Bureaucracy and Foreign Policy* (Baltimore: Johns Hopkins University Press, 1972), 65.

25. Stephen Krasner, "Are Bureaucracies Important? (Or Allison Wonderland)," *Foreign Policy* (summer 1972): 159–76.

26. Ibid., 159.

27. Desmond Ball, "The Blind Men and the Elephant: A Critique of Bureaucratic Politics Theory," *Australian Outlook* 28, no. 1 (April 1974): 83.

28. Desmond Ball, "The Role of Strategic Concepts and Doctrine," in Bernard Brodie, Michael D. Intrilligator, and Roman Kolkowicz, eds., *National Security and International Stability* (Cambridge, MA: Oelgeschlager, Gunn and Hain Publishers, 1982), 61.

29. The issue is more complex than this. The military has sometimes resisted counterforce targeting and the implementation of limited options because they felt that civilian guidance failed to recognize the inherent limitations of nuclear weapons.

30. William Arkin and Peter Pringle, *SIOP: The Secret U.S. Plan for Nuclear War* (New York: W.W. Norton and Company, 1975), 49.

31. John Edwards, *Superweapon: The Making of the MX* (New York: W.W. Norton and Company, 1982), 88.

32. David Rosenberg, "Reality and Responsibility: Power and Process in the Making of United States Nuclear Strategy," *Journal of Strategic Studies* 9, (March 1986): 41.

33. Desmond Ball, "U.S. Strategic Forces: How Would They Be Used?," *International Security* 7, no. 3 (winter 1982/1983): 59.

34. Scott D. Sagan, *Moving Targets: Nuclear Strategy and National Security* (Princeton: Princeton University Press, 1989).

35. Ibid., 55.

36. Ibid., 57.

37. The tensions that policymakers feel regarding plans to use nuclear weapons and the enormous destruction that would result if they were used are captured in Stephen Kull, *Minds at War: Nuclear Reality and the Inner Conflicts of Defense Policymakers* (New York: Basic Books, 1988).

38. This account of the process is put forward by Harold Brown, *Thinking About Foreign Policy: Defense and Foreign Policy in a Dangerous World* (Boulder: Westview, 1983), 83. He writes, "U.S. military planners can be expected to continue the pattern, now three decades old, of deriving force levels and characteristics from perceived needs for retaliatory capability (though the characteristics are also influenced by technological advances) and then creating targeting options for use under various circumstances."

39. See Robert Jervis, "Strategic Theory: What's New and What's True," in Roman Kolkowicz, ed., *The Logic of Nuclear Terror* (Boston: Allen and Unwin, 1987), 69–70.

40. This is based on many sources, including Major General Jerome F. O'Malley, "JSTPS: The Link Between Strategy and Execution," *Air University Review* 27, no 4 (May–June 1977): 38–48; Richard Lee Walker, *Strategic Target Planning: Bridging the Gap Between Theory and Practice*, National Security Affairs

Monograph Series 83-9 (Washington, D.C.: National Defense University, 1983); Desmond Ball, "The Development of the SIOP, 1960–1983," 59–60, in Desmond Ball and Jeffrey Richelson, eds., *Nuclear Strategic Targeting* (Ithaca: Cornell University Press, 1986); Lawrence J. Korb, "National Security Organization and Process in the Carter Administration," 111–37, in Sam C. Sarkesian, ed., *Defense Policy and the Presidency* (Boulder: Westview, 1979); and Edwards, *Superweapon*, 86–94.

41. From the Kennedy through the beginning of the Nixon administration, this was called the National Strategic Targeting and Attack Policy (NSTAP). Charles Hopkins, "Unclassified History of the Joint Strategic Target Planning Staff," prepared by JSTPS, March 15, 1989, 4.

42. We do not see periods where the SIOP appears to change significantly without major civilian input, thus giving further credence to the argument that civilians have indeed controlled nuclear weapons policy.

43. O'Malley, "JSTPS: The Link," 40.

44. For a history of the JSTPS, see *History of the Joint Strategic Target Planning Staff: Background and Programs of SIOP-62*, History and Research Division, Strategic Air Command, sanitized copy declassified by the Office of JCS on April 21, 1980, and Hopkins, "Unclassified History."

45. Walker, *Strategic Target Planning*, 22.

46. O'Malley, "JSTPS: The Link," 43.

47. Ibid.

48. Janne Nolan, *Guardians of the Arsenal* (New York: Basic Books, 1989), 250.

49. Hopkins, "Unclassified History," 7.

50. For more on this and other suggestions, see Walker, *Strategic Target Planning*, 34–37. The organization of SAC and JSTPS was changed in the early1990s. See chapter 6 for these changes.

51. See Werner J. Feld and John K. Wildgren, *Congress and the National Defense: The Politics of the Unthinkable* (New York: Praeger Publishers, 1985), especially chap. 2, "Congressional Organization and Process Regarding Defense Issues."

Chapter 3. The State and U.S. Nuclear Weapons Policy

1. Theda Skocpol, "Bringing the State Back In: Strategies of Analysis in Current Research," in Peter Evans, Dietrich Rueschmayer, and Theda Skocpol, eds., *Bringing the State Back In* (New York: Columbia University Press, 1985), 21.

2. For more on this debate, see Gabriel Almond, "The Return to the State," *American Political Science Review* 82, no. 3 (September 1988), and comments by Eric Nordlinger, Theodore J. Lowi, and Sergio Fabrini, 853–901.

3. Some examples include Stephen Krasner, *Defending the National Interest* (Princeton: Princeton University Press, 1978); Peter J. Katzenstein, *Between Power and Plenty: Foreign Economic Policies of Advanced Industrial States* (Madison: University of Wisconsin Press, 1978): and G. John Ikenberry, *Reasons of State: Oil. Politics and the Capacities of American Government* (Ithaca: Cornell University Press, 1988).

4. Eric Nordlinger, *On the Autonomy of the Democratic State* (Cambridge: Harvard University Press, 1981), 98.

5. Krasner, *Defending the National Interests*, 70.

6. J. P. Nettl, "The State as a Conceptual Variable," *World Politics* 20, no. 4 (July 1968): 654.

7. David Lake, "The State and American Trade Strategy in the Pre-Hegemonic Era," *International Organization* 42, no. 1 (winter 1988): 56.

8. Matthew Evangelista, "Issue-Area and Foreign Policy Revisited," *International Organization* 43, no. 1 (winter 1989): 150.

9. For a similar application, see Ikenberry, *Reasons of State*.

10. Nordlinger, *On the Autonomy*, 10.

11. See Roger Benjamin and Raymond Duvall, "The Capitalist State in Context," in Roger Benjamin and Stephen L. Elkin, eds., *The Democratic State* (Lawrence, Ka.: University Press of Kansas, 1985), 19.

12. Ibid., 26.

13. Stephen Krasner, "Approaches to the State: Alternative Conceptions and Historical Dynamics," *Comparative Politics* 12, no. 2 (January 1984): 223–46.

14. Ibid., 227.

15. It is interesting that those who pay careful attention to the definition of the state do not emphasize structure (Krasner, Nordlinger) while those who think that structure is important do not emphasize the definition of the state (Skocpol and Ikenberry, for example).

16. See G. John Ikenberry, "Conclusion: An Institutional Approach to American Foreign Policy," *International Organization* 42, no. 1 (winter 1988): 219–43.

17. Ibid., 30.

18. See Stephen Skowronek, "National Railroad Regulation and the Problem of State Building: Interests and Institutions in Late Nineteenth-Century America," *Politics and Society* 10, no. 3 (1981): 225–50.

19. Skocpol, *Bringing the State Back In*, 9.

20. Krasner, *Defending the National Interest*, 56–57.

21. Nordlinger, *On the Autonomy*, 11.

22. Lake, "The State and American Trade Policy, 36–37. J. P. Nettl makes a similar point about Congress, asserting "an adequate concept of the state would have to include it [the legislature], "The State as a Conceptual Variable," 570. Katzenstein, in referring to foreign economic policy, also refers to Congress as "a point of entry for society" (*Between Power and Plenty*, 65).

23. For more on this general topic, see Richard Hass, "The Role of Congress in American Security Policy," in *American Defense Policy*, John Reichard and Steven Sturm, eds., 5th ed. (Baltimore: Johns Hopkins University Press, 1982), 546–78.

24. Samuel P. Huntington, *The Common Defense: Strategic Programs in National Politics* (New York: Columbia University Press, 1961), 5.

25. Quoted in Alan Platt, *The U.S. Senate and Strategic Arms Policy* (Boulder: Westview, 1978), 2.

26. For similar conclusions regarding congressional impact on SALT, see Stephen Flanigan, "Congress and the Evolution of U.S. Strategic Arms Limitation Policy: A Study of the Legislature's Role in National Security Affairs, 1955–1979," Ph.D. dissertation, Fletcher School of Law and Diplomacy, April 1979.

27. Some examples of these include James M. Lindsay, *Congress and Nuclear Weapons Policy* (Baltimore: Johns Hopkins University Press, 1991); Daniel Wirls, *Buildup: The Politics of Defense in the Reagan Era* (Ithaca: Cornell University Press, 1992); Paul N. Stockton, "The New Game on the Hill: The Politics of Arms Control and Strategic Force Modernization," *International Security* 16, no. 2 (fall 1991): 146–70.

28. Desmond Ball makes a similar argument in "U.S. Strategic Forces: How Would They Be Used?" *International Security* 7, no. 3 (winter 1982–83): 50.

Chapter 4. The McNamara Years: The Shift to Mad?

1. Confidential interview with high defense department official from the Pentagon who served during the McNamara years.

2. Colin S. Gray, *Strategic Studies and Public Policy: The American Experience* (Lexington: University Press of Kentucky, 1982), 98.

3. Confidential interview with Department of Defense adviser to McNamara.

4. Aaron Friedberg, "A History of the U.S. Strategic Doctrine," *Journal of Strategic Studies* 3, no. 3 (1980): 40.

5. Jeffrey Richelson, "PD-59, NSDD-13 and the Reagan Strategic Modernization Program," *Journal of Strategic Studies* 6, no. 2 (June 1983): 126.

6. David Alan Rosenberg, "The Origins of Overkill: Nuclear Weapons and American Strategy, 1945–1960," *International Security* 7, no. 4 (spring 1983): 16.

7. Ibid., 16.

8. David Alan Rosenberg, "Reality and Responsibility: Power and Process in the Making of United States Nuclear Strategy, 1945–1968," *Journal of Strategic Studies* 9 (March 1986): 39.

9. Richelson, "PD-59," 127.

10. For an account of this period, see William Arkin and Peter Pringle, *SIOP: The Secret U.S. Plan for Nuclear War* (New York: W.W. Norton and Co., 1983), 47–48. For more on LeMay's views, see Richard Kohn and Joseph P. Harahan, eds., "U.S. Strategic Air Power, 1948–1962: Excerpts from an Interview with General Curtis E. LeMay, Leon W. Johnson, David A. Burchinal and Jack J. Catton," *International Security* 12, no. 4 (spring 1988): 75–98.

11. For a thorough review of massive retaliation and the nuclear strategy of Dulles and the Eisenhower administration, see Samuel F. Wells, Jr., "The Origins of Massive Retaliation," *Political Science Quarterly* 96, no. 1 (summer 1981): 31–52.

12. John Lewis Gaddis, *Strategies of Containment: A Critical Appraisal of Postwar American National Security Policy* (New York: Oxford University Press, 1982), especially pp. 352–57.

13. John Foster Dulles, "Policy for Security and Peace," *Foreign Affairs* 32, no. 3 (April 1954): 353–64.

14. Ibid., 358.

15. Wells, "The Origins of Massive Retaliation," 38.

16. Arkin and Pringle, *SIOP*, 44.

17. Much of this summary is based on Captain Mark D. Mariska, "The Single Integrated Operational Plan," *Military Review*, (March 1972): 32–39, and

Charles K. Hopkins, "Unclassified History of the Joint Strategic Target Planning Staff (JSTPS)," JSTPS/JS, March 15, 1989, and *History of the Joint Strategic Target Planning Staff: Background and Preparation of SIOP-62*, sanitized copy declassified by the office of the JCS on April 21, 1980, History and Research Division, Headquarters Strategic Air Command.

18. JSTPS, *History of the Joint Strategic Target Planning Staff*, 4.

19. Memorandum of Conference with the President, August 11, 1960, prepared August 12, 1960, Office of the Secretary of Defense, Freedom of Information Act, National Security Archives.

20. Alain S. Enthoven and K. Wayne Smith, *How Much is Enough: Shaping the Defense Program, 1961–1969* (New York: Harper and Row Publishers, 1971), 55.

21. The DPMs were translated into the public Defense Posture Statements issued to Congress, which will be used in the sections below as one facet of declaratory policy. It appears that William Kaufmann was responsible for this. Interview with former and current defense adviser.

22. Desmond Ball, "Toward a Critique of Strategic Nuclear Targeting, in Desmond Ball and Jeffrey Richelson, eds., *Strategic Nuclear Targeting* (Ithaca: Cornell University Press, 1986), 57.

23. Rosenberg "Reality and Responsibility," 43.

24. Janne Nolan, *Guardians of the Arsenal* (New York: Basic Books, 1989), 71.

25. Scott D. Sagan, "SIOP-62: The Nuclear War Plan Briefing to President Kennedy," *International Security* 12, no. 1 (summer 1987): 36.

26. Desmond Ball, "Déjà Vu: The Return to Counterforce in the Nixon Administration," California Seminar on Arms Control and Foreign Policy," UCLA, November 1974, 11.

27. Gregg Herken, *Counsels of War* (New York: Alfred A. Knopf, 1985), 304.

28. Fred Kaplan, *The Wizards of Armageddon* (New York: Simon and Schuster, 1983), 271.

29. For a full summary of this briefing, see Sagan, "SIOP-62."

30. *Draft Memorandum for the President, Recommended Long Range Nuclear Delivery Vehicles, 1963–1967—Appendix 1*, September 23, 1961, Office of the Secretary of Defense, Freedom of Information Act (cited below as *DPM*, 1961). Table is from p. 5.

31. Kaplan, *Wizards of Armageddon*, 277.

32. Ball, "Toward a Critique of Strategic Nucler Targeting," 66.

33. Ball, "Déjà Vu," 12.

34. Kaplan, *Wizards of Armageddon*, 279.

35. Desmond Ball, *Politics and Force Levels: The Strategic Missile Program of the Kennedy Administration* (Berkeley: University of California Press, 1980), 191.

36. Ball, "Toward a Critique of Strategic Nuclear Targeting," 66.

37. See *DPM*, 1961, 4.

38. *Draft Memorandum for the President: Recommended FY 1964–FY 1968 Strategic Retaliatory Forces*, November 21, 1962, Office of the Secretary of Defense, Freedom of Information Act (cited below as *DPM*, 1962).

39. Speech by the Honorable Robert S. McNamara, Secretary of Defense, Before the Fellows of the American Bar Foundation Dinner, Edgewater Beach Hotel, Chicago, Illinois, Saturday, February 17, 1962. News Release, Department of Defense, Office of Public Affairs, No. 239–62.

40. Robert S. McNamara, *Remarks by Secretary McNamara, NATO Ministerial Meeting*, May 5 1962, Office of the Secretary of Defense, Freedom of Information Act.

41. Confidential interview with former McNamara adviser. This member of the McNamara Pentagon opposed the Athens speech because he thought this was the kind of thing that should be done between the United States and individual allies privately, not at a ministerial meeting.

42. McGeorge Bundy to President, "Memorandum for the President," June 1, 1962, Freedom of Information Act, Office of the Secretary of Defense, National Security Archives.

43. McNamara criticized the development of such forces in his subsequent testimony before Congress. See Congress, Senate, Committee on Armed Services, *Military Procurement Authorization for Fiscal Year 1964*, 88th Cong., 1st sess., March 1963, 111.

44. Nolan, *Guardians of the Arsenal*, 75.

45. For more on this, see Edward A. Kolodziej, *The Uncommon Defense and Congress, 1945–1963* (Columbus: Ohio State University Press, 1966).

46. Paul Boyer, "From Activism to Apathy: The American People and Nuclear Weapons: 1963–1980," *Journal of American History* 70, no. 4 (March 1984): 824.

47. See Henry S. Rowen, *Formulating Strategic Doctrine*, from the Commission on the Organization of the Government for the Conduct of Foreign Policy, The Murphy Commission, Vol. 4, Appendix K, Part III, 1975, 219–34, especially, p. 231.

48. Alton Frye, *A Responsible Congress* (New York: McGraw-Hill, 1975), 10.

49. For more on the heightened public reaction to this new policy, See Nolan, *Guardians of the Arsenal*, 76

50. In a pure policy of MAD, there is no role for damage limitation. In fact, from the perspective of a MAD advocate, the goal of damage limitation is destabilizing.

51. Cited in Ball, "Déjà Vu," 16–17 (emphasis added). This quotation comes from private correspondence between Ball and the secretary. One influential Mcnamara adviser told me, "I still have a bet which if I charged interest it would be a very large sum from an Air Force General who was convinced on the basis of McNamara's posture statements that the SIOP would undergo change. It did not." Confidential interview with former adviser to Robert McNamara.

52. As noted earlier, the DPMs served as the drafts for the annual reports, and are included in this section for that reason.

53. *Draft Memorandum for the President: Recommended FY 1965–FY 1969 Strategic Retaliatory Forces*, December 6, 1963, Office of the Secretary of Defense, Freedom of Information Act, 1–3.

54. Ibid., 1–5 (emphasis added).

55. Ibid., 1–10.

56. Ibid., 34 and 35.

57. *Draft Memorandum for the President, Recommended FY 1967–1971 Strategic Offensive and Defensive Forces*, November 1, 1965, Office of the Secretary of Defense, Freedom of Information Act, 21.

58. Robert McNamara, *Defense Department of Defense Annual Report for Fiscal Year 1967*, January 26, 1966.

59. *Statement of Secretary of Defense Robert S. McNamara, before the Senate Armed Services Committee on the FY 1969–1973 Defense Program and 1969 Defense Budget*, prepared January 22, 1968, 46.

60. Ibid., 47.

61. Ibid., 48, 49, 50. It is interesting to note here that these criteria are a little different than those that were spelled out in the 1964 *DPM*, where MAD

was identified as the capability to destroy 25 percent of the Soviet population and more than two-thirds of its industrial capacity. See *Draft Memorandum for the President, Recommended FY 1966–1970 Programs for Strategic Offensive Forces, and Civil Defense*, December 3, 1964, Office of the Secretary of Defense, Freedom of Information Act, 4 (cited below as DPM, 1964).

62. Congress, Senate, Preparedness Investigating Subcommittee of the Committee on Armed Services, *Status of U.S. Strategic Power*, 90th Cong., 2nd sess., April and May 1968, part I, 6–13.

63. Ibid., 6. It is interesting to note here the controversy over whether it was the military or civilian leadership that favored a counterforce rather than countervalue nuclear weapons policy. First, it is clear that much of the initial counterforce and damage-limitation thinking in the late 1950s and early 1960s came from Rand and civilians there. Though many in the Air Force favored this, there is also ample historical evidence to show that many in the military were skeptical about the limited options that civilians hoped for. They realized that such limits and control would be very difficult to achieve in a nuclear war.

64. Ibid., 60–61.

65. Ibid., 117

66. Ibid., 138.

67. Ibid., 138–139.

68. This point was also made forcefully in a confidential interview with a former Department of Defense official.

69. Ibid., part II, 186.

70. Ibid., 219.

71. Ibid., 238.

72. Ibid., 239.

73. In fact, in *DPM* 1961, McNamara justified turning down the Air Force request for 53 additional B-52 bombers because of the advantages of ballistic missile for counterforce purposes, (12).

74. These numbers are taken from Graham T. Allison and Frederic A. Morris, "The Determinants of Military Weapons," in Daniel J. Kaufman, Jeffrey S. Mikitrick and Thomas J. Levy, eds., *U.S. National Security: A Framework for Analysis* (Boston: Lexington Press, 1983), 307–36.

75. Ball, "Déjà Vu," 12–13.

76. Ibid., 12.

77. Ibid., 22.

78. *DPM*, 1965, 21.

79. For the complete story of the MIRV, see Ted Greenwood, *Making the MIRV: A Study of Defense Decision Making* (Cambridge, MA: Ballinger, 1975).

80. Frye, *A Responsible Congress*, 49.

81. Cited in Ibid., 50. This point was also confirmed to me by a former close adviser to the McNamara Pentagon.

82. See Kaplan, *Wizards of Armageddon*, 363–64.

83. Frye, *A Responsible Congress*, 69.

84. Cited in Ball, "Déjà Vu," 19–20.

85. See *DPM*, 1962, 22.

86. Harvey M. Sapolsky, *The Polaris System Development: Bureaucratic and Programmatic Success in Government* (Cambridge: Harvard University Press, 1972), 221.

87. Ibid., 222

88. *DPM*, 1964, 30. Cited in Graham Spinardi, "Why the U.S. Went for Hard Target Counterforce in Trident II (and Why It Didn't Get There Sooner)," *International Security* 15, no. 2 (fall 1990): 160.

89. Spinardi, "Why the U.S. Went for Hart Target Counterforce," 162.

90. Desmond J. Ball, "The Counterforce Potential of American SLBM Systems," *Journal of Peace Research* 14, no. 1 (1977): 25.

91. Ball, "Déjà Vu," 21.

92. Donald MacKenzie, *Inventing Accuracy: A Historical Sociology of Nuclear Missile Guidance* (Cambridge: MIT Press, 1990), 269.

93. Kaplan, *Wizards of Armageddon*, 125–27.

94. Ibid., 312.

95. Ibid.

96. *DPM*, 1964, 35.

97. Lawrence Freedman, *The Evolution of Nuclear Strategy*, 2nd ed., (New York: St. Martin's Press, 1989), 250–52.

98. Kaplan, *Wizards of Armageddon*, 314.

99.   Confidential interview with official from the McNamara DoD.

100.   Confidential interview with former DoD official.

101.   It should be noted that though McNamara opposed the ABM, he supported a small ABM system for political purposes.

Chapter 5. Shifting Sands?

1.   James Schlesinger, *Planning, Programming, Budgeting*, Inquiry of the Subcommittee on National Security and International Operations, Congress, Senate, Committee on Government Operations, 1970, 133.

2.   See Daniel Ellsberg, "Call to Mutiny," in E. P. Thompson and Dan Smith, eds., *Protest and Survive* (New York: Monthly Review Press, 1981), xi.

3.   Henry Kissinger, *Nuclear Weapons and Foreign Policy* (New York: Harper and Row, 1957).

4.   The same players pop up repeatedly throughout the course of the nuclear age. The names William Kauffman, Fred Ikle, Don Cotter, Leon Sloss, Andy Marshall, Roger Molander, and others were instrumental in more than one of the case studies considered in this study.

5.   These data are from *The Military Balance*, taken from "The Fundamentals of Nuclear Strategy and Arms Control," in *Nuclear Strategy, Arms Control and the Future*, ed. P. Edward Haley and Jack Merritt (Boulder: Westview, 1988), 10–11. The totals were not included in the original chart

6.   Data taken from Tom Gervasi, *The Myth of Soviet Military Supremacy* (New York: Harper and Row, 1987), 411. These figures are also based on *The Military Balance*, supplemented by other sources. These figures include warheads on ICBMs, SLBMs, forward-based medium-range ballistic missiles (MRBMs), long-range bombers, and forward-based bombers.

7.   For more on NSSM-3 and the evolution of U.S. nuclear weapons policy during this period, see Terry Richard Terriff, "The Innovation of U.S. Strategic Policy in the Nixon Administrations, 1969–1974," Ph.D. dissertation, the Department of War Studies, King's College, University of London, September 1991.

8.   Fred Kaplan, *The Wizards of Armageddon* (New York: Simon and Schuster, 1983), 366.

9.   Ibid., 370.

10.   Lynn Etheridge Davis, *Limited Nuclear Options: Deterrence and the New American Doctrine*, (London: International Institute for Strategic Studies, Adelphi Paper 191, 1974), 4.

11. Kaplan, *Wizards of Armageddon*, 367.

12. Janne Nolan, *Guardians of the Arsenal* (New York: Basic Books, 1989), 106.

13. Davis, *Limited Nuclear Options*, 4.

14. Confidential interview with staff member of the Foster panel.

15. William Arkin et al., *The Encyclopedia of the U.S. Military* (Cambridge: Harper and Row, 1990), 487.

16. Desmond Ball, "The Development of the SIOP, 1960-1983," in Desmond Ball and Jeffrey Richelson, eds., *Strategic Nuclear Targeting* (Ithaca: Cornell University Press, 1986), 74.

17. Desmond Ball, "Counterforce Targeting: How New? How Viable?" in John F. Reichert and Steve Sturm, eds., *American Defense Policy*, 5th ed. (Baltimore: Johns Hopkins University Press, 1984), 228 (originally published in *Arms Control Today*, no. 2 [February 1981]).

18. Ibid., 288.

19. Confidential interview with a member of the National Security Council.

20. Confidential interview with a member of Foster panel.

21. Confidential interview with a member of Foster panel and the JCS.

22. Henry Rowen, *Formulating Strategic Doctrine*, from the Commission on the Organization of the Government for the Conduct of Foreign Policy (The Murphy Commission), part III, vol. 4, Appendix K (Washington, DC: GPO, 1975), 223.

23. Nolan, *Guardians of the Arsenal*, 117.

24. Desmond Ball, "U.S. Strategic Forces: How Would They Be Used," *International Security* 7, no.3 (winter 82–83): 36–37.

25. Ball, "The Development of the SIOP," 82–83, from House Appropriations Committee, "Defense Appropriations for 1980," pt. 3, 878; Senate Armed Services Committee, Department of Defense Authorization for Appropriations for Fiscal Year 1980, pt. 3, 1437; Harold Brown, *Department of Defense Annual Report Fiscal Year 1980*, p. 85; and Senate Committee on Armed Services, *Department of Defense Authorization for Appropriations for Fiscal Year 1981*, pt. 2, 544–45.

26. Ibid., 74.

27. Scott Sagan, *Moving Targets* (Princeton: Princeton University Press, 1989), 47–48.

28. Ball, "The Development of the SIOP," 82.

29. Confidential interview with a high Department of Defense official.

30. Richard M. Nixon, *A Report to Congress: U.S. Foreign Policy for the 1970s, A New Strategy for Peace*, February 18, 1970, 122.

31. Richard M. Nixon, *A Report to Congress*, February 25, 1971, 170–71.

32. According to Lynn Davis, "officials in the Defense Department were puzzled and irritated" by this misrepresentation. See Davis, *Limited Nuclear Options*, 3. However, as Kaplan notes, though the people in the Department of Defense knew that the SIOP was more flexible and capable than the Nixon characterization, it also was seen as a recommendation to take such issues more seriously. See Kaplan, *Wizards of Armageddon*, 366. Furthermore, the first Department of Defense Annual Report under then Secretary of Defense Melvin Laird contained similar language. In it he wrote, "[D]eterrence of a deliberate nuclear attack against the United States and its allies remained the first charge on Defense resources in fiscal year 1968. Such deterrence requires that our strategic forces be sufficiently large and versatile to sustain their capability for assured destruction—the ability to inflict at all times and under all foreseeable conditions, decisive damage upon any aggressor." See Melvin Laird, *Department of Defense Annual Report, Fiscal Year 1968*, 18.

33. Congress, House, Armed Services Committee, *Hearings on Military Posture and H.R. 6722*, 1973, 499.

34. Congress, Senate, Committee on Armed Services, *Nomination of James R. Schlesinger to be Secretary of Defense*, 93rd Cong., 1st sess., June 18, 1973, 81.

35. Confidential interview with adviser to James Schlesinger.

36. William Beecher, *Australian Financial Review*, August 7, 1972, cited in Desmond Ball, "Déjà Vu: The Return to Counterforce in the Nixon Administration," California Seminar on Arms Control and Foreign Policy, UCLA, November, 1974.

37. Cited in Ball, "Déjà Vu," 1.

38. Cited in ibid., 4. Note that this description also contributed to the myth of MAD as a description for U.S. policy.

39. Haley and Merritt, *Nuclear Strategy, Arms Control and the Future*, 106.

40. Alan Platt, *The U.S. Senate and Strategic Arms Policy: 1969–1974* (Boulder: Westview, 1978), 76.

41. See James Schlesinger, *Annual Department of Defense Report, Fiscal Year 1975*, March 4, 1974 (cited below as *FY75 Annual Report*).

42. Ibid., 4-5.

43. Ibid., 4.

44. Ibid., 39.

45. Schlesinger sent a special envoy to explain these proposed changes to the European allies (confidential interview with adviser to Schlesinger).

46. Congress, Senate, Subcommittee on Arms Control, International Law and Organization of the Committee on Foreign Relations, *U.S.-U.S.S.R. Strategic Policies*, 93rd Cong., 2nd sess., March 4, 1974, sanitized and made public April 4, 1974, 9.

47. Ibid., 9.

48. Ibid., 26.

49. Ibid., 26–27.

50. Congress, Senate, Committee on Armed Services, *Fiscal Year 1975 Authorization for Military Procurement, Research and Development, and Active Duty, Selected Reserve and Civilian Personnel Strengths*, 93rd Cong., 2nd sess., part 1, February 4, 1974, 10.

51. John W. Finney, "U.S. Retargeting Some Missiles Under New Strategic Concept," *The New York Times*, January 11, 1974, 6.

52. See Michael Getler, "U.S. Studies Re-Targeting of Missiles," *Washington Post*, January 11, 1974, 1 and 16.

53. Secretary of Defense Donald H. Rumsfeld, *Annual Defense Department Report Fiscal Year 1977*, January 27, 1976 (cited below as *FY77 Annual Report*), 47.

54. Confidential interview with a member of the Foster panel.

55. Confidential interview with a member of the National Security Council.

56. Confidential interviews with two members of the Foster panel.

57. Evidence of this emerged in my confidential interviews with various officials from this period.

58. Interview with a high Department of Defense official.

59. Ball, "Déjà Vu," 19.

60. Rumsfeld, *FY77 Annual Report*, 13.

61. Schlesinger, *FY75 Annual Report*, 42.

62. Ibid., 45 (emphasis added).

63. Secretary of Defense James R. Schlesinger, *Annual Defense Department Report, Fiscal Year 1976*, February 5, 1975, section II, 5.

64. Ibid.

65. James M. Lindsay, *Congress and Nuclear Weapons* (Baltimore: Johns Hopkins University Press, 1991), 56–57.

66. Ibid., 57.

67. John M. Collins, "Counterforce and Countervalue Options: A Military Analysis Related to Nuclear Deterrence," Congressional Research Service, Library of Congress, Washington, DC, December 7, 1972, 36.

68. Edward W. Brooke, "Authorization of Appropriation for Military Procurement and Other Purposes," remarks in the Senate (*Congressional Record*, August 27, 1970, 30253, cited in ibid., 38.

69. Platt, *The U.S. Senate and Strategic Arms Policy*, 78.

70. This discussion is based on Collins, "Counterforce and Countervalue Options."

71. Congress, Senate, Armed Services Committee, *Authorizing Appropriations for FY 71 Military Procurement, Research and Development*, July 14, 1970, 82, cited in ibid., 35.

72. Ibid., 41.

73. William Beecher, "Major-War Plans are Being Revised by White House," *The New York Times*, August 5, 1972, 1 and 9, cited in Collins, "Counterforce and Countervalue Options," 43.

74. Ibid., 45.

75. Schlesinger, *FY75 Annual Report*, 51.

76. Ibid., 52.

77. Ibid. To get some sense of the lag involved in getting a program to the operational level, though the MK-12A was approved for funding in this year, it would not actually become operational until June 1980, and not until December 1982 would 300 *Minuteman III* have the new warhead. See Gervasi, *Myth of Soviet Military Supremacy*, 284–85.

78. Schlesinger, *FY75 Annual Report*, 55.

79. Platt, *The U.S. Senate and Strategic Arms Policy*, 82.

80. For a general discussion of this, see Gregory C. Tarbell, "Congress, Counterforce and the Genesis of the MX," master's thesis, Brown University, June 1983, 121–25.

81. Ibid., 131.

82. Confidential interview with a high Department of Defense official.

83. This discussion is based on Graham Spinardi, "Why the U.S. Navy Went for Hard-Target Counterforce in Trident II (And Why it Didn't Get There Sooner), *International Security* 15, no. 2 (fall 1990): 147–90, especially 175–78.

84. Desmond J. Ball, "The Counterforce Potential of American SLBM Systems," *Journal of Peace Research* 14, no.1 (1977): 31 and 35.

85. Spinardi, "Why the U.S. Navy Went," 172.

86. Donald MacKenzie, *Inventing Accuracy: A Historical Sociology of Nuclear Missile Guidance* (Cambridge: MIT Press, 1990), 275.

87. Ibid., 166–67.

88. Schlesinger, *FY75 Annual Report*, 57.

89. See Congress, Senate, Committee on Armed Services, *Authorizing Appropriations for Fiscal Year 1976 and July-September 1976 Transition Period for Military Procurement* 94th Cong., 1st sess., May 19, 1975, 106, cited in Tarbell, "Congress, Counterforce and the MX," 143.

90. *FY 1976 Authorization Hearings*, 6383, cited in Tarbell, ibid., 145.

91. *FY 1977 Authorization Hearings*, 6520, cited in Tarbell, ibid., 146.

92. This discussion of the MX is partially based on Tarbell, ibid., 145–60.

93. Conference Report Authorizing Appropriations for FY 1977 for Military Procurement…, U.S. Congress, #94-1004, June 28, 1976, 40, cited in Tarbell, ibid., 158.

94. Ball, "Déjà Vu," 26.

95. See Donald Latham and John J. Lane, "Management Issues: Planning, Acquisition and Oversight," in Ashton Carter, John Steinbruner, and Charles A. Zraket, eds., *Managing Nuclear Operations* (Washington, DC: Brookings Institution Press, 1988), 640–60.

96. This is reported by Platt, *The U.S. Senate and Strategic Arms Policy*, 109.

97. Confidential interview with a high Defense Department official.

Chapter 6. A Radical Departure? PD-59 and Forward

1. From William Arkin, "SIOP-6," *Bulletin of the Atomic Scientists* (April 1983): 9.

2. Confidential interview with member of Carter's National Security Council.

3. See Richard Burt, "The New Strategy for Nuclear War: How it Evolved," *The New York Times*, August 13, 1980, 35.

4. Harold Brown, *Department of Defense Annual Report—Fiscal Year 1981*, January 29, 1980 (cited below as *FY81 Annual Report*), 37 and 77.

5. Confidential interview with a member of Carter's National Security Council.

6. Confidential interview with a member of Carter's National Security Council.

7. Desmond Ball, "The Development of the SIOP—1960–1983," in Desmond Ball and Jeffrey Richelson, eds., *Strategic Nuclear Targeting* (Ithaca: Cornell University Press, 1986), 76.

8. Janne Nolan, *Guardians of the Arsenal* (New York: Basic Books, 1989), 133.

9. Leon Sloss and Marc Dean Millot, "U.S. Nuclear Strategy in Evolution," *Strategic Review* 12, no. 1 (winter 1984): 24.

10. Confidential interview with a long-time aide to defense policymakers.

11. Sloss and Millot, "U.S. Nuclear Strategy in Evolution," 24.

12. Congress, Senate, Committee on Armed Services, *Department of Defense Authorization for Appropriations for Fiscal Year 1980*. See the testimony of William Perry, 96th Cong., 1st sess., February 1, 1979, 299. It is difficult to interpret the third point since some of Perry's testimony has been deleted from the public record. The third point actually reads, "they concluded that the targeting emphasis should be shifted from a primary emphasis on [deleted] to a primary emphasis on [deleted] targets, and that for that targeting emphasis the priorities should be to maximize the damage to those targets, while at the same time to minimize collateral damage." It is possible that Perry was talking about some type of counterforce damage and avoiding populations, perhaps emphasizing military rather than economic targets, which had been established by NSDM-242.

13. Sloss and Millot, "U.S. Nuclear Strategy in Evolution," 24.

14. Based on Ball, "The Development of the SIOP," 76–77.

15. Ibid., 77. In addition, it was later reported in the press that Secretary of Defense Brown did not think that a presidential directive was necessary, and that the State Department was also skeptical. See Burt, "The New Strategy for Nuclear War," 2 and 3.

16. Ibid., 2.

17. For example, the 1971 SIOP called for the targeting of leadership targets, classified as "Primary Controls," as the second major category in priority order. Milton Leitenberg, "Presidential Directive (PD) 59: United States Nuclear Weapons Targeting Policy," *Journal of Peace Research* 18, no. 4 (1981): 315.

18. Desmond Ball and Robert Toth, "Revising the SIOP: Taking War-Fighting to Dangerous Extremes," *International Security* 14, no. 4 (spring 1990): 67.

19. William Beecher, "U.S. Drafts New N-War Strategy vs. Soviets," *Boston Globe*, July 27, 1980, 1 and 12, cited in Jeffrey Richelson, "PD-59, NSDD-13 and the Reagan Strategic Modernization Program," *Journal of Strategic Studies* 6, no.2 (June 1983): 129.

20. Desmond Ball, "Counterforce Targeting: How New, How Viable?" *Arms Control Today* 11, no. 2 (February 1981): 7.

21. Richelson, "PD-59," 130

22. John Edwards, *Superweapon: The Making of MX* (New York: W.W. Norton and Company, 1982), 172 and 174.

23. Ball, "The Development of the SIOP," 17.

24. Confidential interview with an aide to the Department of Defense.

25. See Harold Brown, *Department of Defense Annual Report—for Fiscal Year 1982,* January 19, 1981, 39.

26. Confidential interview with a defense policymaker for the Carter Administration.

27. Richelson, "PD-59," 131.

28. "Nuclear Weapons Employment Policy," NSDD-12, NSC F 83-1129, Freedom of Information Act (emphasis added).

29. Congress, Senate, Committee on Foreign Relations, *U.S. Strategic Doctrine*, 97th Cong., 2nd sess., December 14, 1982, 100. Cited in Scott Sagan, *Moving Targets: Nuclear Strategy and National Security* (Princeton: Princeton University Press, 1989), 199, note 112.

30. Ball, "The Development of the SIOP," 79–80.

31. Congress, Senate, Committee on Armed Services, *Consideration of Mr. Paul C. Warnke to be Director of the U.S. Arms Control and Disarmament Agency and Ambassador*, 95th Cong., 1st sess., February 1977, 129.

32. Ibid, 129.

33. Ibid,. 130.

34. Ibid., 264.

35. Desmond Ball, "Developments in U.S. Strategic Nuclear Policy Under the Carter Administration," Center for International and Strategic Affairs, UCLA, CISA Working Paper No. 21, February, 1980, from *The New York Times*, December 16, 1977.

36. Ibid., 4.

37. Harold Brown, Secretary of Defense, *Department of Defense Annual Report—Fiscal Year 1979*, February 2, 1978, 42.

38. Ibid., 54.

39. Cited in Ball, "Developments," 5.

40. Dellums mischaracterized the historical nature of U.S. nuclear weapons policy. Congress, House, Committee on Armed Services, *Hearings on Military Posture and H.R. 1872 and HR 2575*, Part 1 of 6, 96th Cong., 1st Sess., 512–13.

41. Ibid., 512.

42. Harold Brown, Secretary of Defense, *Department of Defense Annual Report—Fiscal Year 1980*, January 25, 1979, 15.

43. Ibid.

44. Ibid., 75.

45. Ibid., 77.

46. U.S. Congress, Senate, *Department of Defense Authorization for Appropriations for Fiscal Year 1980*, 96th Cong., 1st sess., part 3, March, April, and May 1979, 101.

47. Brown, *FY81 Annual Report*, 66.

48. Ibid., 66.

49. Though it is hard to say why the policy came out when it did and the way it did, many of the policymakers that I interviewed thought that the leak came from either Brzezinski or his assistant, General Odom. I have no direct evidence to support this claim.

50. Michael Getler, "Carter Directive Modifies Strategy for a Nuclear War," *Washington Post*, August 6, 1980, A10. Because the review process had gone on for so long, there were occasional leaks to the press over the years regarding the new strategy. For examples, see George C. Wilson, "Defense Orders New Study on Limited Nuclear War," *Washington Post*, November 11, 1978, 10, and Walter C. Pincus, "Thinking the Unthinkable: Studying New Approaches to a Nuclear War," *Washington Post*, February 11, 1979, A21.

51. See "Aiming Missiles, and Dodging Them," *The New York Times*, August 13, 1980, p. 25. There are two other important aspects to this report. First, the *Times* editorial was negative about these changes in the arsenal. Second, this editorial also criticized PD-58, also leaked, which focused on the evacuation and safe keeping of government leaders in the event of a nuclear war to help improve the chances for continuity in government. The reasons as to why these leaks all took place in the middle of the election campaign remain conjecture.

52. Looking back, Brown said that the delay took place because "other events in Iran and Afghanistan took priority." See Harold Brown, "Domestic Consensus and Nuclear Deterrence," from *Defense and Consensus: The Domestic Aspects of Western Security* (London: International Institute for Strategic Studies, Adelphi Paper 183, 1983), 21.

53. See Harold Brown, "The Flexibility of Our Plans: Strategic Nuclear Policy," delivered at the U.S. Naval War College, August 20, 1980, in *Vital Speeches of the Day*, October 21, 1980, 743.

54. Ibid., 743.

55. See Melinda Beck with David C. Martin, "A New View of Nuclear War," *Newsweek*, August 18, 1980, 39. To be fair, the authors do note later in the article that the idea of surgical strikes actually began with Schlesinger.

56. Congress, Senate, Committee on Foreign Relations, *Presidential Directive 59—Nuclear War Strategy*, 96th Cong., 2nd sess., September 16, 1980, 29.

57. Of those within the administration, Brown seemed to be particularly skeptical about the prospects for a limited nuclear war, and continually said throughout this testimony that he did not think that the United States could win a nuclear war, but that the important thing was that since the Soviet Union had indicated that it thought it could, we had to base our deterrence posture on such a belief. Ibid., 9.

58. "Slocombe Clarifies PD 59 Policy: Industrial Targets Still Important," *Defense Week*, November 17, 1980, 10.

59. Interview with adviser to the Carter National Security Council.

60. Confidential interview with a high official of the Carter National Security Council.

61. State of the Union Address, 1979.

62. Confidential interview with Reagan Defense Department officials.

63. See Charles W. Cordery, "Reagan Apparently Towing Carter's Nuclear Line," *Baltimore Sun*, August 3, 1981, 6.

64. Caspar Weinberger, Secretary of Defense, *Department of Defense Annual Report to Congress—Fiscal Year 1983*, January 31, 1982, I-18.

65. Ibid.

66. Congress, Senate, Subcommittee on Strategic and Theater Nuclear Forces of the Committee on Armed Services, *Strategic Force Modernization Programs*, 97th Cong., 1st sess., 1981, 281–82.

67. Bernard Gwertzman, "Haig Cites a Standing NATO Plan Envisioning a Warning A-Blast," *The New York Times*, November 5, 1981, 1.

68. Charles W. Cordery, "Weinberger Contradicts Haig's Nuclear-Shot Testimony," *Baltimore Sun*, November 6, 1981, 1; Walter Pincus and George C. Wilson, "Nuclear Warning Shot Plan Disputed," *Washington Post*, November 6, 1981, 20; and Richard Halloran, "Haig Is Disputed By Weinberger on A-Blast Plan," *The New York Times*, November 6, 1981.

69. Cordery, "Weinberger Contradicts Haig," 1.

70. Charles W. Cordery, "Reagan Repeats A-War Stand," *Baltimore Sun*, November 11, 1981, 1.

71. Richard Halloran, "Pentagon Draws up First Strategy for Fighting a Long Nuclear War," *The New York Times*, May 30, 1982, 1. Halloran states that the view here on protracted nuclear war is different than that put forward by the Carter administration, but that is not clear. After all, PD-18 asked defense policymakers to examine the notion of protracted nuclear war. See Sloss and Millot, "U.S. Nuclear Strategy in Evolution," 24.

72. *FY 1984–1988 Defense Guidance*, 34-35, quoted in Richard Halloran, "50 Legislators Protest Extended A-War Policy," *The New York Times*, July 22, 1982, 6.

73. The Defense Guidance had been greatly expanded by the Reagan administration as a bureaucratic tool, and its themes are usually contained in the Defense annual reports that are issued to Congress. See Sloss and Millot, "U.S. Nuclear Strategy in Evolution," 25.

74. Michael Getler, "Pentagon Acts to Clarify Position on Nuclear War," *Washington Post*, June 4, 1982, 4.

75. Ibid.

76. Richard Halloran, "Weinberger Angered by Reports on War Strategy," *The New York Times*, August 24, 1982, 8.

77. George C. Wilson, "Weinberger Lobbies Editors on War Policy," *Washington Post*, August 25, 1982, 9.

78. See Robert G. Kaiser, "Pentagon Official Retreats, Calls A-War Unwinnable," *Washington Post*, April 1, 1982, 1.

79. See "Weinberger Drops Disputed Words in Revision of '82 Arms Proposal," *The New York Times*, March 18, 1983, A30; and Richard Barnard, "Less Talk of Nuclear War in Weinberger's New Defense Guidance," *Defense Week*, March 14, 1983, 1.

80. David Wood, "Pentagon Tames Rhetoric to Offer a Softer Image," *Los Angeles Times*, March 20, 1983, 1.

81. David Meyer, *A Winter of Discontent: The Nuclear Freeze and American Politics* (New York: Praeger Publishers, 1990), 15.

82. Ibid., 125. For an analyis of this from a social movements perspective, see David Meyer, "Protest Cycles and Political Process: American Peace Movements in the Nuclear Age," *Political Research Quarterly* 46, no. 3 (September 1993): 451–80.

83. Frances B. McCrea and Gerald E. Markle, *Minutes to Midnight: Nuclear Weapons Protest in America* (Newbury Park, CA: Sage Publications, 1989), 143.

84. This is based on many Gallup Polls, including: *The Gallup Poll*, 1982, Survey #188-G, p. 77; *The Gallup Poll*, 1984, #231-G, p. 71 and Survey #240-G, p. 144 ; *The Gallup Poll*, 1985, Survey #249-G, p. 52; *The Gallup Poll*, 1990, Survey #6092207, p. 38; *The Gallup Poll*, 1992, Survey #603220115, p. 84.

85. *The Gallup Poll*, December 22, 1983, Survey #227-G, p. 265.

86. *The Gallup Poll*, 1990, 54.

87. Ibid., 88.

88. Study cited in McCrea and Markle, Minutes to Midnight, 140, from M. Milburn, P. Watanaba, and B. Kramer, "The Nature and Sources of Attitudes Toward a Nuclear Freeze," *Political Psychology* 7 (1986): 661–74.

89. Ibid., 89.

90. Adam Garfinkle, *The Politics of the Nuclear Freeze* (Philadelphia: Foreign Policy Research Institute, 1984), 10.

91. Interview with Jerome Grossman, president of Council for a Livable World.

92. Richard Stengle, "Freezing Nukes, Banning Bottles," *Time*, November 15, 1982, 35.

93.   For an inside account of this, see Douglas Waller, *Congress and the Nuclear Freeze: An Inside Look at the Politics of a Mass Movement* (Amherst: University of Massachusetts Press, 1987).

94.   Much of this summary is based on Rob Leavitt, "Freezing the Arms Race: The Genesis of a Mass Movement," Kennedy School of Government Case Program, Harvard University, 1983, unpublished manuscript.

95.   See Pam Solo, *From Protest to Policy: Beyond the Freeze to Common Security* (Cambridge, MA: Ballinger, 1988), 79.

96.   For a compelling argument that the SDI was a response to domestic political circumstances, see Daniel Wirls, *The Politics of Defense in the Reagen Era* (Ithaca: Cornell University Press, 1992), 133–68.

97.   Congress, Senate, Subcommittee on Strategy and Theater Nuclear Force of the Committee on Armed Services, *Strategic Force Modernization Programs*, 1981, 75.

98.   During this testimony Edward C. Aldridge, Jr., undersecretary of the Air Force defined the following terms for the committee—this is interesting as the emphasis here was clearly on trying to justify improvements in the accuracy of U.S. strategic nuclear forces. Hard-Target Capability: the ability to destroy hard targets (economic and military) with high probability. Counterforce Capability: the ability to destroy military targets—hard or soft—usually forces, but also including support elements, with high probability. Hard-Target Counterforce Capability: the ability to destroy hardened military targets with high probability. See Ibid., 2123.

99.   Congress, Senate, Committee on Armed Services, *Fiscal Year 1978 Authorization for Military Procurement, and Active Duty, Selected Reserve and Civilian Personnel Strengths*, 94th Cong., 2nd sess., part 2, March 1976, 6253.

100.   Tom Gervasi, *The Myth of Soviet Military Supremacy* (New York: Harper and Row, 1987), 284–85.

101.   Congress, *FY 1978 Authorization*, part 2, 6444–45.

102.   Congress, Senate, Committee on Armed Services, *Department of Defense Authorization for Appropriations for Fiscal Year 1981*, 96th Cong., 2nd sess., part 2, 506.

103.   Lauren H. Holland and Robert A. Hoover, *The MX Decision: A New Direction in U.S. Weapons Procurement Policy?* (Boulder: Westview, 1985), 123.

104.   John Edwards, *Superweapon: The Making of MX* (New York: W.W. Norton and Company, 1982), 134.

105.   Holland and Hoover, *The MX Decision*, 78.

106. Ibid., 79.

107. Confidential interview with a Reagan Defense Department official.

108. Holland and Hoover, *The MX Decision*, 228.

109. Ibid., 242.

110. "The MX Missile," factsheet, Council for a Livable World, January 1985, 2.

111. Ibid., 3.

112. James Lindsay, *Congress and Nuclear Weapons Policy* (Baltimore: Johns Hopkins Unversity Press, 1991), 69.

113. Holland and Hoover, *The MX Decision*, 216.

114. For more on the grass roots efforts against the MX missile, see John Isaacs, "MX: Reagan's Pyrrhic Victory," *Bulletin of the Atomic Scientists* (June–July 1985): 46.

115. Colin S. Gray, *The MX ICBM and National Security* (New York: Praeger Publishers, 1981), 27.

116. Richelson, "PD-59," 139.

117. Ibid.

118. Congress, Senate, Subcommittee on Strategic and Theater Nuclear Forces of the Committee on Armed Services, *Strategic Force Modernization Programs*, 73.

119. Ibid., 86.

120. Ibid., 86–87.

121. Congress, Senate, Committee on Armed Services, *Research and Development*, 94th Cong., 1st sess., March 1975, 2831.

122. Congress, House, Committee on Armed Services, *Hearings on Military Posture*, 96th Cong., 1st sess., 1979, 513.

123. Joel S. Witt, "American SLBMs: Counterforce Options and Strategic Implications," *Survival* 24 (July–August 1982): 165.

124. D. Douglas Dalgleish and Larry Schweikart, *Trident* (Carbondale: Southern Illinois University Press, 1984), 104.

125. Cited in Witt, "American SLBMs," 168.

126. See Richard Halloran, "Weinberger Said to Offer Reagan Plan to Regain Atomic Superiority," *The New York Times*, August 14, 1981, 1.

127.   Cited in Witt, "American SLBMs," 162.

128.   Cited in Ibid., 103.

129.   Congress, Senate, Subcommittee on Strategic and Theater Nuclear Forces of the Committee on Armed Services, *Strategic Force Modernization Programs*, 116.

130.   Cited by William M. Arkin, "Sleight of Hand with Trident II," *Bulletin of the Atomic Scientists* (December 1984): 5.

131.   The D-5 would not become operational until March 1990. See "Trident 1.5?" *Bulletin of the Atomic Scientists* (July–August 1990): 48.

132.   Graham Spinardi, "Why the U.S. Went for Hard Target Counterforce in Trident II (and Why It Didn't Get There Sooner)," *International Security* 15, no. 2 (fall 1990): 178.

133.   "The Trident II Missile," factsheet by Council for a Livable World, February 1985.

134.   It appeared that the MX might be more expensive. In 1980, it was estimated that the *Trident* missiles (not including the new submarines themselves) would cost $8.5 billion. Others had estimated the total cost of the program to be $50 billion. See "First Strike Weapons at Sea: The Trident II and the Sea-Launched Cruise Missile," *Defense Monitor* 16, no. 6 (1987): 4.

135.   For the best single study of this, see Lindsay, *Congress and Nuclear Policy*.

136.   Ibid., 61.

137.   Ibid.

138.   Ball and Toth, "Revising the SIOP," 65–92.

139.   This warning is clearly voiced in Robert Toth, "U.S. Shifts Nuclear Response Strategy: New Formula Designed to Eliminate Soviet Leadership Early in Conflict," *Los Angeles Times*, July 23, 1989, 16.

140.   Though the Bush administration did not make a declaratory statement regarding these changes, it clearly was sensitive to societal reaction to an announcement of major changes to the SIOP. For example, as guidance was prepared for the new SIOP, it was generally referred to as SIOP 7. However, out of a fear of possible reactions to the desire to target leadership more seriously, the Bush administration decided to label the new SIOP 6F, to communicate its continuity with the existing SIOP 6. See Toth and Ball, "Revising the SIOP," 66, citing General John T Chain, CINCSAC from Richard Halloran, "U.S. Revises its War Plan for a New Age," *The New York Times*, November 2, 1988, A7.

141.   See Ball and Toth, "Revising the SIOP," 79–81.

142.   Robert C. Toth, "U.S. Scratches Nuclear Targets in Soviet Bloc," *Los Angeles Times*, April 19, 1991, 1.

143.   R. Jeffrey Smith, "U.S. Trims List of Targets in Soviet Union," *Washington Post*, July 21, 1991, 1.

144.   My report on the nonpublic version of this is based on press reports. These include R. Jeffrey Smith, "U.S. Urged to Cut 50 percent of A-Arms," *Washington Post*, January 6, 1992, 1; and "Strategic Study Endorses SSBNs," *Navy News and Undersea Technology*, January 13, 1992, 3.

145.   Smith, "U.S. Urged to Cut 50% of A-Arms," 1.

146.   "Strategic Study Endorses SSBNs," 3.

147.   Thomas C. Reed and Michael O. Wheeler, "The Role of Nuclear Weapons in the New World Order," statement presented to the Committee on Armed Services, U.S. Senate, January 23, 1992.

148.   Ibid., 9.

149.   Ibid., 14.

150.   Confidential interview with a Carter national security adviser.

Chapter 7. Conclusion: State, Society, and U.S. Nuclear Weapons Policy

1.   Harold Brown, *Defense and Consensus: The Domestic Aspects of Western Security* (London: International Institute for Strategic Studies, Adelphi Paper 183 1983), 19 and 25.

2.   Desmond Ball and Robert Toth, "Revising the SIOP: Taking War-Fighting to Dangerous Extremes," *International Security* 14, no. 4 (spring 1990): 67.

3.   Donald MacKenzie, *Inventing Accuracy: A Historical Sociology of Nuclear Missile Guidance* (Cambridge: MIT Press, 1990), 438–29.

4.   Eric Nordlinger, *On the Autonomy of the Democratic State* (Cambridge: Harvard University Press, 1981), 83.

5.   Of course, whether the state was ever really able to procure such capabilities remains a matter for conjecture, though the belief during this latter period was that they had come closer to doing so.

6.   Morton Halperin and Arnold Kanter, eds., *Readings in American Foreign Policy: A Bureaucratic Perspective* (Boston: Little Brown and Company, 1973), 33.

7. Graham T. Allison and Morton H. Halperin, "Bureaucratic Politics: A Paradigm and Some Policy Implications," *World Politics* 24, supplement (1972): 43.

8. Dan Caldwell, "Bureaucratic Foreign Policy-Making," *American Behavioral Science* (September–October 1977): 96.

9. Morton H. Halperin, *Bureaucratic Politics and Foreign Policy* (Washington, DC: Brookings Institution, 1974), 5.

10. Matthew Evangelista, "Issue-Area and Foreign Policy Revisited," *International Organization* 43, no. 1 (winter 1989): 150.

11. Ibid.

12. Halperin and Kanter, *Readings in American Foreign Policy*, 3.

13. Of course, one might respond to this by stating that I am constructing a pluralist model for the study of security policy. Such a claim overstates the case. Instead, the arguments in this study may properly be seen as a step in this direction, as an attempt to focus on the state and its relationship to society, rather than on society itself. This analysis is more consistent with a statist than a pluralist approach. Nonetheless, this study leaves off where a pluralist approach may now be appropriate for the study of U.S. nuclear weapons policy.

14. Halperin and Kanter, *Readings in American Foreign Policy*, 3.

15. For some examples of this, see Judith Goldstein, "The Impact of Ideas on Trade Policy: The Origins of U.S. Agricultural and Manufacturing Policies," *International Organization* 43, no. 1 (winter 1989): 31–71; Peter M. Haas, "Do Regimes Matter? Epistemic Communities and Mediterranean Pollution Control," *International Organization* 43, no. 3 (smmer 1989): 377–403; and the special issue of *International Organization* 46, no. 1 (winter 1992), edited by Peter Haas, "Knowledge, Power and International Policy Coordination." Other examples of this literature include Judith Goldstein and Robert Keohane, eds., *Ideas and Foreign Policy* (Ithaca: Cornell University Press, 1994); and Jeff Checkel, "Ideas, Interests and Gorbachev's Foreign Policy Revolution," *World Politics* 45, no. 2 (1993): 271–300.

16. G. John Ikenberry, "Conclusion: An Institutional Approach to American Foreign Economic Policy," *International Organization* 42, no. 1 (winter 1988): 242.

17. For a treatment of this, see Richard Melanson, *Reconstituting Consensus: Foreign Policy Since the Vietnam War* (New York: St. Martin's Press, 1991).

18. Colin Gray, *War, Peace and Victory: Strategy and Statecraft for the Next Century* (New York: Simon and Schuster, 1990), 299.

19. William Broad, "Reduced Goals Set on Reagan's Plan for Space Defense," *The New York Times*, December 13, 1984, 1.

20. For a discussion of this, see Michael Howard, *War in European History* (Great Britain: Oxford University Press, 1976), 49.

21. Though this is a bit beyond the scope of this study, it is worth noting here that this link may be severed as a result of the Gulf War, a war that the United States could fight but have other countries pay for. The need to extract resources from society was minimized, and thus eliminated one source of control that society may have over the state.

22. See Stephen Krasner, "Are Bureaucracies Important?" *Foreign Policy* 7 (summer 1972), especially 160–61.

Bibliography

"Aiming Missiles, and Dodging Them," *The New York Times*, August 13, 1980, 25.

Allison, Graham T. *Essence of Decision.* Boston: Little Brown and Company, 1971.

Allison, Graham T. and Morton H. Halperin. "Bureaucratic Politics: A Paradigm and Some Policy Implications." *World Politics*, 24, supplement (1972): 40–79.

Allison, Graham T. and Frederic A. Morris. "The Determinants of Military Weapons," in *U.S. National Security: A Framework for Analysis*, ed., Daniel J. Kaufman, Jeffrey S. Mikitrick and Thomas J. Levy. Boston: Lexington Press, 1983.

Almond, Gabriel. *The American People and Foreign Policy.* New York: Praeger Publishers, 1960.

Almond, Gabriel. "The Return to the State." *American Political Science Review* 82, no. 3 (September 1988) with commentaries by Eric Nordlinger, Theodore J. Lowi and Sergio Fabrini, 853–901.

Arkin, William. "SIOP-6." *Bulletin of the Atomic Scientists* (April 1983): 9.

———. "Slight of Hand with Trident II." *Bulletin of the Atomic Scientists* (December 1984): 5.

Arkin, William and Peter Pringle. *SIOP: The Secret U.S. Plan for Nuclear War.* New York: W.W. Norton and Company, 1983.

Arkin, William et. al. *The Encyclopedia of the U.S. Military.* Cambridge: Harper and Row, 1990.

Armacost, Michael H. *The Politics of Weapons Innovation: The Thor-Jupiter Controversy.* New York: Columbia University Press, 1969.

Arms Control Association. *Star Wars Quotes.* July 1986.

Art, Robert. "Bureaucratic Politics and American Foreign Policy." *Policy Sciences* 4 (1973): 467–90.

Ball, Desmond. "The Blind Men and the Elephant: A Critique of Bureaucratic Politics Theory." *Australian Outlook* 28, no. 1 (April 1974): 83.

———. "Déjà Vu: The Return to Counterforce in the Nixon Administration." California Seminar on Arms Control and Foreign Policy, UCLA, November 1974.

——. The Counterforce Potential of American SLBM Systems." *Journal of Peace Research* 14, no. 1 (1977): 23–40.

——. "Developments in U.S. Strategic Policy Under the Carter Administration." CISA Working Paper No. 21, Center for International and Strategic Affairs, UCLA, February 1980.

——. *Politics and Force Levels: The Strategic Missile Program of the Kennedy Administration.* Berkeley: University of California Press, 1980.

——. "Counterforce Targeting: How New, How Viable?" *Arms Control Today* 11, no. 2 (February 1981): 4–7.

——. "The Role of Strategic Concepts and Doctrine," *National Security and International Stability*, ed. Bernard Brodie, Michael D. Intrilligator, and Roman Kolkowicz. Cambridge, MA: Oelgeschleger, Gunn and Hain Publishers, 1982.

——. "U.S. Strategic Forces: How Would They Be Used?" *International Security* 7, no. 3 (winter 82–83): 31–60.

——. "Counterforce Targeting: How New? How Viable?" in *American Defense Policy*, ed. John F. Reichert and Steve Sturm. Baltimore: Johns Hopkins University Press, 1984.

——. "The Development of the SIOP, 1960–1983," and "Toward a Critique of Strategic Nuclear Targeting," in *Strategic Nuclear Targeting*, ed. Desmond Ball and Jeffrey Richelson. Ithaca: Cornell University Press, 1986.

Ball, Desmond, and Robert Toth. "Revising the SIOP: Taking War-Fighting to Dangerous Extremes." *International Security* 14, no. 4 (spring 1990): 65–92.

Beard, Edmund. *Developing the ICBM: A Study in Bureaucratic Politics.* New York: Columbia University Press, 1976.

Beck, Melinda, and David C. Martin. "A New View of Nuclear War." *Newsweek*, August 18, 1980.

Beecher, William. "U.S. Drafts New N-War Strategy vs. Soviets." *Boston Globe*, July 27, 1980, 1 and 12.

Bender, Jonathen and Thomas Hammond. "Rethinking Allison's Models." *American Political Science Review* 86, no. 2 (June 1992): 301–22.

Benjamin, Roger, and Raymond Duvall. "The Capitalist State in Context," in *The Democratic State*, ed. Roger Benjamin and Stephen L. Elkin. Lawrence, Ka.: University of Kansas Press, 1985.

Bernard, Richard. "Less Talk of Nuclear War in Weinberger's New Defense Guidance." *Defense Week*, March 14, 1983, 1.

Betts, Richard. "Nuclear Peace: Mythology and Futurology." *Journal of Strategic Studies* 2, no. 1 (May 1979): 83–101.

Boyer, Paul. "From Action to Apathy: The American People and Nuclear Weapons, 1963-1980," *The Journal of American History*, 70, no. 4 (March 1984): 219–34.

Broad, William. "Reduced Goals Set on Reagan's Plan for Space Defense." *The New York Times*, December 13, 1984, 1.

Brown, Harold. "The Flexibility of Our Plans: Strategic Nuclear Policy." *Vital Speeches of the Day*, October 21, 1980, 741–44.

——. *Thinking About Foreign Policy: Defense and Foreign Policy in a Dangerous World*. Boulder: Westview, 1983.

——. "Domestic Consensus and Nuclear Deterrence." In *Defense and Consensus: The Domestic Politics of Western Security*. London: International Institute for Strategic Studies, Adelphi Paper, 183, 1983.

Builder, Carl. "Why Not First Strike Counterforce Capabilities?" *Strategic Review* (spring 1979): 32–39.

Burt, Richard. "The New Strategy for Nuclear War: How it Evolved." *The New York Times*, August 13, 1980, 35.

Caldwell, Dan. "Bureaucratic Foreign Policy-Making." *American Behavioral Science* (September–October 1977): 87–110.

Checkel, Jeff. "Ideas, Interests and Gorbachev's Foreign Policy Revolution." *World Politics* 45, no. 2 (1993): 271–300.

Cordery, Charles W. "Reagan Apparently Towing Carter's Nuclear Line." *Baltimore Sun*, August 3, 1981, 6.

——. "Weinberger Contradicts Haig's Nuclear-Shot Testimony." *Baltimore Sun*, November 6, 1981, 1.

——. "Reagan Repeats A-War Stand." *Baltimore Sun*, November 11, 1981, 1.

Council for a Livable World. "The MX Missile." January 1985.

——. "The Trident II Missile." February, 1985.

Dahl, Robert. *Controlling Nuclear Weapons: Democracy Versus Guardianship*. Syracuse: Syracuse University Press, 1985.

Dalgleish, D. Douglas and Larry Schweikart. *Trident*. Carbondale: Southern Illinois University Press, 1984.

Davis, Lynn Etheridge. *Limited Nuclear Options: Deterrence and the New American Doctrine*. London: International Institute for Strategic Studies, Adelphi Paper 191, 1974.

Dulles, John Foster. "Policy for Security and Peace." *Foreign Affairs* 32, no. 3 (April 1954): 353–64.

Eckstein, Harry. "Case Study in Theory and Political Science," in *Handbook of Political Science: Strategies of Inquiry*, ed. Fred Greenstein. Reading, MA: Addison-Wesley Publishing Company, 1975.

Edwards, John. *Superweapon: The Making of the MX*. New York: W.W. Norton and Company, 1982.

Ellsberg, Daniel. "Call to Mutiny," in *Protest and Survive*, ed. E. P. Thompson and Dan Smith. New York: Monthly Review Press, 1981.

Enthoven, Alain S., and Wayne K. Smith. *How Much Is Enough: Shaping the Defense Program, 1961–1969*. New York: Harper and Row Publishers, 1971.

Evangelista, Matthew. "Issue-Area and Foreign Policy Revisited." *International Organization* 43, no. 1 (winter 1989): 147–71.

Feld, Werner J. and John K. Wildgren. *Congress and the National Defense: The Politics of the Unthinkable*. New York: Praeger Publishers, 1985.

Finney, John W. "U.S. Retargeting Some Missiles Under New Strategic Concept." *The New York Times*, January 11, 1974, 6.

"First Strike Weapons at Sea: The Trident II and the Sea-Launched Cruise Missile." *Defense Monitor* 16, no. 6 (1987).

Flanigan, Stephen. "Congress and the Evolution of U.S. Strategic Arms Limitation Policy: A Study of the Legislature's Role in National Security Affairs, 1955-1979." Ph.D. dissertation, Fletcher School of Law and Diplomacy, April 1979.

Foster, Richard. "From Assured Destruction to Assured Survival." *Comparative Strategy* 2, no. 1 (1980): 53–74.

Freedman, Lawrence. *The Evolution of U.S. Nuclear Weapons Policy*. 2nd ed. New York: St. Martin's Press, 1989.

Friedberg, Aaron. "A History of U.S. Strategic Doctrine." *Journal of Strategic Studies* 3 no. 3 (March 1980): 37–71.

Frye, Alton. *A Responsible Congress*. New York: McGraw-Hill, 1975.

Gaddis, John Lewis. *Strategies of Containment: A Critical Appraisal of Postwar American National Security Policy*. New York: Oxford University Press, 1982.

——. "Expanding the Data Base: Historians, Political Scientists and the Enrichment of Security Studies." *International Security* 12, no, 1 (summer 1987): 3–21.

Garfinkle, Adam. *The Politics of the Nuclear Freeze*. Philadelphia: Foreign Policy Research Institute, 1984.

Gelb, Leslie, Anthony Lake and I. M. Destler. *Our Own Worst Enemy*. New York: Simon and Schuster, 1984.

George, Alexander, and Richard Smoke. *Deterrence in American Foreign Policy: Theory and Practice*. New York: Columbia University Press, 1974.

——. "Case Studies and Theory Development," in *Diplomacy: New Approaches in History, Theory and Policy*, ed. P. Lauren. New York: Free Press, 1979.

——. "The Causal Nexus Between Cognitive Beliefs and Decisions-Making Behavior: The 'Operational Code' Belief System," in *Psychological Models and International Politics*, ed., Lawrence Falkowski. Boulder: Westview, 1979.

George, Alexander and Timothy McKeown. "Case Studies and Theories of Organizational Decision Making," in *Advances in Information Processing in Organizations, Research on Public Organizations*, vol. 2, ed. R. Coulam and R. Smith. Greenwich, CT: JAI Press, 1985.

Gervasi, Tom. *The Myth of Soviet Military Supremacy*. New York: Harper and Row, 1987.

Getler, Michael. "U.S. Studies Re-Targeting of Missiles." *Washington Post*, January 11, 1974, 1 and 16.

——. "Carter Directive Modifies Strategy for a Nuclear War." *Washington Post*, August 6, 1980, A10.

——. "Pentagon Acts to Clarify Position on Nuclear War." *Washington Post*, June 4, 1982, 4.

Glaser, Charles. "Why Do Strategists Disagree about the Requirements of Strategic Nuclear Deterrence," in *Nuclear Arguments: Understanding the Strategic Nuclear Arms and Arms Control Debates*, ed. Lynn Eden and Steven Miller. Ithaca: Cornell University Press, 1989.

Goldberg, Alfred. "A Brief Survey of the Evolution of Ideas about Counterforce." Santa Monica: Rand Corporation, October 1967.

Goldstein, Judith. "The Impact of Ideas on Trade Policy: The Origins of U.S. Agricultural and Manufacturing Policies." *International Organization* 43, no. 1 (winter 1989): 31–71.

Goldstein, Judith and Robert Keohane, ed. *Ideas and Foreign Policy*. Ithaca: Cornell University Press, 1994.

Gray, Colin. "Nuclear Strategy: A Case for a Theory of Victory." *International Security* 1, no. 3 (summer 1979): 66–90.

———. "Targeting Problems for Central War." *Naval War College Review*, (January–February 1980): 3–21.

———. *The MX ICBM and National Security*. New York: Praeger Publishers, 1981.

———. "Warfighting for Deterrence." *Journal of Strategic Studies*, 7 (March 1984): 5–28

———. *Strategic Studies and Public Policy: The American Experience*. Lexington: University Press of Kentucky, 1982.

———. *War, Peace and Victory: Strategy and Statecraft for the Next Century*. New York: Simon and Schuster, 1990.

Gray, Colin, and Keith Payne. "Victory Is Possible." *Foreign Policy* 39 (summer 1980): 14–27.

Greenwood, Ted. *Making the MIRV: A Study in Defense Decision Making*. Cambridge, MA: Ballinger, 1975.

Gwertzman, Bernard. "Haig Cites a Standing NATO Plan Envisioning a Warning A-Blast." *The New York Times*, November 5, 1981, 1.

Haas, Peter M. "Do Regimes Matter? Epistemic Communities and Mediterranean Pollution Control." *International Organization* 43, no. 3 (summer 1989): 377–403.

Haley, P. Edward, and Jack Merritt, ed. *Nuclear Strategy, Arms Control and the Future*. Boulder: Westview, 1988.

Hall, John A., and G. John Ikenberry. *The State*. Minneapolis: University of Minnesota Press, 1989.

Halliday, Fred. "State and Society in International Relations." *Millennium: Journal of International Studies* 16, no. 2 (summer 1987): 215–29.

Halloran, Richard. "Weinberger Said to Offer Reagan Plan to Regain Atomic Superiority." *The New York Times*, August 14, 1981, 1.

———. "Haig Is Disputed by Weinberger on A-Blast Plan." *The New York Times*, November 6, 1981, 1.

———. "Pentagon Draws Up First Strategy for Fighting a Long Nuclear War." *The New York Times*, May 30, 1982, 1.

———. "Weinberger Denies US Plans for Protracted War." *The New York Times*, June 21, 1982, 1.

——. "50 Legislators Protest Extended A-War Policy." *The New York Times*, July 22, 1982, 6.

——. "Weinberger Angered by Reports on War Strategy." *The New York Times*, August 24, 1982, 3.

——. "U.S. Revises Its War Plan for a New Age." *The New York Times*, November 2, 1988, A7.

Halperin, Morton H. *Bureaucratic Politics and Foreign Policy*. Washington, DC: Brookings Institution, 1974.

——. *National Security Policy-Making: Analyses, Cases and Proposals*. Lexington, MA: D.C. Heath and Company, 1975.

Halperin, Morton and Arnold Kanter, ed. *Readings in American Foreign Policy: A Bureaucratic Perspective*. Boston: Little Brown and Company, 1973.

Hass, Richard. "The Role of Congress in American Security Policy," in *American Defense Policy*, 5th ed., ed. John Reichard and Steven Sturm. Baltimore: Johns Hopkins University Press, 1982.

Herken, Gregg. *Counsels of War*. New York: Alfred A. Knopf, 1985.

Holland, Lauren. "Explaining Weapons Procurement: Weaving Old Conceptual Threads into New Theory." Presented at the annual meeting of the American Political Science Association, September 3–6, 1987.

Holland, Lauren H., and Robert Hoover. *The MX Decision: A New Direction in U.S. Weapons Procurement Policy*. Boulder: Westview, 1985.

Howard, Michael. *War in European History*. Great Britain: Oxford University Press, 1976.

Huntington, Samuel. *The Common Defense: Strategic Programs in National Politics*. New York: Columbia University Press, 1961.

Ikenberry, G. John. "Conclusion: An Institutional Approach to American Foreign Policy." *International Organization* 42, no. 1 (winter 1988): 219–43.

——. *Reasons of State: Oil, Politics and the Capacities of American Government*. Ithaca: Cornell University Press, 1988.

Isaacs, John. "MX: Reagan's Pyrrhic Victory." *Bulletin of the Atomic Scientists* (June–July 1985): 46.

Jervis, Robert. *Perception and Misperception in International Politics*. Princeton: Princeton University Press, 1976.

——. "Security Regimes." *International Organization* 36, no. 2 (spring 1982): 90–120.

———. *The Illogic of American Nuclear Strategy.* Ithaca: Cornell University Press, 1984.

———. "Strategic Theory: What's New and What's True," in *The Logic of Nuclear Terror,* ed. Roman Kolkowicz. Boston: Allen and Unwin, 1987.

———. *The Meaning of the Nuclear Revolution.* Ithaca: Cornell University Press, 1989.

Joseph, Paul. "Making Threats: Minimal Deterrence, Extended Deterrence and Nuclear Warfighting." *Sociological Quarterly* 26, no. 3 (1985): 293–310.

Kaiser, Robert G. "Pentagon Official Retreats, Calls A-War Unwinnable." *Washington Post,* April 1, 1982, 1.

Kanter, Arnold. "Congress and the Defense Budget: 1960–1970." *American Political Science Review* 66, no. 1 (March 1972): 129–43.

Kaplan, Fred. "Going Native Without a Field Map: The Press Plunges into Limited Nuclear War." *Columbia Journalism Review* (January–February 1981): 23–29.

———. *The Wizards of Armageddon.* New York: Simon and Schuster, 1983.

Katzenstein, Peter J. *Between Power and Plenty: Foreign Economic Policies of Advanced Industrial States.* Madison: University of Wisconsin Press, 1978.

Keeny, Spurgeon and Wolfgang Panofsky. "From MAD to NUTS." *Foreign Affairs* 60, no. 2 (winter 1981–82): 287–304.

Keohane, Robert and Joseph Nye. *Power and Interdependence: World Politics in Transition.* Boston: Little Brown and Company, 1977.

Kissinger, Henry. *Nuclear Weapons and Foreign Policy.* New York: Harper and Row, 1957.

———. "NATO: The Next Thirty Years." *Survival* 21, no. 6 (November–December 1979): 264–68.

Kohn, Richard and Joseph P. Harahan., ed., "U.S. Strategic Air Power, 1948-1962: Excerpts from an interview with General Curtis E. Lemay, Leon W. Johnson, David A. Burchinal and Jack J. Catton." *International Security* 12, no. 4 (spring 1988): 78–95.

Kolodziej, Edward A. *The Uncommon Defense and Congress, 1945–1963.* Columbus: Ohio State University Press, 1966.

Korb, Lawrence. "National Security Organization and Process in the Carter Administration," in *Defense Policy and the Presidency,* ed. Sam C. Sarkesian. Boulder: Westview, 1979.

Krasner, Stephen. "Are Bureaucracies Important? (Or Allison in Wonderland)." *Foreign Policy* (summer 1972): 159–76.

——. "United States Commercial and Monetary Policy: Unraveling the Paradox of External Strength and Internal Weakness," in *Between Power and Plenty: Foreign Economic Policies of Advanced Industrial States*, ed. Peter J. Katzenstein. Madison: University of Wisconsin Press, 1978.

——. *Defending the National Interest*. Princeton: Princeton University Press, 1978.

——. "Approaches to the State: Alternative Conceptions and Historical Dynamics." *Comparative Politics* 12, no. 2 (January 1984): 223–46.

Kull, Stephen. *Minds at War: Nuclear Reality and the Inner Conflicts of Defense Policy Makers*. New York: Basic Books, 1988.

Lake, David. "The State and American Trade Strategy in the pre-Hegemonic Era." *International Organization* 42, no. 1 (winter 1988): 35–58.

Latham, Donald, and John J. Lane. "Management Issues: Planning, Acquisitions and Oversight," in *Managing Nuclear Operations*, ed. Ashton Carter, John Steinbruner, and Charles A. Zraket. Washington, DC: Brookings Institution Press, 1988.

Lawrence, Philip. "Strategy, the State and the Weberian Legacy." *Review of International Studies* 13, no. 4 (October, 1987): 295–310.

Lawrence, Philip. *Preparing for Armageddon: A Critique of Western Strategy*. New York: St. Martins Press, 1988.

Leavitt, Rob. "Freezing the Arms Race: The Genesis of a Mass Movement." Kennedy School of Government Case Program. Harvard University, 1983. Unpublished manuscript.

Leitenberg, Milton. "Presidential Directive (PD) 59: United States Nuclear Weapons Targeting Policy." *Journal of Peace Research* 18, no. 4 (1981): 309–17.

Levy, Jack S. "The Diversionary Theory of War: A Critique," in *Handbook of War Studies*, ed. Manus I. Midlarsky. London: Allen and Unwin, 1989.

Lewis, Kevin N. "Managing the Current Transition in Strategic Nuclear Affairs P-7096." Santa Monica: Rand Corporation, March 1985.

Lindsay, James. *Congress and Nuclear Weapons*. Baltimore: Johns Hopkins University Press, 1991.

Luttwak, Edward A. *The Grand Strategy of the Soviet Union*. New York: St. Martin's Press, 1983.

McCrea, Frances B. and Gerald E. Markle. *Minutes to Midnight: Nuclear Weapons Protests in America*. Newbury Park, CA: Sage Publications, 1989.

Mackenzie, Donald A. _Inventing Accuracy: A Historical Sociology of Nuclear Missile Guidance_. Cambridge: MIT Press,1990.

Mandelbaum, Michael. _The Fate of Nations: The Search for National Security in the Nineteenth and Twentieth Centuries_. New York: Cambridge University Press, 1988.

Mariska, Mark D. "The Single Integrated Operational Plan." _Military Review_ (March 1972): 32–39.

Melanson, Richard. _Reconstituting Consensus: Foreign Policy Since the Vietnam War_. New York: St. Martin's Press, 1991.

Meyer, David. _A Winter of Discontent: The Nuclear Freeze and American Politics_. New York: Praeger Publishers, 1990.

———. "Protest Cycles and Political Process: American Peace Movements in the Nuclear Age." _Political Research Quarterly_ 46, no. 3 (September 1993): 451–80.

Nacht, Michael. _The Age of Vulnerability: Threats to the Nuclear Stalemate_. Washington, DC: Brookings Institution, 1985.

Nettl, J. P. "The State as a Conceptual Variable." _World Politics_ 20, no. 4 (July 1968): 559–92.

Nitze, Paul. "Atoms, Strategy and Foreign Policy." _Foreign Affairs_ 34, no. 2 (January 1956): 187–98.

Nolan, Janne. _Guardians of the Arsenal: The Politics of Nuclear Strategy_. New York: Basic Books, 1989.

Nordlinger, Eric. _On the Autonomy of the Democratic State_. Cambridge: Harvard University Press, 1981.

Nye, Joseph S., Jr. and Sean M. Lynn-Jones. "International Security Studies: A Report of a Conference on the State of the Field." _International Security_ 12, no. 4 (spring 1988): 5–27.

O'Malley, Jerome F. "JSTPS: The Link Between Strategy and Execution." _Air University Review_ 27, no. 4 (May–June 1977): 38–48

Paarlberg, Ron. "Forgetting About the Unthinkable." _Foreign Policy_ 10 (1973): 132–46.

Payne, Christopher. "Disarming Congress." _Bulletin of the Atomic Scientists_ (June/July 1985): 6

Pincus, Walter C. "Thinking the Unthinkable: Studying New Approaches to a Nuclear War." _Washington Post_, February 11, 1979, A21.

Pincus, Walter, and George C. Wilson. "Nuclear Warning Shot Plan Disputed." *Washington Post*, November 6, 1981.

Pines, Burton. "Rethinking the Unthinkable: Carter Revises the New Game Plan for Fighting a Nuclear War." *Time*, August 25, 1980, 30.

Platt, Alan. *The U.S. Senate and Strategic Arms Policy: 1969–1974.* Boulder: Westview, 1978.

Posen, Barry. *The Sources of Military Doctrine.* Ithaca: Cornell University Press, 1984.

Rhodes, Edward. *Power and MADness.* New York: Columbia University Press, 1989.

——. "Hawks, Doves, Owls and Loons: Extended Deterrence without Flexible Response." *Millenium: The Journal of International Studies* 19, no. 1 (1990): 37–57.

Richelson, Jeffrey. "PD-59, NSDD-13, and the Reagan Strategic Modernization Program." *Journal of Strategic Studies* 6, no. 2 (June 1983): 125–46.

Rosenau, James. "Toward Single Country Theories of Foreign Policy," in *New Directions in the Study of Foreign Policy*, ed., Charles Hermann, Charles Kegley, and James Rosenau. Boston: Allen and Unwin, 1987.

Rosenberg, David Alan. "A Smoking Radiating Ruin at the End of Two Hours: Documents on American Plans for Nuclear War with the Soviet Union." *International Security* 6, no. 3 (winter 81–82): 3–38.

Rosenberg, David Alan. "The Origins of Overkill: Nuclear Weapons and American Strategy, 1945–1960," *International Security* 7, no. 4 (spring 1983): 3–69.

——. "Reality and Responsibility: Power and Process in the Making of United States Nuclear Strategy, 1945–1968," *Journal of Strategic Studies* 9, no. 3 (March 1986): 35–51.

——. "U.S. Nuclear Strategy: Theory vs. Practice." *Bulletin of the Atomic Scientists* (March 1987): 20–26.

Rourke, Francis E. *Bureaucracy and Foreign Policy.* Baltimore: Johns Hopkins University Press, 1972.

Russett, Bruce. "International Interactions and Processes: The Internal vs. the External Debate Revisited," in *Political Science: The State of the Discipline*, ed. Ada W. Finifter. Washington, DC: American Political Science Association, 1983.

———. "The Democratic Governance of Nuclear Weapons." Draft, January 1, 1987 (unpublished manuscript.)

Russett, Bruce. *Controlling the Sword: The Democratic Governance of National Security.* Cambridge: Harvard University Press, 1990.

Sagan, Scott D. "SIOP-62: The Nuclear War Plan Briefing to President Kennedy." *International Security* 12, no. 1 (summer 1987): 22–51.

———. *Moving Targets: Nuclear Strategy and National Security.* Princeton: Princeton University Press, 1989.

Sapolsky, Harvey. *The Polaris System Development: Bureaucratic and Programmatic Success in Government.* Cambridge: Harvard University Press, 1972.

Schattsneider, E. E. *The Semi-Sovereign People.* New York: Holt, Rinehart and Winston, 1960.

Schelling, Thomas. *Arms and Influence.* New Haven: Yale University Press, 1966.

Skocpol, Theda. "Bringing the State Back In: Strategies of Analysis in Current Research," in *Bringing the State Back In,* ed. Peter Evans, Dietrich Rueschmayer and Theda Skocpol. New York: Columbia University Press, 1985.

Skowronek, Stephen. "National Railroad Regulation and the Problem of State Building: Interests and Institutions in Late Nineteenth-Century America." *Politics and Society* 10, no. 3 (1981): 225–50.

"Slocombe Clarifies PD 59 Policy: Industrial Targets Still Important." *Defense Week,* November 17, 1980, 10.

Sloss, Leon, and Marc Dean Millot. "U.S. Nuclear Strategy in Evolution." *Strategic Review* 12, no. 1 (winter 1984): 19–28.

Smith, R. Jeffrey. "U.S. Trims List of Targets in Soviet Union," *Washington Post,* July 21, 1991, 1.

———. "U.S. Urged to Cut 50% of A-Arms," *Washington Post,* Jaunary 6, 1992, 1.

Snyder, Glenn. *Deterrence and Defense: Toward a Theory of National Security.* Princeton: Princeton University Press, 1961.

Solo, Pam. *From Protest to Policy: Beyond the Freeze to Common Security.* Cambridge, MA: Ballinger, 1988.

Spinardi, Graham. "Why the U.S. Went for Hard Target Counterforce in Trident II (And Why It Didn't Get There Sooner.") *International Security* 15, no. 2 (fall 1990): 147–90.

Stein, Arthur. "Strategy as Politics, Politics as Strategy: Domestic Debates, Statecraft and Star Wars," in *The Logic of Nuclear Deterrence,* ed. Roman Kolkowicz. Winchester, MA: Allen and Unwin, 1987.

Stengle, Richard. "Freezing Nukes, Banning Bottles." *Time*, November 15, 1982, 35.

Stockton, Paul N. "The New Game on the Hill: The Politics of Arms Control and Strategic Force Modernization." *International Security* 16, no. 2 (fall 1991): 146–70.

"Strategic Study Endorses SSBNs," *Navy News and Undersea Technology*, January 13, 1993, 3.

Tarbell, Gregory. "Congress, Counterforce and the Genesis of the MX." Master's thesis, Brown University, June 1983.

Terriff, Terry Richard. "The Innovation of U.S. Strategic Policy in the Nixon Administration, 1969–1974. Ph.D. dissertation, the Department of War Studies, Kings College, University of London, September 1991.

Toth, Robert. "U.S. Shifts Nuclear Response Strategy: New Formula Designed to Eliminate Soviet Leadership Early in Conflict," *Los Angeles Times*, July 23, 1989, 16.

———. "U.S. Scratches Nuclear Targets in Soviet Bloc," *Los Angeles Times*, April 19, 1991, 1.

"Trident I.5?" *Bulletin of the Atomic Scientists* (July–August 1990): 48.

Tucker, Robert. *The Nuclear Debate: Deterrence and the Lapse of Faith.* New York: H. M. Holmes and Meier, 1985.

Van Evera, Stephen. "The Cult of the Offensive and the Origins of the First World War." *International Security* 9, no. 1 (summer 1984): 58–107.

Wagstaff, Peter C. "An Analysis of the Cities-Avoidance Theory." *Stanford Journal of International Studies* 7, no. 1 (1987): 162–72.

Walker, Richard Lee. *Strategic Target Planning: Bridging the Gap Between Theory and Practice.* National Security Affairs Monograph Series. Washington, D.C.: National Defense University, 1983.

Waller, Douglas. *Congress and the Nuclear Freeze: An Inside Look at the Politics of a Mass Movement.* Amherst: University of Massachusetts Press, 1987.

Wallop, Malcolm. "Opportunities and Imperatives of Ballistic Missile Defense." *Strategic Review* 7, no. 4 (fall 1979): 3–21.

"Weinberger Drops Disputed Words in Revision of '82 Arm's Proposal," *The New York Times*, March 18, 1983, A30.

Welch, David A. "The Organizational Process and Bureaucratic Process Paradigms: Retrospect and Prospect." *International Security* 17, no. 2 (fall 1992): 112–146.

Wells, Samuel, Jr. "The Origins of Massive Retaliation." *Political Science Quarterly* 96, no. 1 (summer 1981): 31–52.

Whiteside, Thomas. "Annals of the Cold War: The Yellow-Rain Complex-I." *The New Yorker*, February 11, 1991.

Williamson, Samuel, R., and Steven L. Rearden. *The Origins of U.S. Nuclear Strategy, 1945–1953*. New York: St. Martins Press, 1993.

Wilson, George C. "Defense Orders New Study on Limited Nuclear War." *Washington Post*, November 11, 1978, 10.

——. "Weinberger Lobbies Editors on War Policy." *Washington Post*, August 25, 1982, 9.

Wirls, Daniel. *Buildup: The Politics of Defense in the Reagan Era*. Ithaca: Cornell University Press, 1992.

Witt, Joel S. "American SLBMs: Counterforce Options and Strategic Implications." *Survival*, 24 (July–August, 1982): 163–74.

Wood, David. "Pentagon Tames Rhetoric to Offer a Softer Image." *Los Angeles Times*, March 20, 1983, 1.

Government Documents

Brown, Harold. *Department of Defense Annual Report—Fiscal Year 1979*. February 2, 1978.

——. *Department of Defense Annual Report—Fiscal Year 1980*. January 25, 1979.

——. *Department of Defense Annual Report—Fiscal Year 1981*. January 29, 1980.

——. *Department of Defense Annual Report—Fiscal Year 1982*. January 19, 1981.

Bundy, McGeorge. "Memorandum for the President," June 1, 1962, Freedom of Information Act, Office of the Secretary of Defense, National Security Archives.

Collins, John M. "Counterforce and Countervalue Options Compared: A Military Analysis Related to Nuclear Deterrence." Congressional Research Service, Library of Congress. Washington, DC, December 7, 1972.

Draft Memorandum for the President, Recommended Long Range Nuclear Delivery Vehicles, 1963–1967—Appendix 1. September 23, 1961, Office of the Secretary of Defense, Freedom of Information Act.

Draft Memorandum for the President, Recommended FY 1964–FY 1968 Strategic Retaliatory Forces. November 21, 1962, Office of the Secretary of Defense, Freedom of Information Act.

Draft Memorandum for the President, Recommended FY 1965–FY 1969 Strategic Retaliatory Forces. December 6, 1963, Office of the Secretary of Defense, Freedom of Information Act.

Draft Memorandum for the President, Recommended FY 1966–1970 Programs for Strategic Offensive Forces, Continental Air and Missile Defense Forces, and Civil Defense. December 3, 1964, Office of the Secretary of Defense, Freedom of Information Act.

Draft Memorandum for the President, Recommended FY 1967–1971 Strategic Offensive and Defensive Forces. November 1, 1965, Office of the Secretary of Defense, Freedom of Information Act.

Draft Memorandum for the President, Recommended FY68–72, Strategic Offensive and Defensive Forces. November 9, 1966, Office of the Secretary of Defense, Freedom of Information Act.

Draft Memorandum for the President, Strategic Offensive and Defensive Forces. January 15, 1968, Office of the Secretary of Defense, Freedom of Information Act.

Draft Presidential Memorandum on Strategic Offensive and Defensive Forces. January 9, 1969, Office of the Secretary of Defense, Freedom of Information Act.

History and Research Division, Strategic Air Command. *History of the Joint Strategic Target Planning Staff: Background and Programs of SIOP-62.* Sanitized copy declassified by the Office of the Joint Chiefs of Staff, April 21, 1980.

Hopkins, Charles. "Unclassified History of the Joint Strategic Target Planning Staff," prepared by JSTPS, March 15, 1989.

Laird, Melvin. *Annual Defense Department Report—Fiscal Year 1973—National Security Strategy of Realistic Deterrence.* February 15, 1972.

——. *Department of Defense Annual Report—Fiscal Year 1968.* February 14, 1967.

McNamara, Robert. Speech before the Fellows of the American Bar Foundation Dinner, Edgewater Beach Hotel, Chicago, Illinois, Saturday, February 17, 1962. News Release, Department of Defense, Office of Public Affairs, No. 239-62, National Security Archives.

——. *Remarks by Secretary McNamara, NATO Ministerial Meeting.* Ministerial Meeting, May 5, 1962. Office of the Secretary of Defense, Freedom of Information Act, National Security Archives.

——. *Remarks of Secretary of Defense Robert S. McNamara at the Commencement Exercises, University of Michigan, Ann Arbor, Michigan.* Department of Defense, Office of Public Affairs, June 16, 1962.

——. *Defense Department Annual Report for Fiscal Year 1967*, including reports of the Secretary of Defense, Secretary of the Army, Navy and Air Force. January 26, 1966.

Memorandum of Conference with the President, August 11, 1960, prepared August 12, 1960. Office of the Secretary of Defense, Freedom of Information Act, National Security Archives.

Nixon, Richard. *A Report to Congress: U.S. Foreign Policy for the 1970s: A New Strategy for Peace*. February 18, 1970.

——. *A Report to Congress*. February 25, 1971.

"Nuclear Weapons Employment Policy." NSDD 12, NSC F 83-1129, Freedom of Information Act.

Reed, Thomas C. and Michael O. Wheeler. "The Role of Nuclear Weapons in the New World Order," statement presented to the Committee on Armed Services, U.S. Senate, Janaury 23, 1992.

Rowen, Henry S. *Formulating Strategic Doctrine*, from the Commission on the Organization of the Government for the Conduct of Foreign Policy (The Murphy Commission), Part III, Vol. 4, Appendix K. Washington, DC: U.S. GPO, 1975.

Rumsfeld, Donald H. *Annual Defense Department Report—Fiscal Year 1977*. January 27, 1976.

——. *Annual Defense Department Report—Fiscal Year 1978*. January 17, 1977.

Schlesinger, James. *Planning, Programming, Budgeting*. Inquiry of the Subcommittee on National Security and International Operations. U.S. Congress. Senate. Committee on Government Operations. 1970.

——. *Annual Defense Department Report—Fiscal Year 1976*. February 5, 1975.

——. *Annual Department of Defense Report—Fiscal Year 1975*. March 4, 1974.

——. *Annual Department of Defense Report—Fiscal Year 1976*. February 5, 1975.

U.S. Congress. House. Armed Services Committee. *Defense Report: On President Nixon's Strategy for Peace: Toward a National Security Strategy of Realistic Deterrence*. Statement of Secretary of Defense Melvin R. Laird on the FY72–76 Defense Program and 1972 Defense Budget. 92nd Cong, 2nd sess., March 9, 1971.

——. *Hearings on Military Posture and H.R. 6722*. 93rd Cong., 1st sess., 1973.

——. *Hearings on Military Posture and H.R. 1872 and H.R. 2575*. 96th Cong., 1st sess, February 14–April 2, 1979.

——. *Hearings on Military Posture.* 96th Cong., 1st sess., 1979.

——. *Hearings on Military Posture and H.R. 6495.* 96th Cong., 2nd sess., part 4, February 7, 12, 18, 19, 20, 21, 26, and 27 and March 3, 4, 5, 6, and 11, 1980.

U.S. Congress. Senate. Committee on Armed Services. *Military Procurement Authorization for Fiscal Year 1964.* Senate. Committee on Foreign Relations. 88th Cong., 1st sess, 1963.

——. *Military Procurement Authorization for Fiscal Year 1964.* 88th Cong., 1st sess., March 1, 4, 5, 6, 7, and 8, 1963.

——. *Statement of Secretary of Defense Robert McNamara before the Senate Armed Services Committee on the FY 1969–1973 Defense Program and 1969 Defense Budget.* January 22, 1968.

——. Preparedness Investigating Committee. *Status of U.S. Strategic Power.* 90th Cong., 2nd sess., parts I and II, April 23, 24, 26, 1968, and part II, April 30, May 1, 8, 10, 1968.

——. *Nomination of James R. Schlesinger to be Secretary of Defense.* 93rd Cong, 1st sess., June 18, 1973.

——. *Fiscal Year 1975 Authorization for Military Procurement, Research and Development, and Active Duty, Selected Reserve and Civilian Personnel Strengths.* 93rd Cong., 2nd sess., part 1, February 4, 1974.

——. *Research and Development.* 94th Cong., 1st sess., part 4, February 25, 27, March 4 and 5, 1975, and part 6, March 11, 17, 19, 21 and 25, 1975.

——. *Fiscal Year 1977 Authorization for Military Procurement, Research and Development, and Active Duty, Selected Reserve and Civilian Personnel Strengths.* 94th Cong., 2nd sess., part 2, March 9, 11, 15, 17, 19, 1976.

——. *Fiscal Year 1978 Authorization for Military Procurement, and Active Duty, Selected Reserve and Civilian Personnel Strengths.* 95th Cong., 1st sess., January 25, February 24, 1977.

——. *Consideration of Mr. Paul C. Warnke to be Director of the U.S. Arms Control and Disarmament Agency and Ambassador.* 95th Cong, 1st sess., February 22, 23, 28, 1977.

——. *Department of Defense Authorization for Appropriations for Fiscal Year 1980.* 96th Cong., 1st sess., January 25, 30, February 1, 1979.

——. *Department of Defense Authorization for Appropriations for Fiscal Year 1980.* 96th Cong, 1st sess., part 3, March 7, 8, 20 and 28; April 2, 5, May 10, 15, 1979.

——. *Department of Defense Authorization for Appropriations for Fiscal Year 1981.* 96th Cong., 2nd sess., Part 5, March 1980.

——. *Department of Defense Authorization for Appropriations for FY 1981.* 96th Cong., 2nd sess., March 11, 12, 13, 14, 25, 1980.

——. Subcommittee on Strategic and Theater Nuclear Forces. *Strategic Force Modernization Programs.* 97th Cong., 1st sess., October 26–29, 30 and November 3, 4, 10, 12, 13, 1981.

——. Committee on Foreign Relations. *Nuclear War Strategy.* 96th Cong., 2nd sess., September 16, 1980.

——. *U.S. Strategic Doctrine.* 97th Cong., 2nd sess., December 14, 1982.

——. *The SALT II Treaty.* 96th Cong., 1st sess., part 4, pp. 61–63, 1983.

——. Subcommittee on Arms Control, International Law and Organization. *ABM, MIRV, SALT, and the the Nuclear Arms Race.* 91st Cong., 2nd sess., March 16, April 8, 9, 13 and 14, May 13 and 28, June 4 and 29, 1970.

——. Subcommittee on Arms Control, International Law and Organization. *U.S.-U.S.S.R. Strategic Policies.* 93rd Cong., 2nd sess., March 4, 1974, sanitized and made public April 4, 1974.

Weinberger, Caspar. *Department of Defense Annual Report to Congress—Fiscal Year 1983.* January 31, 1982.

Index

Aaron, David, 89

ABMs. *See* Anti-ballistic missiles

Accuracy: of ballistic missiles, 24, 74, 76, 77, 134–35, 152–53, 156; enhancements to, 106–7; and flexibility, 100, 102; of *Minutemen* ICBMs, 73, 104; of MIRVs, 74, 80; in PD-18, 116; of *Poseidon* missile systems, 73, 104; role in counterforce, 76, 101; of SLBMs, 106, 140

Action policy, 49; definition of, 2; disjunction with declaratory policy, 4, 27–29, 51, 55, 58, 82; and force development policy, 118; in Kennedy administration, 152; NUTs in, 27

Advanced Ballistic Re-Entry System (ABRES), 103–4, 134

Air Force, 89; and creation of JSTPS, 60, 61; ICBM force of, 76–77; nuclear weapons policy of, 23, 61; requests for MX missiles, 135

Air-launched cruise missiles (ALCMs), 139

Allison, Graham, 9, 20, 21–22, 24–29, 160, 161

Almond, Gabriel, 162

Anti-ballistic missiles (ABMs), 23–24, 82; Congressional debate on, 46, 74, 155, 156; role in damage limitation, 69; of Soviet Union, 78–79. *See also* Ballistic missiles

Anti-Ballistic Missile Treaty, 107, 140

Appropriations Committees (U. S. Congress), 33. *See also* Congress, U.S.

Arkin, William, 27

Armacost, Michael H., 22

Armed forces: conscription into, 170; coordination of policy among, 59–60; effect of nuclear war on, 36; nuclear weapons policy of, 22–23, 27; position on MAD, 12; reaction to NUWEP-1, 90–91; role in decision-making, 160; role in targeting, 31

Armed Services Committee (House), 33; and MAD policies, 120–21; and *Trident* submarine, 107; weapons procurement debate in, 104, 106

Armed Services Committee (Senate), 33; in MX missile debate, 108, 137; nuclear policy hearings of, 72–75, 122; Research and Development Subcommittee of, 107–8; and *Trident II* missile, 140, 142

Arms Control and Disarmament Agency (ACDA), 88, 119

Arms Control Association, 45

Arms Control Subcommittee (Senate), 105–6, 107–9

Art, Robert, 25

Assured destruction. *See* Mutual Assured Destruction (MAD)

Autonomy: and balance of power, 51; effect of state capacity on, 41; in foreign policy, 4–5, 52, 166; realist paradigm of, 38; role in national security, 37–38, 168. *See also* State autonomy

Balance of power, 40, 50, 114, 166; during Nixon administration, 86–87, 95, 112; in post-Cold War era, 168; role of state autonomy in, 51

Ball, Desmond, 26, 27, 28; on MAD, 120; on Nixon administration, 95; and revisions to SIOP, 145; on SLBM system, 106; on weapons procurement, 153

Ball, George, 131

Ballistic missiles, 79; accuracy of, 24, 76, 77, 134–35; intermediate-range, 22; MIRVing of, 87. *See also* Antiballistic missiles; Intercontinental ballistic missiles; Submarine-launched ballistic missiles

B-1 bomber, 133

B-2 bomber, 107, 144, 145

Beard, Edmund, 22–23

Benjamin, Roger, 39

Bingham, Jonathan, 132

Bomb shelters, 68

Boyer, Paul, 67

Bravo targets, 57

Breem, John, 106

Broiler (Joint Outline Emergency War Plan), 56

Brooke, Edward, 96, 102–3, 111

Brown, Harold, 149; address to Naval War College, 123, 124–25, 166; as Air Force secretary, 74–75; countervailing strategy of, 114, 166; on declaratory policy, 4; and MAD, 119–22; and MX missile controversy, 135; and PD-59, 14–15, 116–17, 121, 129; and Senate Foreign Relations Committee, 124–25; and *Trident II*, 140

Brzezinski, Zbigniew, 114, 115, 116

Buckley, James, 104

Builder, Carl, 10

Bundy, McGeorge, 66–67

Bureaucracies: influence of, 25; relationships among, 160–61

Bureaucratic politics: approach to international relations, 48; competition in, 160, 163; critiques of, 24–29; and Executive Branch of government, 25, 26, 159–60; role in

decision-making, 24, 160–61; role in nuclear weapons policy, 1, 21–29, 50, 53, 112; role in targeting, 29–30; role in weapons procurement, 22–24; role of domestic politics in, 162–63; and role of state, 39, 43; and society, 34; and statist paradigm, 48–49, 158–65

Burke, Arleigh, 60

Bush, George: in MX missile debate, 137; strategic defense cuts by, 143

Bush administration: SDI in, 168; strategic budget cuts by, 143–45; study of nuclear weapons policy, 145–46

Byrd, Robert, 106

Caldicott, Helen, 131

Caldwell, Dan, 25

Carter, Jimmy, 14–15, 113–14; approval of MX missile, 136; involvement in SIOP, 160; signing of PD-59, 123

Carter administration, 13, 113–14; command and control structure in, 115, 116, 118, 133, 148; counterforce policies of, 14–15, 115, 119–25, 133; declaratory policy of, 116, 118–25, 148; differences of opinion within, 159; force development in, 133; MX missile during, 107, 136; NUTs during, 119; SIOP during, 115–18; targeting policies of, 30, 31, 122, 128; and *Trident* missile, 140

Case studies, methodology of, 15–16

Center for Defense Information, 45

Central Intelligence Agency (CIA), 88

China: nuclear policy towards, 62, 63, 64; nuclear threat from, 24; targeting of, 89, 147

CINCSAC. *See* Commander in chief of Strategic Air Command

Circular error probable (CEP), 134, 138, 152–53; improvement of, 74, 75, 77; of *Minuteman III*, 104

Cities: avoidance of, 13, 14, 47, 55, 65–66, 81, 96; as "bad" targets, 99; destruction of, 11; targeting of, 56, 121, 122. *See also* McNamara, Robert

Civil defense, 68, 69, 155; during Johnson administration, 71; role in weapons procurement strategy, 80–81

Civilian control of nuclear policy, 27, 28, 30, 31, 51, 61, 153–54, 163, 173; in Carter administration, 117–18; in Kennedy administration, 64, 76, 82, 83; McNamara's role in, 55–56; in Nixon administration, 89; in 1950s, 57

Clifford, Clark, 98

Clinton administration, 147–48

Cold War. *See* Post-Cold War era

Collateral damage. *See* Populations

Command and control structure: in Carter administration, 115, 116, 118, 133, 148; in Reagan administration, 127, 138–39, 148; role in force development, 109–10, 116; role of flexibility in, 101

Command Data Buffer System, 105

Commander in chief of Strategic Air Command (CINCSAC), 31; and coordination of nuclear policy, 59

Committee on the Present Danger, 114, 119

Congress, U. S.: ABM debates of, 46, 74, 155, 156; conflict with Executive Branch, 49, 155–56; and declaratory policies, 12; effect of bureaucratic politics on, 34; funding of weapons procurement, 102–10, 136–38; as gatekeeper to state, 44, 48, 155–56, 161; and limited nuclear policy, 96, 97–98, 112, 149; MIRV debate in, 78–79, 102–3; nuclear freeze proponents in, 132; role in counterforce policies, 33, 156; role in defense policy, 33, 44–47, 154; role in nuclear

weapons policy, 67–68, 72–75, 102–10, 142, 156, 161–62, 166; and SLBM policy, 22; societal input to, 49; and the state, 43–44; and *Trident II* missile, 140–42

Congressional Budget and Impoundment Act (1974), 44–45

Congressional Budget Office (CBO), 45

Congressional Research Service (CRS), 45

Conte, Silvio, 132

Coordinated Reconnaissance Plan (CRP), 32

Council for a Livable World, 45

Counterforce policies: of Carter Administration, 14–15, 115, 119–25, 133; of Kennedy-Johnson administrations, 11–12, 53, 63, 75–76, 82, 83, 152; in 1940s, 56–57; in 1950s, 57, 59; of Nixon administration, 89–99; in post-Cold War era, 145, 149; public opinion on, 17; of Rand Corporation, 163; of Reagan administration, 9, 114, 126, 148; of Robert McNamara, 11–12, 63, 66–67, 74; role of accuracy in, 76; role of Congress in, 33, 156; role of MIRV in, 102; in SIOP, 62, 81, 93, 112; weapons procurement in, 70, 102–10. *See also* Nuclear Utilization theory (NUTs)

Countervalue policies, 7, 8; in declaratory policy, 14, 15; flexibility in, 100; in Kennedy administration, 63; in Nixon administration, 99; in SIOP, 14. *See also* Populations, targeting of

Crowe, William T., 146

Cruise missile, 133, 135

C-3 systems. *See* Command and control structure

Cuban missile crisis, 21, 68; role of domestic politics in, 25

Dahl, Robert, 17, 40
Damage-limitation strategies
(Kennedy-Johnson administrations), 69–75, 77, 81, 85; abandonment of, 97
Davis, Bernard, 113, 126–27
Davis, Lynn, 115
Decision-making, 160–61; for ballistic
missiles, 27; by Defense Department, 62; investigation of, 16;
models of, 21–22, 24, 25, 26; role of
bureaucratic politics in, 160–61; role
of secretaries of defense in, 160;
unintended consequences of, 29
Declaratory policies, 49, 166; of Carter
administration, 118–25; countervalue targeting in, 14, 15; definition
of, 2; disjunction with action policy,
4, 8, 27–29, 51, 55, 58, 82; effect on
weapons procurement, 27, 31, 148;
history of, 94; of Kennedy administration, 65–67; massive retaliation
in, 57–59; during post-Cold War era,
147; of Reagan administration,
125–30; role of Congress in, 12, 33;
role of MAD in, 3–4, 8, 51; and SIOP,
17; strategic aspects of, 46
DeConcini, Dennis, 113
Defense Guidance statement, 31,
128–30, 154
Defense Posture Statements
(Department of Defense), 2
Defense Reorganization Act (1958), 60
DeGaulle, Charles, 67
Dellums, Ron, 12, 120; and *Trident II*
development, 139–40
Department of Defense (DoD), 44;
cancellation of stellar inertial
guidance systems, 103; civilian
control over, 61, 154; decision-
making process of, 62; Defense
Posture Statements of, 2; and MX
missile, 108, 110; in Nixon administration, 101; revisions to SIOP, 88;
role in targeting, 30

D-5 missile. *See Trident II* missile
"Doctrine of Sufficiency" (Nixon
administration), 93
Domestic politics: role in bureaucratic
politics, 162; role in nuclear
weapons policy, 4–5, 19–20, 23,
47–48, 51, 83, 153–54, 157; statist
perspective of, 83, 163
Downey, Tom, 142
Draft Presidential Memorandums
(DPMs), 83, 154; origin of, 61–62; of
Robert McNamara, 63–64, 65, 69–70,
77–78
Dropshot war plan, 56–57
Dulles, John Foster: massive retalia-
tion policy of, 4, 13, 57–59, 67
Duvall, Raymond, 39

E-48 airborne command posts, 139
Eastern Europe: nuclear policy
towards, 62, 63, 64; targeting of, 32,
89, 146
Eisenhower, Dwight: New Look
policy of, 67, 171; on nuclear
coordination, 60
Eisenhower administration: civil
defense during, 80; coordination of
policy during, 59–60; massive
retaliation policy of, 4, 13, 57–59, 67
Ellsberg, Daniel, 64
Enthoven, Alain, 61–62, 64, 73–74
Escalation control: role of flexibility in,
101; in SIOP-5, 92
Essence of Decision (Allison), 21–22
Europe, nuclear deterrence for, 97, 112,
127–28, 158, 171
Evangelista, Matthew, 38
Executive Branch of government:
bureaucratic perspective of, 159–60;
counterforce concerns of, 109;
nuclear objectives of, 23, 27–28;
relationship with bureaucracy, 25,
26; relations with Congress, 49,
155–56; role in policy disjunctions,

51; role in targeting, 30–31; role in the state, 43; and shaping of public opinion, 156–57; statist perspective of, 159–60

First-strike capabilities, 104; in Kennedy administration, 62, 63, 67, 70; of Soviet Union, 116, 124
Fleet Ballistic Missile (FBM) program, 79
Flexibility: and accuracy, 100, 102; in nuclear weapons policy, 92, 95, 118, 119–20, 148; role in command and control structure, 101; role in countervalue policies, 100, 111; in SIOP, 116; in targeting policies, 112
Force development policy, 49, 166; and action policy, 118; in Carter administration, 133; command and control structure in, 109–10, 116; definition of, 2; disjunctions with declaratory policy, 8; effect of NSDM-242 on, 91, 152; evolution of, 152–53; of Kennedy-Johnson administration, 75–81; in limited options policy, 101; of Nixon administration, 99–110; of Reagan administration, 125–26, 133–35; role of damage limitation in, 73–74; structural aspects of, 46. *See also* Weapons procurement
Ford administration, weapons targeting during, 30
Foreign policy: autonomy in, 166; decision-making process in, 21, 161–62; and democratic process, 17, 173; effect of domestic policy on, 44; role of public interest groups in, 45, 165; secret, 169; and state autonomy, 4–5, 52
Foreign Relations Committee (Senate), 33, 127; and MAD policies, 124–25; in MIRV debate, 102

Foster, John, 88–89, 100; on damage limitation, 72–73; on MIRVs, 78, 79
Foster, Richard, 10
Foster Panel, 88–89; on force development, 100
Freedom of Information Act (FOIA), 16
Freeze movement, 130–33, 138, 151
Friedberg, Aaron, 3
Frolic war plan, 56

Gaither Committee Report, 80
Gates, Robert, 31
Gates, Thomas, 60–61
General Accounting Office (GAO), 45
George, Alexander, 16
Getler, Michael, 123
Global Protection Against Limited Strikes (GPALS), 144
Goodpaster, Andrew, 60
Gorbachev, Mikhail, 143
Gore, Al, 132
Gray, Colin, 138
Greenwood, Ted, 23
Griffith, Charles H., 141
Ground zeros, 62; in SIOP, 32

Haig, Alexander, 127–28
Half-Moon war plan, 56
Hall, John A., 20
Halperin, Morton, 20, 21–22, 23, 25, 159; on bureaucratic politics, 160, 161, 163; on international affairs, 162
Halsted, Thomas, 46
Hard-target capability, 102, 133; "good" targets in, 99; of ICBMs, 107; kill capacity of, 103, 111, 135, 136, 138, 140, 141, 142; of SLBMs, 80, 81, 106; of SS-18, 114
Hart, Gary, 119, 132
Hatfield, Mark, 132
Helms, Jesse, 119
Holland, Lauren, 24

Holloway, Bruce, 60
Humphrey, Hubert H., 103, 111
Huntington, Samuel, 45, 115

Ikenberry, G. John, 20, 40, 42, 164
Ikle, Fred, 118, 134, 139
Improved Accuracy Program
  (SLBMs), 106
Industrial targets, 8, 62, 121; during
  Carter administration, 122, 124;
  during Kennedy administration, 63,
  73; of SIOP-5, 91, 92
Intercontinental ballistic missiles
  (ICBMs): accuracy of, 74, 152, 156;
  Air Force use of, 11; decision-
  making process for, 22–23; hard-
  target capabilities of, 107; during
  1960s, 66, 76, 82; Soviet build-up of,
  96; targeting of, 102; vulnerability
  of, 114–15, 121, 134, 168
Intermediate-range ballistic missiles
  (IRBMs), 22, 102. *See also* Ballistic
  missiles
International relations: bureaucratic
  approach to, 48; effect of domestic
  politics on, 20, 162; statist approach
  to, 49
International system: role of state in,
  47–48, 52, 173; role of United States
  in, 169
Iran, 92

Jackson, Henry, 119
Jervis, Robert, 3, 6
Johnson, Lyndon, 23, 170
Johnson administration: damage
  limitation during, 70–71, 77;
  weapons targeting during, 30. *See
  also* McNamara, Robert
Joint Chiefs of Staff (JCS), 44; and
  limited nuclear options, 88; and
  MAD policies, 70, 72; in 1950s, 57;
  and NUWEP-1, 90–91; role in
  targeting, 32

Joint Coordination Centers, formation
  of, 59
Joint Strategic Capabilities Plan
  (JSCP): Annex C of, 31, 32–33; and
  PD-59, 127
Joint Strategic Target Planning Staff
  (JSTPS), 2; civilian understanding
  of, 33; creation of, 31, 60–61, 154;
  execution of policy by, 91; growth
  of, 32; and NUWEP-1, 90–91; and
  PD-59, 127; in post-Cold War era,
  146; role in targeting, 20, 154
Jones, T. K., 129
Jordan crisis (1970), 88

Kanter, Arnold, 159, 162, 163
Kaplan, Fred, 62–63, 80
Kauffman, William, 97
Kendall, James T., 72–75
Kennan, George, 131
Kennedy, Edward, 132
Kennedy, John F.: campaign issues of,
  61; on cities-avoidance doctrine,
  66–67; on civil defense, 80–81; in
  Cuban missile crisis, 25; and SIOP,
  63, 160
Kennedy, Robert, 80
Kennedy administration: civil defense
  in 80-81, 155, 156; damage-
  limitation policies of, 69–75;
  declaratory policy of, 65–67, 68, 152;
  force development policy of, 75–81;
  SIOP during, 53, 61–67, 82; weapons
  targeting during, 30. *See also*
  McNamara, Robert
Keyworth, George, 167
Kill capabilities, 73, 103, 111, 135, 141,
  142; of MX missile, 138, 140
Kissinger, Henry, 12, 86; and limited
  nuclear options, 89; NSSMs of, 88
Korean War, 85
Krasner, Stephen, 37, 39, 163; on
  bureaucratic paradigm, 26; on state
  structure, 40, 42, 43

La Berge, Walter, 108
Laird, Melvin, 80, 86; limited options policies of, 98; and *Poseidon* funding, 106
Lake, David, 37–38, 44
Laroque, Gene, 113
Laxalt, Paul, 136
LeMay, Curtis, 57
Lemnitzer, Lyman, 63
Levin, Carl, 122
Limited Test Ban Treaty (1963), 67, 68
Lindsay, James, 102, 137–38, 142
Lippman, Walter, 162
Lodge, Henry Cabot, 131
Luttwack, Edward, 10

MacKenzie, Donald, 24
MAD. *See* Mutual Assured Destruction
Maneuvering re-entry vehicle (MARV), 134; development of, 105, 156
Mansfield, Mike, 78–79
Markey, Edward, 132
Marxism, 36; theories of the state, 39
Massive retaliation policies, 4, 85; of John Foster Dulles, 13, 57–59, 63
McIntyre, Thomas, 106, 107, 108, 111
McNamara, Robert, 13; Ann Arbor speech of, 66–67, 69, 72, 81, 96; anti-ballistic missile policy of, 23–24; appointment of, 61; cities-avoidance policy of, 14, 47, 65–66, 68, 69, 77, 82, 100, 155; civil defense policies of, 81; and civilian control of defense, 55–56, 61, 83; counter-force policies of, 11–12, 70–71, 98, 148; DPMs of, 63–65, 69–70, 77–79, 154; MAD policies of, 9, 71–72, 81, 119, 120, 152; and SIOP-62, 14, 62–67, 69, 152
Medium-range ballistic missiles (MRBMs), 102. *See also* Ballistic missiles

Members of Congress for Peace through Law, 45
Midgetman missile, 137, 143
Military Procurement Authorization Bill (1972), 103
Miller, Jack, 74
Minuteman, 77, 109; accuracy of, 73; decision-making process for, 27; hard-target kill capability of, 81; silos of, 136, 143; vulnerability of, 108, 121
Minuteman, Improved, 79
Minuteman II, 78; accuracy of, 152
Minuteman III, accuracy of, 104, 152; improvements to, 104–5, 134; MIRVs on, 78, 79
MIRVs. *See* Multiple independently targetable re-entry vehicles
Missile gap, 61, 115
MK-500 *Evader*, 139–40
Molander, Roger, 113
Moorer, Thomas, 12
Morris, Frederic, 9
Multiple independently targetable re-entry vehicles (MIRVs), 23, 82; accuracy of, 74, 80; Congressional debates on, 78–79; decision-making process for, 27; development of, 76, 156; hard-target kill capability of, 81; purpose of, 107, 109; role in counterforce, 77–79
Multiple protective shelter (MPS) basing mode, 136, 140, 143
Muskie, Edmund, 96, 111; and PD-59, 123
Mutual Assured Destruction (MAD), 2–4, 166; acceptance by society, 173–74; advocates of, 5–6, 106, 155; during Carter administration, 119–22; continuum with NUTs, 5–9, 68, 112, 119, 152, 156–57; declaratory policies of, 8, 51, 81, 112, 153, 167, 172; Joint Chiefs of Staff on, 70; during Kennedy-Johnson admin-istrations, 55, 69–75; military

position on, 12; misperceptions of,
9–12, 59, 81–82, 94, 148, 157; in
Nixon administration, 93–94; in
post-Cold War era, 147; public
perception of, 11–12; and Robert
McNamara, 9, 71–72, 81, 119, 120,
152; weapons systems for, 27
MX missile, 15; accuracy of, 152; and
command and control issues, 148;
controversial aspects of, 135, 138,
142, 149; freeze efforts against, 133;
funding for, 107–9, 136–38, 141;
procurement of, 115; purpose of,
107–9; during Reagan administration, 107, 135–42; vulnerability of,
138; warheads of, 108

National Nuclear Strategic Targeting
and Attack Plan (NSTAP), 88–89
National Security Action Memorandums (NSAMs), 30
National Security Council (NSC), 44,
88, 89; and flexible nuclear options,
95; in 1950s, 57; and PD-59, 125
National Security Decision Directives
(NSDDs), 30, 31, 166; NSDD-12, 118,
138–39; NSDD-13, 133, 134, 146;
NSDD-14, 144
National Security Decision Memor-
andums (NSDMs), 30
—NSDM-242, 89–93, 91, 100, 115,
117, 166; command and control
in, 152; public presentation of,
134
National Security Study Memoran-
dums (NSSMs), 30; NSSM-3, 88;
NSSM-169, 89, 100
National Strategic Target Data Base,
32
National Strategic Target List (NSTL),
32; growth of, 117
NATO. *See* North Atlantic Treaty
Organization

Naval War College (Newport, R. I.),
123, 124–25
Navy: and creation of JSTPS, 60; role
in counterforce strategy, 80
Neo-Realism, 20
Net-Evaluation Sub-Committee
(NESC), 77
Nettl, J. P., 37
New Look policy, 67, 171
Newman, Paul, 131
Nitze, Paul, 4
Nixon, Richard M., 61; involvement in
SIOP, 89, 160; on limited nuclear
options, 93; 1972 campaign of, 112
Nixon administration, 85; changes to
SIOP, 87–89; counterforce policies
of, 89–93; declaratory policy of,
93–99; force development policy of,
91, 99–110; national security during,
86; use of MAD, 92, 93–94; weapons
targeting during, 30
Nordlinger, Eric, 37, 42–43, 157
North Atlantic Treaty Organization
(NATO), 13; *Pershing II* policies of,
130; warning-shot policy of, 127–28
Nuclear deterrence, 2–3; in Carter
administration, 120, 122; for
Europe, 97, 112, 127–28, 158, 171;
role of Executive Branch in, 27; role
of MAD in, 5–6; role of NUTs in,
6–7; role of SDI in, 168; theoretical
literature of, 19
Nuclear Targeting Policy Review
(NTPR), 116, 117
Nuclear test ban, 67, 68
Nuclear Utilization theory (NUTs), 3,
29; action policies of, 26–27; advocates of, 6–7, 155; during Carter
administration, 119; component
policies of, 7; continuum with
MAD, 5–9, 68, 112, 119, 152, 156–57;
and declaratory policy, 148; involvement of society in, 172; and MX
controversy, 138; during 1960s, 68,
82; in Reagan administration, 114,
126. *See also* Counterforce policies

Nuclear Weapons Employment Policy
(NUWEP), 31; NUWEP-1, 89–90,
115; NUWEP-80, 116–17;
NUWEP-82, 118; and PD-59, 127
Nunn, Sam, 132, 134

Odom, William, 116
Office of Technology Assessment
(OTA), 45
Offut Air Force Base (Omaha,
Nebraska), 31
O'Malley, Jerome F., 32

Packard, David, 80, 109
Parker, Edward, 60
Patriot missiles, 144
Peace dividend, 169
Pell, Claiborne, 12
Perle, Richard, 129
Perry, William, 135
Pershing II missiles, 127, 130
Persian Gulf War, 144, 172
Physicians for Social Responsibility,
131
Pines, Burton, 11–12
Platt, Alan, 46
Pluralism: concept of state in, 39, 40,
42, 43, 158; and policy-making, 165,
166–67
Polaris submarine, 22, 109; accuracy of,
152; MIRVs on, 79, 80
Populations: role in nuclear warfare,
170–71, 172. *See also* Civilians
Populations, targeting of, 5, 8, 11, 104,
172; during Carter administration,
122; in Kennedy administration, 67;
during 1940s, 56–57; in Nixon
administration, 92, 93, 94, 99. *See
also* Countervalue policies
Poseidon missile systems, 22, 73;
accuracy of, 73, 104; counterforce
capabilities of, 79–80; kill capability
of, 142

Post-Cold War era, 113, 143; counter-
force policies in, 149; declaratory
policy during, 147; MAD in, 147;
nuclear weapons policy in, 15,
145–48, 168–69
Presidential Decision Memorandums
(PDMs), 30–31, 166
Presidential Directives (PDs), 31;
PD-18, 115–16, 118, 135; PD-53, 117;
PD-57, 117
—PD-59, 12, 13, 14–15, 47, 116–17,
121; declaration of, 123–25;
public opinion on, 124; in
Reagan administration, 125,
126–28; targeting in, 118; and
weapons procurement, 134
Presidential Review Memorandums
(PRMs), 30; PRM-10, 115
Pringle, Peter, 27
Process-tracing procedures, 16
Public interest groups, role in foreign
policy, 45, 165
Public opinion, 49; on counterforce
policies, 17, 68; effect on bur-
eaucracy, 25; influence on foreign
policy, 162; of MAD, 11–12; of
NUTs, 13; of PD-59, 124; in post-
Cold War era, 145; and Reagan
administration policies, 130–33; role
in nuclear weapons policy, 83, 151,
154–55; shaping by Executive
Branch, 156–57

Quayle, Dan, 144

Rand Corporation, 61, 86, 163
Reagan, Ronald, 12; involvement in
SIOP, 160; political career of, 114;
presidential campaign of, 123, 126;
and SDI, 167; and warning-shot
policy, 128
Reagan administration: command and
control issues in, 110, 118, 138–39,
148; counterforce policies of, 14, 148;

declaratory policies of, 125–30, 134,
148; Defense Guidance of, 128–30,
154; force development policies of,
125–26, 133–42; MX missile during,
107, 135–42; nuclear protests
during, 130–33, 151; nuclear
weapons policy of, 113, 114–15;
PD-59 in, 125, 126–28; strategic
modernization plan of, 143–45;
weapons targeting during, 31
Realist paradigm, 4; conception of
international relations, 20, 163; of
decision-making, 21; of state
autonomy, 38
Reed, Thomas, 146
Richardson, Elliot, 86; limited options
policies of, 98; on targeting, 94
Rockefeller, Nelson, 80
Rosenberg, David, 28, 56
Rostow, Eugene, 119
Rostow, Walt, 63
Rourke, Francis, 25
Rowen, Henry, 64, 91
Rumsfeld, Donald, 86; on flexibility,
101; and MX missiles, 107
Russell, Richard, 68

Sagan, Carl, 131
SALT II. *See* Strategic Arms
Limitation Talks
Sagan, Scott, 11, 28–29
SANE, 131–32
Sapolsky, Harvey, 22
Schlesinger, James, 13; declaratory
policy of, 86; and flexibility of
options, 92, 148; limited nuclear
policy of, 14, 47, 89, 94–99, 110–11,
166; on *Minuteman III*, 104; and MX
missile funding, 107; 1974 speech of,
93, 94, 95–96, 99, 166; and nuclear
command structure, 110; targeting
policy of, 95, 110; testimony before
Congress, 96, 97–98; weapons
procurement policies of, 99,
100–102, 110–11, 134

Scowcroft, Brent, 136
Scud missiles, 144
SDI. *See* Strategic Defense Initiative
Selin, Ivan, 86, 88
Senate, U. S.: and limited nuclear
policy, 96, 97; role in arms control,
46. *See also* Congress, U. S.; Armed
Services Committee
Silos, hardened, 136, 138
Single Integrated Operational Plan
(SIOP), 2, 3, 166; during Carter
administration, 115–18; counterforce policies in, 81, 93, 112;
countervalue targeting in, 14;
creation of, 30, 62, 154; decision-
making process for, 160; and
declaratory policy, 17; flexibility in,
100; and JSTPS, 32; during
Kennedy-Johnson administrations,
53, 75–76; limited options in, 89,
91–92, 113, 158; in 1990s, 147; during
Nixon administration, 87–89, 91; in
post-Cold War era, 145–47; in
Reagan administration, 141–42;
replacement with Systems of
Integrated Operational Plans, 147;
revisions to, 152; under Robert
McNamara, 14, 62–67, 69, 152;
"withholds" in, 92. *See also*
Targeting policies
  —SIOP-5, 90–93, 152; implemen-
    tation of, 91; targeting of
    populations in, 92, 93
  —SIOP-5F, 62, 63, 152
  —SIOP-6, 118, 160
  —SIOP-6F, 145, 152
  —SIOP-62, 62, 63, 152, 153
  —SIOP-63, 152; targeting options
    in, 65, 66, 81
Skocpol, Theda, 41, 42, 163
Slay, Alton, 107–8
Slocombe, Walter, 125
Sloss, Leon, 116
Smith, Margaret Chase, 68

Society: acceptance of MAD, 173–74;
access of state to, 154; anti-nuclear
sentiments of, 131; knowledge of
nuclear weapon systems, 173;
opposition to nuclear policies, 51,
143–45, 165; in policy-making
process, 48; role in national security,
163; role in nuclear weapons policy,
83, 111, 149, 155, 165–67, 173; role in
waging of war, 170; role in
bureaucratic politics, 34; as source
of public policy, 36; and state
power, 42; in statist paradigm, 167.
See also State autonomy;
State-society relationship
Sorenson, Theodore, 80
Soviet Union: ABMs of, 78–79, 107;
assured destruction of, 70; conventional capability of, 56; detente
with, 112; economic recovery
targets of, 108, 116, 128; first-strike
capabilities of, 116, 124; hardened
facilities of, 90; hard-target kill
capability of, 87, 136; ICBM build-
up of, 96; industrial targets in, 73,
91, 92, 121, 124, 128; MAD policies
of, 10–11; military targets in, 3, 8, 56,
63, 90, 95, 116; nuclear arsenal of, 73,
76, 87, 91; nuclear parity with, 5,
47–48, 50, 52, 111, 112, 114, 158, 169;
NUTs policies of, 11; second-strike
capability of, 95–96; targeting of, 32,
89, 152; tension with United States,
68, 135. *See also* Targeting policies
Special Coordination Committee
(Carter administration), 115
Spinardi, Graham, 106–7, 141
Standard operating procedures
(SOPs), 23; role of defense
establishment in, 112
State: access to society, 154; concepts
of, 39–40; decision-making
apparatus of, 163; effect of policy
disjunction on, 8; extractions from
society, 170, 171–72; interests of,
163–65; policy-making agencies of,
42–43; political theories of, 36–38;
Realist view of, 20; role in international system, 47–48; role of ideas
in, 164; role of legislation in, 43–44;
strong/weak distinctions in, 42;
structural components of, 40–41, 43
State autonomy, 1–2, 164–65; and
balance of power, 51; during Carter
administration, 15; determinants of,
41–42; effect of declaratory policy
on, 81; effect of Vietnam War on,
164–65, 167; fluctuations in, 52; in
foreign policy, 4–5, 52, 166; loss of,
16, 33, 38, 118, 149, 152, 174; and
national security, 38, 162, 168; in
Nixon administration, 112; and
nuclear superiority, 157; and public
policy, 36; resistance to, 41; and
state structure, 42. *See also*
Autonomy
State capacity, and autonomy, 41–43
State Department, 43
State-society relationship, 4–5, 37, 166;
effect of nuclear weapons on, 35–36,
111, 149, 153, 157–59, 170–71; in
post-Cold War era, 168; statist
concept of, 40; and three-level
nuclear policy, 16, 17, 35. *See also*
Society
Statist paradigm, 34, 36–37, 39–40,
50–51; autonomy in, 37; and
bureaucratic politics, 48–49, 158–65;
and democratic control of weapons,
173; and domestic political structure, 83, 163; and evolution of
nuclear policy, 52–53, 149, 159;
foreign policy in, 42; and
McNamara policies, 55; and Realist
paradigm, 38; role of Congress in,
161–62; role of society in, 167; role
of strategy in, 82; and state-society
relationship, 40
Stellar inertial guidance systems, 103,
106–7; kill capability of, 142

Stennis, John, 104, 106
STOP legislation, 132
Strategic Air Command (SAC), 23;
  bombers of, 109; dominance in
  nuclear policy, 61; requests for
  Minutemen, 76; role in targeting, 31,
  56
Strategic Arms Limitation Talks (SALT
  II), 12, 47, 88; effect of counterforce
  funding on, 103, 105; and MX
  missile, 136; and Nuclear Targeting
  Policy Review, 116; Paul Warnke in,
  119
Strategic Arms Reduction Treaty
  (START), 145
Strategic Defense Initiative (SDI), 133;
  in Bush administration, 144;
  declaratory goals of, 167–68
Strategic Defense Initiative Organi-
  zation (SDIO), 144
Strategic Modernization Program, 114
Submarine launched ballistic missiles
  (SLBMs), 22, 81; accuracy of, 140,
  141, 152–53; decision-making
  process for, 27; during 1960s, 76; use
  on hard targets, 80, 81, 106. *See also*
  Ballistic missiles
Symington, Stuart, 98
Systems of Integrated Operational
  Plans, 147

Targeting policies, 3–4; balance in, 31;
  of Carter administration, 30, 31, 122,
  128; civilian review of, 117–18;
  continuity in, 152; coordination of,
  59–60; disjunctions within, 8;
  flexibility in, 112; in limited options
  policy, 101; in MAD, 6, 7–8, 153;
  under NUWEP-1, 90; in PD-59,
  116–17, 121, 128, 152; phases of,
  30–33; policy-making process of, 19;
  in post-Cold War era, 146–47;
  pre-nuclear, 164; role of weapons
  procurement in, 134; of SIOP-5, 91.

See also Single Integrated Operational Plan; Soviet Union
Taylor, Maxwell, 63, 64
Technology, role in nuclear weapons
  policy, 82, 153
Third World, nuclear proliferation in,
  147
Thor-Jupiter intermediate-range
  ballistic missiles, 22
Triad, nuclear: establishment of, 166;
  land-based leg of, 87, 120, 135, 140;
  in Reagan administration, 134;
  Soviet, 114; submarine-based leg of,
  143, 147
Trident I missile, 135, 140
Trident II missile, 133, 139–43; and
  command and control issues, 148;
  funding of, 140–41, 142; testing of,
  143
Trident submarine, 107, 133; accuracy
  of, 152–53
Trinkle, Frank, 64
Twining, N. F., 60

United States: first-strike capability of,
  140; institutional structures of, 41;
  nuclear superiority of, 10, 56, 82, 85,
  87, 112, 157, 158; role in international system, 169; second-strike
  capabilities of, 121; tension with
  Soviet Union, 68, 135; as weak state,
  42

Vance, Cyrus, 114; and MX missile
  controversy, 135
Van Evera, Stephen, 9–10
Vietnam War, 44, 45; effect on nuclear
  weapons policy, 85; effect on state
  autonomy, 164–65, 167; societal
  opposition to, 170

Wade, James P., Jr., 139, 141
Wagstaff, Peter, 13

Walker, Richard Lee, 32, 33
Wallop, Malcolm, 12
Walsh, John, 108
War-fighting policies. *See*
Counterforce policies; Nuclear
Utilization theory (NUTs)
Warheads: MK-12A, 105, 115, 134, 135,
139; of MX missile, 108; number of,
87; re-entry vehicles for, 105;
second-strike capabilities of, 121;
yield-to-weight ratios in, 102
Warner, John, 132, 139; on kill
capability, 141
Warnke, Paul, 113; and anti-nuclear
movement, 131; and MX missile
controversy, 135; in SALT
negotiations, 119
Watergate scandal, 86
Watson, Thomas, Jr., 131
Weapons procurement, 49;
bureaucratic approach to, 22–24, 26;
in counterforce policies, 70, 104;

funding for, 102–10, 111; in limited
nuclear policy, 99, 100–102, 148, 158;
in MAD policy, 76, 81; and no-cities
doctrine, 77; role of civil defense in,
80–81; role of Congress in, 102–10.
See also Force development policy
Weinberger, Caspar, 118, 126, 129; and
warning-shot policy, 127–28
Weiss, Seymour, 89
Weiss, Ted, 142
Welch, Jasper, 116
Wells, Samuel, Jr., 59
Wheeler, Earle, 72
Willens, Harold, 131
Williams, William A., III, 141
Worldwide Coordination conferences,
59–60

Yeltsin, Boris, 143

Zeiberg, Seymour, 140